JOHN ENGLISH is a member of the Department of History at the University of Waterloo.

The first two decades of this century saw dramatic changes in the shape of Canadian politics. During that turbulent period the contours of the modern party system were formed. *The Decline of Politics* examines the forces which led to change and describes the impact of those changes on the party system in general and the Conservative party in particular.

The war and the recognition of the divisions which it created in Canadian society were important factors, but Professor English demonstrates that many changes arose from general trends in pre-war political developments. A growing national awareness inspired widespread demands by a most articulate element of the population for a national party system which reflected national considerations rather than local prejudices.

The Union government created in 1917 drew upon these arguments and, as a result, rejected the 'brokerage politics' or 'politics of national unity' which had characterized the past. Unionist supporters called for an 'end to politics' which, once in power, they could not effect. The dream of an activist, dominant central government crumbled after the war, and the diversity of the Canadian political tradition returned. Yet the Conservative party was to bear the mark of the Unionist experiment. The party's difficulties in French Canada and among non-Anglo-Saxon Canadians, Professor English argues, were very much caused by 1917.

Skilfully sorting out a complexity of issues and events, he provides an important contribution to the history of Canadian parties and politics.

CANADIAN GOVERNMENT SERIES

General Editors

R. MACG. DAWSON, 1946-58 / J.A. CORRY, 1958-61
C.B. MACPHERSON, 1961-75 / S.J.R. NOEL, 1975-

JOHN ENGLISH

The Decline of Politics:
The Conservatives and
the Party System
1901-20

UNIVERSITY OF TORONTO PRESS
Toronto and Buffalo

©University of Toronto Press 1977
Toronto and Buffalo
Printed in Canada

Canadian Cataloguing in Publication Data

English, John, 1945-
The decline of politics

(Canadian government series; 19 ISSN 0068-8835)

Includes index.
ISBN 0-8020-5386-6

1. Progressive Conservative Party (Canada) —
History. 2. Canada — Politics and government —
1896-1911.* 3. Canada — Politics and government —
1911-1921.* 4. Borden, Robert Laird, Sir, 1954-
1937. I. Title. II. Series.

JL197.P67E54   329.9'71   C77-001370-8

This book has been published during the
Sesquicentennial year of the University of Toronto

To Hilde

Preface

The first two decades of this century have been justly termed an age of transformation when Canadian social and economic institutions responded to the various tensions of immigration, urbanization, intellectual uncertainty, and war. This book explores how the party system and, in particular, the Conservative party reflected and influenced these changes. It therefore assumes that the party system and the political system are not epiphenomenal, mere reflections of the economic structures of society and independent of the wills of men. They are, rather, independent actors in the complex drama of historical change. The title of the book describes what contemporaries believed they were witnessing. They were of course incorrect: politics did not decline; they merely took on new forms. The Union government did not, as it claimed, mark an end to politics; what it did was redefine for many what politics were and should be. Whether Union government succeeded is at least debatable, but that it, along with diverse economic, social, and intellectual pressures, fundamentally disturbed the Canadian party system is undeniable.

My debts in writing this book are acknowledged in part in the numerous notes. But several debts require more formal acknowledgment. Like so many other younger scholars, I have benefited greatly from association with Professors Craig Brown and Ramsay Cook, models in every sense of what senior scholars should be. Professor Brown and Mr Henry Borden have also kindly permitted me full use of Sir Robert Borden's diary. Dean H.J. Hanham guided this work in thesis form; his comments were always stimulating, and his sympathy much appreciated. Good friends have influenced this book in less direct but nevertheless real ways. In this regard, I am most grateful to Bob Bothwell, Norm Hillmer, Veronica Strong-Boag, Jim Reed, Ron Freeman, and, of course, my colleagues at the University of Waterloo. Rik Davidson, Gerald Hallowell, and S.J.R. Noel have been, in their separate capacities, superb editors, and the faults which remain in this book are mine, not theirs. My greatest debt, that to my wife, is only barely acknowledged in the dedication to her of this book.

Canada Council Doctoral Fellowships and Harvard Graduate Prize Fellowships supported the research work for this book. Its publication is made possible by grants from the Social Science Research Council of Canada, using funds provided by the Canada Council, and from the Publications Fund of the University of Toronto Press.

JE

Contents

THE DECLINE OF POLITICS:
THE CONSERVATIVES AND THE PARTY SYSTEM
1901-20

Introduction

It is in politics as in horses: when a man has a beast that's near about up to the notch, he'd better not swap him; if he does, he's een amost sure to get one not so good as his own. My rule is, I'd rather keep a critter whose faults I do know than change him for a beast whose faults I don't know.
T.C. Haliburton, *Sam Slick*

Like Sam Slick, Canadian politicians have rarely changed their 'critter'; but on some occasions when a party has become decrepit and no longer appears likely to reach its destination, the politician has no choice. Such was the situation confronting Robert Laird Borden, a relatively obscure and inexperienced Nova Scotia member of Parliament, when he became leader of the Conservative party of Canada in 1901. Borden's efforts to restructure Macdonald Conservatism, which was far along 'the low road to extinction' by 1901,[1] is the main subject of this book.

Recent works on the first two decades of this century have emphasized the profound impact of industrialization, urbanization, and immigration upon Canadian development. Indeed, Robert Craig Brown and Ramsay Cook have entitled their Centenary Series volume *Canada, 1896-1921: A Nation Transformed.* Other more specialized studies have confirmed that Canadian political institutions and the relationship between federal and provincial governments were fundamentally altered during this period.[2] Naturally the party system was not

---

1 'Domino' (Augustus Bridle), *The Masques of Ottawa* (Toronto, 1921), 31.
2 H.V. Nelles, *The Politics of Development: Forests, Mines & Hydro-Electric Power in Ontario, 1849-1941* (Toronto, 1974); and Christopher Armstrong, 'The Politics of Federalism: Ontario's Relations with the Federal Government, 1896-1941,' unpublished PhD thesis, University of Toronto, 1972.

immune to these changes. Parties acquired new functions, lost old ones, and in general reflected in their internal disruption the pressures and turmoil of the larger society of which they were an important part. While the historian of Canadian party development does not have the range of psephological data the political scientist employs when analysing contemporary political culture, he does have access to rich collections of primary material which illuminate the nature of political leadership, the character of party organization, and the process of political change. In short, these materials permit the historian of Canada's Conservative party to enquire to what extent the party's leaders directed the changes occurring about them.

The Conservative party under Sir Robert Borden has received little attention from Canadian historians who have preferred the earlier, more successful, years under Sir John A. Macdonald and the later, less complicated, post–First World War period. For this reason, it has been necessary to include a narrative of the development of the Conservative party from 1901 to 1920. This gap in the historiography of the party is curious, since many commentators have portrayed that turbulent and sometimes tragic period as perhaps the most significant in Canadian political history, the decades when the contours of the modern party system were shaped.[3] J.W. Dafoe, an observer of both the pre-war and post-war systems from his editor's desk at the *Manitoba Free Press*, claimed that the year 1917 marked 'both an end and a beginning in Canada's political development' and 'brought to a definite close what might be called the era of the Great Parties.'[4] While accepting this clear distinction between party life before and after the war, it will be argued that the break was not so precipitous as supposed – nor was the cause merely the war. Nineteen-seventeen, that traumatic year of 'the clash,' was not a unique, almost inexplicable, occurrence, but in many ways the logical outgrowth of the attempt to define national goals undertaken by many of Canada's political leaders after 1900.

3 The interest in the Macdonald period is undoubtedly a product of Donald Creighton's splendid biography of Canada's first prime minister, *John A. Macdonald: The Old Chieftain* (Toronto, 1955). The best monograph on the Conservative party, but one written within a narrow compass, is J.L. Granatstein, *The Politics of Survival: The Conservative Party of Canada, 1939-1945* (Toronto, 1967). Much inferior but of wider scope is J.R. Williams, *The Conservative Party in Canada, 1920-1949* (Durham, NC, 1956). Curiously, the only study of the party's overall development is by the Conservative member of Parliament Heath Macquarrie, *The Conservative Party* (Toronto, 1965). The best source of material on the party between 1901 and 1914 is Robert Craig Brown's *Robert Laird Borden: A Biography, 1854-1914* (Toronto, 1975), I.
4 *Laurier: A Study in Canadian Politics* (Toronto, 1922), 176.

Chapter 2 presents the structure for the argument developed in succeeding chapters. Until 1896 the national party system was primarily concerned with the integration and survival of the political community created by Confederation, while, at this same time, the political system of the new nation was congealing, to use Gad Horowitz's apt metaphor. This process led to the formation of an appropriate national party system, one which defined few national goals and which found its locus of energy at the local level. By 1900 this type of party system had become the focus of increasing criticism. The billowing optimism arising from economic prosperity, the apparent end of the struggle for survival, and a growing national feeling inspired widespread demands by a most articulate element of the population for a national party system which reflected national considerations and did not merely pander to local prejudice. Stephen Leacock expressed this sentiment when he wrote in 1907: 'Our politics, our public life and thought, rise not to the level of our opportunity.'[5] Businessmen whose corner workshops had swollen into national industries, journalists who had out-grown the constraints of the local party organ, and professionals who followed, with interest and admiration, the ambitious national polities of Canada's mother country and her great southern neighbour's 'age of reform,' for all these diverse individuals, the boundaries of political identity had expanded. For them, the significant election issue was not a local bridge or post office, but the future direction of the nation. Of course, not all agreed upon the correct course. For example, two who called for a national party system which concerned itself with larger questions were Henri Bourassa, whose goal was a bicultural, independent nation,[6] and Stephen Leacock, who called for a 'Greater Canada' within a more closely knit British Empire. Part of Bourassa's pessimism may have arisen from his knowledge that, in this clamour raised by the articulate and influential por-tion of the nation, the French-Canadian voice was very faint indeed.

Borden, unlike his great antagonist Sir Wilfrid Laurier, sympathized with this demand for a more national and creative party system, one which would involve Canadians more closely in shaping the future of their land. He argued in 1910 that democracy was impossible unless the individual citizen 'accepts his duty to the state.'[7] Similarly, Sir Clifford Sifton believed that the 'new era' would bring a 'national superstructure' which would expunge the evils of vice, corruption,

5 'Greater Canada: An Appeal,' *University Magazine,* VI (April 1907), 136.
6 'The Nationalist Movement in Quebec,' *Addresses Delivered before the Canadian Club of Toronto, 1906-7* (Toronto, 1907), 56-62.
7 'An Ideal of a Continental Relationship,' Public Archives of Canada (PAC), Borden Papers (BP), v. 300.

poverty, and disease.[8] It is this common belief in the possibility and the efficacy of national action in spheres where the state had never previously trod which united these various groupings. A national interest was both definable and attainable, and political parties must be an important instrument for this end.

This perception of political development led Robert Borden increasingly to shun the compromises and the limits supposedly required of Canadian political leaders. 'Brokerage politics,' or the 'politics of national unity,' which minimizes differences, avoids conflict, and makes politics an end in itself, was rejected by Borden and many of his contemporaries. Historians and political scientists have often treated this as an aberration, puzzling in terms of the models usually applied in the interpretation of the Canadian party system. Brokerage politics, many claim, are inevitable so long as regionalism remains predominant.[9] More recently, a political scientist has explained the persistence of brokerage by referring to certain representational tendencies inherent in the Canadian electoral system.[10] Another seems to blame the absence of 'creative' politics in Canada upon the long tenure of William Lyon Mackenzie King, the rebel's grandson, who would

Do nothing by halves
Which can be done by quarters.

Canada's lack of ideology, of vision, and of political maturity are attributed to King's peculiar style:

---

8 'The Foundations of the New Era,' in J.O. Miller, ed., *The New Era in Canada: Essays Dealing with the Upbuilding of the Canadian Commonwealth* (London, Paris, Toronto, 1917), 37.

9 One finds this thesis throughout studies of the Canadian political system. A variation of it stresses the cleavage resulting from the racial differences in Canada. For the general statement see R. MacGregor Dawson, *The Government of Canada*, revised by Norman Ward (5th ed., Toronto, 1970), 430-2; Jack McLeod, 'Party Structure and Party Reform,' in Abraham Rotstein, ed., *The Prospect of Change* (Toronto, 1967), 4-9; Alexander Brady, *Democracy in the Dominions* (2nd ed., Toronto, 1952), 110-12; Bernard Crick, *In Defence of Politics* (Harmondsworth, 1964), 86-7; and F.H. Underhill, *Canadian Political Parties*, Canadian Historical Association, booklet no. 8 (1956). For the variation see André Siegfried, *The Race Question in Canada*, trans. E. Nash (1907), ed. Frank Underhill (Toronto, 1966); and H.Blair Neatby, *Laurier and a Liberal Quebec* (Toronto, 1973).

10 Alan C. Cairns, 'The Electoral System and the Party System in Canada, 1921-1965,' *Canadian Journal of Political Science*, I (March 1968), 55-80.

We had no shape
Because he never took sides,
And no sides
Because he never allowed them to take shape.[11]

All these insights possess a certain validity, but it can be argued that History, or, more specifically, the political experience of Canada between 1901 and 1920, is an equally significant factor in the explanation of the character of the contemporary Canadian party system.

Too often modern critics forget that there was once an attempt to make vision, conflict, and 'creativity' the central features of Canadian politics, and that attempt was a failure, even in the minds of its authors. Upon the party system it left as little visible impression as 'a sword-cut in the water.'[12] Yet surely it is no accident that young Mackenzie King received most of his political education in those early decades of this century when the traditional constraints upon Canadian political leadership were broken. King then learned that politics was like poetry, in that innate lyricism must accept formal limits. The Canadian party system may be, as its critics charge, a bud which never opened, a flower which bore no fruit. But for the Canadian electorate, as for King, that brief moment of political fury over half a century ago left an impression profound and enduring. In the future they preferred safety to danger, Augustus to Caesar, the mundane home to the heavenly city. Like Sam Slick, they retained the flawed yet familiar.

11 Frank R. Scott, 'W.L.M.K.,' in Scott and A.J.M. Smith, eds., *The Blasted Pine* (Toronto, 1967), 36-7. Gad Horowitz makes this argument in *Canadian Labour in Politics* (Toronto, 1968), chap. 1.
12 Dafoe, *Laurier*, 180.

1

Politics and corruption

Corruption pervades every tissue of our society.
Sir Wilfrid Laurier

There is no better description of Canadian political life before the Great War
than André Siegfried's perspicacious and often prophetic *The Race Question in
Canada*. Siegfried, a young French political sociologist, devoted the largest single
portion of his study to the Canadian political parties whose activities he
observed during the 1904 general election. This concern is a reflection of a
remarkable international interest in political parties at the time and of the great
significance which Canadian thinkers themselves attached to the role of parties
in national life. His section on parties therefore attracted the majority of
contemporary comment on his book, comment largely in praise of the 'lucidity'
and accuracy of the analysis. Siegfried has accordingly acquired an importance
beyond the inherent merit of his observations and has become a Canadian
Tocqueville who expressed what Canadians sensed but could not and did not
themselves articulate.

To Siegfried, the Canadian political party was at best an anachronism, at
worst 'a machine for winning elections.' Unlike the parties of Third Republic
France or of western Europe generally, Canadian parties deliberately and
energetically shunned ideas and doctrines. In Siegfried's view, this tendency had
ominous results:

In the absence of ideas or doctrines to divide the voters, there remain only
questions of material interest, collective or individual. Against their pressure the
candidate cannot maintain his integrity, for he knows that his opponent will not
show the same self-restraint. The result is that the same promises are made on
both sides, following an absolutely identical conception of the meaning of

power. Posed in this way, the issue of an election manifestly changes. Whoever may be the winner, everyone knows that the country will be administered in the same way, or almost the same.

Canadian parties were no more than Tweedledum and Tweedledee, seeking in devious ways an empty ring signifying power. Only when 'some great wave of opinion sweeps over the whole country, covering under its waters all the political pygmies,' did Canadian public life rise above 'the sordid preoccupations of patronage or connection.' But such crises, 'violent no doubt but at bottom healthy,' occurred infrequently and Canadian statesmen devoted themselves 'to weakening such movements rather than encouraging them or availing themselves of them.' Canadian parties, then, were utterly meaningless and without fundamental difference on any major subject — in a word, corrupt.

Canadian historians since Siegfried have usually accepted these conclusions. Indeed, Frank Underhill, sixty years after Siegfried wrote, called his analysis of Canadian parties 'unanswerable.'[1] Generally, the historian's indictment of Macdonald Conservatism has echoed that of Sir John Willison: 'it carried out a great constructive Canadian policy by bad political methods and gross corruption in the constituencies.'[2] From Siegfried to Peter Waite's *Arduous Destiny*,[3] corruption has been a valuable spice to enliven a fairly bland portion of Canadian history. For this reason it is, as a study of the Canadian bureaucracy points out, 'somewhat curious that the practice of patronage has never been the subject of sustained analysis on the part of Canadian social scientists and historians.'[4]

1 *The Race Question in Canada*, trans. E. Nash (1907, Toronto, 1966), 113, and Frank H. Underhill's introduction, 1 and 9. For contemporary comment see F.P. Walton, 'Recent Books on Canada,' *University Magazine*, VI (April 1907), 247-53; and W.L. Grant, 'Review of Siegfried: Le Canada, les deux races,' *Review of Historical Publications relating to Canada*, XI (1906), 144-8.
2 Quoted in E.M. Saunders, *Life and Letters of Sir Charles Tupper* (Toronto, 1921), II, 253.
3 *Canada, 1874-1896: Arduous Destiny* (Toronto, 1971).
4 J.E. Hodgetts, William McCloskey, Reginald Whitaker, and V. Seymour Wilson, *The Biography of an Institution: The Civil Service Commission of Canada, 1908-1967* (Montreal and London, 1972), 8. See also D.G.G. Kerr, 'The 1867 Elections in Ontario: The Rules of the Game,' *Canadian Historical Review*, LI (Dec. 1970), 369-85, which begins: 'It is generally and quite correctly assumed that a good deal of corruption was involved in Canadian elections in the years before and for some time after Confederation.' And see David Smith, *Prairie Liberalism: The Liberal Party in Saskatchewan, 1905-71* (Toronto, 1975), especially chap. 2.

The problem is not solely Canadian. One student of corruption has warned that 'any attempt to analyse the concept of corruption must contend with the fact that in English and other languages the word *corruption* has a history of vastly different meanings and connotations.' Although this study shows that social scientists still employ a wide variety of definitions, the majority 'relate their definitions of political corruption to concepts concerning the duties of public office.'[5] What is corrupt is not only what is illegal. This modern approach, although more analytical and precise, is remarkably similar to that of turn-of-the-century Canadian writers such as Sandford Fleming who in his 1892 compilation, *An Appeal to the Canadian Institute on the Rectification of Parliament*, sets out a concept of duty for the holders of public office. In Fleming's view, and that of other Canadian contributors such as Goldwin Smith and Edward Blake, the allegiance and responsibility of the office holder must be to the 'commonwealth,' not to private interests or individuals. Whenever this is not the case, the political system is, in Smith's word, 'defective.'

These writings reflected the moral righteousness characteristic of the period, but, more importantly, they also posited a model, one drawn from British and Prussian political theory and practice. In this ideal state the loyalty of the officeholder would be devoted to what Max Weber termed 'impersonal and functional purposes.'[6] Thus the bureaucracy would serve the commonwealth, not a faction, and the result would be both efficiency and probity. The member of Parliament, elected in 'clean' elections where no votes were bought with liquor, promises of favour, or deception, would truly be the representative of the people as contemporary political theory asserted he should be.[7] The system would be rationalized; it would become what it professed to be.

However much Fleming's definition of corruption parallels that of the modern social scientist, neither he, nor his associates, nor the overwhelming majority of his contemporary authorities would have accepted the belief of some modern social scientists that, in certain situations, corruption could itself be functional. Some, it is true, did regard corruption as 'a necessary evil' associated

5 A. Heidenheimer, ed., *Political Corruption* (New York, 1970), 3, 4.
6 'Bureaucracy,' in H.H. Gerth and C. Wright Mills, eds., *From Max Weber* (New York, 1958), 199.
7 Goldwin Smith — and many others — was led to call for the abolition of parties, 'a fine name for faction of which the ties are passion and corruption.' 'The Decline of Party Government,' *Macmillan's Magazine*, XXXVI (1877), 298-306. See also Carl Berger, *The Sense of Power: Studies in the Ideas of Canadian Imperialism, 1867-1914* (Toronto, 1970), chap. 8.

with democratic and popular government.[8] Yet even these Canadians would have been astounded and outraged by Robert Merton's suggestion that the political machine satisfies 'basic latent functions.' According to Merton 'the functional deficiencies of the official structure generate an alternative [unofficial] structure to fulfill existing needs somewhat more effectively.'[9] Historically, one must accept that Merton's insight is more useful in explaining the persistence of corruption than the analyses of turn-of-the-century writers, who all too often substituted moral righteousness for analysis and institutional explanations for societal ones.

Does Merton's perception offer assistance to the student of the Canadian party system before the First World War? To answer this question, the remainder of this chapter will discuss pre-war electoral, legislative, and administrative corruption, and the post-1896 party system in general, a topic which must be examined first.

THE PARTY SYSTEM

The 1896 general election is one of those rare political events which deserves to be called a 'turning point.' In that election Sir Wilfrid Laurier led a phalanx of Liberal provincial premiers in the overthrow of the long-besieged Macdonald Conservatives. Both W.S. Fielding, Nova Scotian premier and former secessionist, and Oliver Mowat, the Ontario nationalist, became members of the new federal cabinet, symbolizing by their presence that Confederation was no longer an issue in Canadian politics. According to W.L. Morton it was after this election that the national party system 'reached its fullest and most solid development.'[10] And it was this full and solid, though most peculiar, system that André Siegfried observed during the 1904 general election.

To Siegfried the election and the party system were almost inexplicable. At the national level the election seemed quite meaningless; at the constituency level it was everything. He was struck by the 'fury and enthusiasm' in the constituencies which he thought was unparalleled anywhere else in the world. The domination of an election by the Liberals and Conservatives made French

---

8 Herbert Ames, 'Electoral Management,' *Canadian Magazine*, XXV (May 1905), 26. Ames noted this sentiment and then went on to show that such a supposition was unwarranted. That Sir John A. Macdonald shared the belief that corruption was a 'necessary evil' of a democratic system is made clear in Waite, *Canada, 1874-1896*, 20.

9 *Social Theory and Social Structure* (New York, 1968), 126-7; see also Edward Banfield and James Q. Wilson, *City Politics* (Cambridge, Mass., 1963), chap. 9.

10 *The Progressive Party in Canada* (Toronto, 1950), 5.

political contests seem anarchic. The gusto, the rigidity of party discipline, and the devotion of party workers were incredible. Yet for all this sound and fury the election ultimately changed nothing. It was only a contest 'between a government and an opposition, or between two parties equally Conservative.'[11]

Siegfried never resolved this paradox he presented. Being French, he was disposed towards the doctrinal parties of France where a party's national characteristics and activities were mirrored at the local level.[12] In Canada, however, the argument from composition was fallacious – the surface of the Canadian party system did not reflect its core. The Liberal worker in Assiniboia West constituency in Saskatchewan, the back bench member from that constituency, and Sir Wilfrid Laurier did not share the same view of politics and parties. A student of party politics in Victorian Britain has sounded the same note: 'elections considered as national politics were frivolous and primitive: considered as local politics, serious and rational.'[13] Such an interpretation applied to pre-war Canadian politics offers the possibility of resolution of the striking paradox so apparent in *The Race Question in Canada* and many other documents of the time.[14]

The uppermost layer of the complex tissue of Canadian parties was the parliamentary party. It defined and presumably represented the entire party structure, and was consequently the focus of national press attention. In 1900, however, the most striking impression made by the parliamentary party was one of simplicity. The parliamentary chamber and the cloakrooms were characteristically marked by somnolence. To be sure, the debates were replete with rough and tumble, but this very rarely spilled beyond the Commons chamber. Hector Charlesworth, a newspaper and magazine editor, saw the parliamentary struggle as a poker game. The players had 'an eye on the winnings, but they did not mind playing tricks on each other. After the election was over and the chips counted, so to speak, the participants did not mind exchanging confidences as to the merry devices they had adopted to over-reach the other fellow.'[15]

11 *The Race Question in Canada*, 117, 118, and 164.
12 This trait has persisted in French political sociologists examining North American party systems. Maurice Duverger in *Political Parties*, trans. Barbara and Robert North (New York, 1954), regards American party systems as undeveloped and anachronistic and the European party is regarded as a norm. For a critique of Duverger's methodology, see Aaron Wildavsky, 'A Methodological Critique of Duverger's Political Parties,' *Journal of Politics* (May 1959), 303-18.
13 John Vincent, *The Formation of the Liberal Party, 1857-1868* (London, 1966), xv.
14 Siegfried's point of view is reflected at least in part in many works which discuss the pre-war party system, notably Frank Underhill's numerous articles on the Canadian party system. Two other important books which share many of his assumptions are J.W. Dafoe, *Laurier: A Study in Canadian Politics* (Toronto, 1922), and Henry Borden, ed., *Robert Laird Borden: His Memoirs* (Toronto, 1938).
15 *More Candid Chronicles* (Toronto, 1928), 124.

Sessions were short and the work of Parliament devolved upon a few. For the rest who lived nearby in Montreal or in Ontario, most of the time was spent at home. For those less fortunate (or perhaps more fortunate, depending on one's viewpoint in such matters), the Russell Hotel, or some similar Ottawa watering place, alive with political gossip and intrigue, was some consolation. But the excitement of a world capital, a London, or a Paris, or even a Washington, was absent. To Rupert Brooke, a pre-war tourist, Canada's capital possessed 'an air of civilization' without the 'sense of strain or tightness in the atmosphere' which one felt in Montreal. It was a world of 'safeness and honour and massive buildings and well-shaded walks.'[16]

It was in this world of moderate scale that the business of Canadian government was conducted, and party structure received definition and nourishment. The bureaucracy was small and the demands made on it were generally few. Because of this, a great deal of everyday decision-making was in the hands of the party leader and a few subordinates. Moreover, unlike Westminister where the Public Accounts Committee exercised careful scrutiny of executive management and expenditure, the Canadian Parliament had failed 'to establish a system in which Parliament examined the affairs of the executive on behalf of the public, as distinct from a system in which the Opposition examined the Government's affairs for its own purposes.'[17] Indeed, even senior members often knew surprisingly little about government or party affairs. Borden, for example, announced his Halifax Platform, a wide-ranging policy declaration, without consultation of the party caucus, much less the rank and file of his party. It is also known that Laurier took two of the most significant decisions during his period as prime minister without consulting the appropriate minister. The negotiations about and the decision to go ahead with a second transcontinental railway were carried out with little reference to the minister of railways and canals, Andrew G. Blair. Nor was the leading western minister, Sir Clifford Sifton, informed of the changes relating to separate schools in the Autonomy Bills of 1905 which set up the provinces of Alberta and Saskatchewan.[18] Such lack of consultation on issues

16 *Letters from America* (Toronto, 1916), 54-6.
17 Norman Ward, *The Public Purse: A Study in Canadian Democracy* (Toronto, 1962), 142.
18 C.F. Hamilton to J.S. Willison, 20 Sept. 1907, Public Archives of Canada (PAC), Willison Papers, v. 36. The consultation cited in Borden's *Memoirs*, I, 192, was with outsiders such as Willison and Joseph Flavelle, not with members of his caucus. On Laurier, see John Willison, *Sir Wilfrid Laurier* (Toronto, 1927), chap. 28; J.W. Dafoe, *Clifford Sifton in Relation to His Times* (Toronto, 1931), chap. 10; O.D. Skelton, *Life and Letters of Sir Wilfrid Laurier* (Toronto, 1921), II, 188-95, 226-47; and David Hall, 'A Divergence of Principle: Clifford Sifton, Sir Wilfrid Laurier and the North West Autonomy Bills, 1905,' *Laurentian University Review / Revue de l'Université Laurentienne*, VII (Nov. 1974), 3-24.

of major importance was regarded as going too far, and both of the outraged ministers resigned; but on most matters decisions by the party leader were the rule rather than the exception.

What permitted this centralization of power was the relatively few decisions that had to be made. One is struck by the evidence in the Laurier Papers that Laurier himself had to deal with the most minor matters, such as a request for assistance in obtaining a post office or a disagreement with a neighbour, matters which today would be handled or, more likely, dismissed by lower level clerks. But at the turn of the century such clerks were few and there was no real need for them. In 1900 federal government spending was only $55 million of which $24 million was allocated to transportation, a field which was largely entrusted to private companies rather than to governmental agencies. The estimated gross national product in 1900 was $1057 million, and federal government spending as a percentage of GNP was therefore slightly over 5 per cent in contrast to over 20 per cent in 1970.[19] While expenditures increased rapidly in the years before 1914, the touch of pre-war national government remained light. There were, of course, certain groups, like those engaged in the transportation industry and in resource development, which were greatly affected by governmental decision, and since the locus of power was well known, these interests swarmed around the leader and sometimes overwhelmed him and his entourage, leaving a sordid impression in their wake. But the overall scope of government was so limited that the vast majority of the population was not much affected by its activities.

Like governmental policy, party policy and organizational control was concentrated in the hands of a few, with the party leader himself responsible for an extraordinary amount of party work. In the parties, as with the government, the process of bureaucratization had not gone far. Parties lacked both mass organization as well as a cadre of permanent officials who provided experience and discipline.[20] By 1900, however, the increasing demands of government itself or, in the case of the opposition leader, activities in the House of Commons, as well as a general recognition that strident press and public attacks upon patronage and favouritism had made it very dangerous for a leader to seem too closely involved with party 'wirepulling,' had led to delegation of some of the leader's power within the party. Already there had arisen the cultivation of an appearance

19 M.C. Urquhart and K.H. Buckley, eds., *Historical Statistics of Canada* (Toronto, 1965), 130, 141, 201, 202.
20 See Reinhard Bendix, *Max Weber: An Intellectual Portrait* (Garden City, NY, 1962), 445. This is not to suggest that certain individuals, especially at the local level, did not act as full-time party agents. Some did, but in nearly every case they were not party officials *de jure* but rather individuals whose position, most likely as civil servants, enabled them to devote full time to party interest. Nevertheless, no formal bureaucratization had occurred.

of indifference to and innocence of internal party affairs which was to emerge as a highly developed native Canadian art with the masterful Mackenzie King in the 1930s. The manner in which this was accomplished in the age of Borden and Laurier was to give responsibility for organization within an area to the most prominent or the most competent minister from that area or, if in opposition, to the most knowledgeable member. Thus some politicians became particularly identified as 'machine politicians,' a breed which achieved its quintessence in pre-war Canada in such powerful individuals as Joseph Israel Tarte, Clifford Sifton, and Robert Rogers, who waged memorable struggles with consummate skill and dubious means.

The mention of 'Bob' Rogers points to the most important but least known aspect of party organization after 1896, the close relationship which Borden and Laurier established between most provincial and federal parties.[21] In 1904, 1908, and 1911 Rogers remained a provincial minister in the Manitoba government while conducting the federal campaigns in western Canada. This apparent anomaly can be traced to many factors but it is ultimately both product and reflection of the pre-eminence of the national party system after 1896. The 'loose fish' and independents had by 1904 become very rare in the House of Commons. In 1903 Richard McBride's formation of a very partisan Conservative government brought non-partisan government in British Columbia to an end. Two years later when the new provinces of Alberta and Saskatchewan were carved from the old Northwest Territories, the federal parties quickly extended their hold on this previously non-partisan preserve. The national party system had embraced all Canadian political life, and, superficially at least, political existence beyond it seemed impossible to sustain.

The achievement of this goal, a hegemonic national party system — which had long ago been espoused by Macdonald who saw its value as a national cement — was largely the work of Laurier and Borden. Both these leaders created close ties with the provincial branches of their parties, and they had good reasons. As Christopher Armstrong has written, 'everywhere [urbanization and industrialization] enhanced both the role and the status of provincial governments so that they became semi-independent principalities treating with one another and the federal government.'[22] As provincial governments became stronger so too did provincial parties and the patronage available to them became a much richer

---

21 For proof that this was not always the case with the Conservatives, see Charles Tanner, leader of the opposition in Nova Scotia, to Borden, 3 Dec. 1909, PAC, Borden Papers (BP), v. 352. Laurier's concern with close provincial ties is shown in H.B. Neatby, *Laurier and a Liberal Quebec* (Toronto, 1973). See also Christopher Armstrong, 'The Politics of Federalism: Ontario's Relations with the Federal Government, 1896-1941,' unpublished PhD thesis, University of Toronto, 1972, 411-12.
22 *Ibid.*, 2.

lode. The lesson of the Liberal victory in 1896 was not lost upon Borden. In the campaign of 1908 Laurier ridiculed the phalanx of provincial premiers that took its place in the front lines of the national Conservative campaign, but he knew how threatening the new Conservative alliance was.[23] In 1911, Premiers McBride of British Columbia, Rodmond P. Roblin of Manitoba, Sir James P. Whitney of Ontario, and J. Douglas Hazen of New Brunswick threw the full force of their provincial organizations into the national campaign with such remarkable success that the fifteen-year-old Laurier government fell. Like Laurier in 1896, Borden turned in gratitude to the provinces for talent for his first cabinet. Although McBride and Whitney refused to leave their provinces, their influence secured cabinet positions for Martin Burrell, McBride's former personal secretary, and Frank Cochrane, an important member of Whitney's cabinet. Premier Hazen did enter the new cabinet, and the legendary Robert Rogers became the Manitoba provincial government's unique contribution to the national Conservative government.[24]

Yet, in a certain sense, this consolidation of the national party structure occurred at the apex of the party system not at its roots where Siegfried correctly discerned that a traditional or, in his words, anarchic pattern still persisted. The task of Borden and Laurier, as these leaders themselves interpreted it, was to create greater uniformity throughout the party structure. This implied the elimination of a great variety of separate political cultures within individual provinces or constituencies. In a sense, this goal was not unlike the one faced by political leaders in 'Third World' nations today. In such states, Colin Leys argues, 'neither attitudes nor material conditions ... are focused on the support of a single concept of the national interest or of the official purposes of state and local offices and institutions which would promote that interest.'[25] Instead, a strong counter-conception of the nature of public office and of the role of

23 Laurier reportedly said: 'Wolves, it is said, hunt in packs; the lion hunts alone.' Cited in J.C. Hopkins, ed., *Canadian Annual Review, 1908* (Toronto, 1909), 160.
24 Whitney to Donald McLellan, 17 Oct. 1911, Provincial Archives of Ontario (PAO), Whitney Papers, v. 21; George Perley to McBride, 17 Oct. 1911, Public Archives of British Columbia (PABC), McBride Papers, Letters Inward, 1911. The information on Burrell was obtained in an interview with McBride's daughter, Mrs M. Macintosh, Oct. 1970. See also Roger Graham, 'The Cabinet of 1911,' in F. Gibson, ed., *Cabinet Formation and Bicultural Relations* (Ottawa, 1970), 47-62; Heath Macquarrie, 'The Formation of Borden's First Cabinet,' *Canadian Journal of Economics and Political Science*, XXIII (Feb. 1957), 90-104; and R.C. Brown, *Robert Laird Borden: A Biography, 1854-1914* (Toronto, 1975), I, chap. 10.
25 'What Is the Problem about Corruption?' *Journal of Modern African Studies*, III (1965), 224.

elected officials exists within tribes or local areas. The legislator is primarily a delegate not a trustee. There is strong evidence to confirm that Canadian members of Parliament thought of themselves in this fashion.

In 1962 Alan Kornberg asked 165 members how they conceived of their functions, offering them three categories to choose from: trustee, delegate, or 'politico,' that is, 'one who tries to span the chasm between independent thinking and constituency control.' They were also asked what geographic area they believed they represented. The former Kornberg termed 'representational style,' the latter 'representational focus.' The results are both striking and important: only 15 per cent of the respondents saw themselves as 'trustees,' 36 per cent chose 'politico,' and fully 49 per cent declared themselves to be 'delegates'; 47 per cent felt they were representing 'national' interests, 19 per cent 'national-local,' and 34 per cent 'local.' Kornberg's research further indicates that members without advanced education, from rural ridings, and in non-ideological parties tended to prefer the delegate orientation and to focus upon their constituency more than their better educated urban colleagues.[26]

The member of Parliament in 1902, sixty years before Kornberg's survey, was less likely to possess a college degree, and more likely to represent a rural constituency. Moreover, the population of that constituency was considerably smaller, and of that population a large percentage was ineligible to vote. In 1900 there were 214 members and 1,167,402 voters; the average constituency had merely 5455 voters of whom an average of 4443 chose to exercise their ballot.[27] Knowing all of one's electors was not a politician's wistful dream, but probably in many cases a reality. Considering all these factors, it can be argued that the 1902 member exhibited an even stronger tendency to see himself as a 'delegate' and to feel that his principal task was to represent his constituents in caucus and in Parliament while clarifying and justifying his party's stand to his constituents. Compromise is an inevitable product of such a system; so, too, is 'corruption,' which is a means of purchasing party discipline and success both at the national and local level when a clear sense of public and common interest is absent.

---

26 *Canadian Legislative Behaviour* (New York, 1967), 108-9. The 1911 redistribution still left almost 70 per cent of Canadian parliamentary seats rural. On the educational background of members, see Kornberg, chap. 3, and Norman Ward, *The Canadian House of Commons: Representation* (Toronto, 1950), chap. 7. There was, of course, no socialist grouping in the House of Commons before 1914 and therefore no 'ideological' members in the sense which Kornberg uses that term.

27 Urquhart and Buckley, eds., *Historical Statistics*, 616, 618.

CORRUPTION

O.D. Skelton, Laurier's official biographer, noted that Sir Wilfrid considered patronage 'the most important single function of government. No other subject bulked so large in correspondence, no other purpose brought so many visitors to Ottawa.'[28] For Laurier, preoccupied with national affairs, patronage was an endless nuisance; for the ordinary member of Parliament it was the lifeblood of political existence. Through it, he nurtured the intricate system which had brought him political success. Charles G. Power, whose father was a prominent Quebec City Liberal, remembered that before the First World War 'it was generally accepted that the sitting member was the source from which all material blessings flowed,'[29] and an erratic rate of flow could rapidly assure one's political doom.

An excellent description of the lack of appeal of national issues and the penalty for ignoring local 'needs' during a political campaign is given in Sara Jeannette Duncan's novel, *The Imperialist*, published in 1904. In this novel Lorne Murchison, a wealthy businessman running in a by-election in the Ontario constituency of 'South Fox,' found the Canadian party system incapable of accepting unadulterated doses of his 'great idea,' the supreme national interest, imperialism:

His [Murchison's] mind accepted the old working formulas for dealing with an average electorate, but to his eager apprehending heart it seemed unbelievable that the great imperial possibility, the dramatic chance for the race that hung even now, in the history of the world, between the rising and the setting of the sun, should fail to be perceived and acknowledged as the paramount issue, the contingency which made the by-election of South Fox an extraordinary and momentous affair. He believed in the Idea; he saw it, with Wallingham [Chamberlain], not only a glorious prospect, but an educative force; and never had he a moment of such despondency that it confounded him upon his horizon in the faded colours of some old Elizabethan mirage.

The 'great idea' could never be relevant to the political life of South Fox constituency, absorbed as it was with the politics of 'box-cars and canals.' The continual reference to 'the Idea' in his speeches caused his audiences to dwindle. Soon he noticed that the 'political leaders' of the constituency were showing 'a

28 Skelton, *Laurier*, II, 270-1.
29 *A Party Politician: The Memoirs of Chubby Power*, ed. Norman Ward (Toronto, 1966), 18.

special reticence' and that 'his arrival would sometimes have a disintegrating effect upon a group in the post-office or at a street corner.' Murchison, of course, lost the election.[30]

What were the devices which he deigned not to use? In the case of South Fox, electoral corruption, which Murchison eschewed in favour of an 'intellectual' approach, would have been of great assistance. In Canada, as elsewhere, this type of corruption took many forms, the most common of which was bribery. Indeed, so prevalent was this practice that one of Canada's most distinguished jurists, J.D. Armour, could seriously inquire in 1884: 'Is not bribery the cornerstone of Party Government?'[31] Canadians will nevertheless be reassured to learn that they did not sell themselves, or rather their votes, cheaply. While legend has it that Americans sold their votes for one dollar, there is abundant evidence that the Canadian price could be as high as seven dollars.[32] No less a figure than Sir Richard Cartwright, scion of one of Canada's most eminent families, admitted that he had, on occasion, bought votes. The relatively small electorate undoubtedly made bribery very effective in winning elections. But it was not only within the constituency that the prudent, corrupt candidate looked: Canadians who had emigrated to the United States often returned to their native land on election day where they found their ballot more valuable, at least in a monetary sense, than in their adopted land. A reformer wrote in despair in 1905 of one of the most notorious instances of this practice:

Then there was the Sault Ste. Marie election. Here the incredible effrontery of the affair showed it was conducted by men who were accustomed to defy the law with impunity. A well known agent of the machine engaged a tug boat, the famous Minnie M., to carry a number of American 'pluggers' from the American side of the Sault, to personate voters on behalf of the Liberal candidate at two remote stations in the constituency. Attorney-General [J.M.] Gibson, who was at the Sault the night before the election, was informed of the project by a letter read on the public platform and was requested to take steps to prevent its being carried out. It is almost incredible that a Cabinet minister should have failed to

30 *The Imperialist* (Toronto, 1961), 226, 260.
31 Armour made this statement when trying a conspiracy case. He added that he personally believed that 'men are party men for the spoils.' Cited in the Toronto *Globe*, 5 Dec. 1884.
32 See Thomas Hodgins, *Election Cases* (Toronto, 1883), 560; James Cappon, 'The Responsibility of Political Parties,' *Queen's Quarterly*, XII (Jan. 1905), 307-13; and Ward, *Canadian House of Commons*, 252n. For a description of how expensive an election could be because of bribery, see A Candidate in the Late Elections, 'Electoral Management (A Reply to Mr. Ames),' *Canadian Magazine*, XXV (Aug. 1905), 316-19.

perceive what was the only decent or even sensible course for him to take. But his reply shows the depths to which politics in Canada has fallen. Instead of asking for proofs and declaring that he would stop such an expedition at any cost, he said he was not a policeman. He was only a Cabinet minister whose word was all powerful with every Liberal functionary and every official in the district; he was only Attorney-General with the whole legal machinery of the Province at his command. The Minnie M. sailed with her pluggers on board and helped to win a much needed seat for the Government. It reads like a page from the history of a rotten South American republic.[33]

Another popular technique, especially in larger ridings with a 'considerable floating population,' was impersonation. According to Herbert B. Ames, a Montreal MP, 'there is so little likelihood of detection, the attendant risk is so insignificant, the price paid for passing false votes is so tempting, that unless severe measures are employed, there will always be persons willing to undertake the business.'[34] Better known, perhaps because it was more obvious, was the practice of 'treating' for liquor, which, at the low price of Canadian spirits, was much cheaper than purchasing votes outright. So prevalent was this that Norman Ward, with characteristic wit and pardonable exaggeration, claims that 'there is considerable evidence to suggest that a large portion of the history of Canadian politics could be written in terms of its alcoholic content.'[35] Rather oddly, treating was not an indictable offence so long as one was 'a habitual treater at a constant rate.' Treating, bribery, and personation were, of course, accompanied by candidates' promises of positions, contracts, and other benefits in exchange for support in the polling booth.[36]

All these devices made pre-war elections exasperating and expensive affairs. Sir Richard Cartwright described the problem: '... [theoretically] the people should come out of their own accord; practically, they have to be driven or

33 Cappon, 'The Responsibility of Political Parties,' 310; see also Brian Tennyson, 'The Cruise of the Minnie M.,' *Ontario History*, LXIX (June 1967), 125-8.
34 'Electoral Management,' 30.
35 *Canadian House of Commons*, 245.
36 Any acceleration in the rate of treating led to conviction. Accordingly, known inebriates were usually employed for the purpose. See PAC, Sifton Papers, v. 278, 'Election 1908,' for a description of a hotel at election time in Brandon, Manitoba. A 'negro' was employed by the organization as a treater. Such promises were not illegal if made in a 'general' way. A candidate's promise to lay sidewalks in a municipality at his own expense was, however, considered by the courts sufficient grounds to void an election. See C.O. Ermatinger, *Canadian Franchise and Election Laws* (Toronto, 1886), 243, 244.

spurred up, and unless considerable pains have been taken in the interval between any two general elections, or unless some burning question has sprung up,
which is not often the case, it requires a very great outlay, even if the expenditure is confined to purely legitimate purposes, to organize such an immense
force at short notice.'[37] The candidate himself had to find most of these funds
within the constituency, although the central organization contributed varying
amounts as well. According to a candidate in the 1904 general election, the cost
of an election in an urban Ontario seat was never less than $3000 to $4000 and
in some cases went as high as $15,000 to $20,000. Since the average vote for a
winning candidate in Ontario in this election was approximately three thousand,
it is clear that every vote cost the candidate at least one dollar and perhaps even
six dollars. This amount is much higher than the current per voter cost of an
election campaign.[38] The difference is that one dollar was normally the equivalent of a full day's wages in 1904; in the 1970s it is equal to, roughly, fifteen
minutes working time. The implications of this for the party system were
immense.

Unfortunately, in discussing the extent of corruption, we must rely on
impressionistic evidence. H.J. Hanham's claim that, for Britain, election petitions
are the best indicator of the scale of corruption[39] is not so valid for Canada, even
though the procedure was similar. Under the provisions of the Controverted
Elections Act of 1874 petitions against a candidate's election were tried before a
single judge who reported to the House of Commons, which could then take
action. Normally, the House failed to act. Like the election agent, required by
the same act and so crucial in electoral reform in other nations, the election
petition was scandalously abused in Canada, with many innocent candidates
being victimized and notorious rascals escaping unscathed.[40] Petitions were
costly – a thousand dollar deposit was required – and if the judges' scrutiny was

37 *Reminiscences* (Toronto, 1912), 125-6.
38 A Candidate in the Late Elections, 'Electoral Management,' 316-18. See also H.B. Ames,
   'The Organization of Political Parties in Canada,' American Political Science
   Association, *Proceedings* (27-30 Dec. 1911), 183-5. On contemporary elections, see
   Canada, *Report of the Committee on Election Expenses* (Ottawa, 1966), especially the
   special studies.
39 *Elections and Party Management: Politics in the Age of Gladstone and Disraeli* (London, 1959), 262.
40 The courts were largely responsible for weakening the potential good of the provision
   that an agent be appointed through whom all donations and expenditures must pass. See
   Ward, *Canadian House of Commons*, chap. 15; and Canada, *Report of the Committee on
   Election Expenses*, 15-25. As Ward remarks (p. 259), 'almost from the beginning the
   provisions of the law have been reasonably adequate, and have been uniformly
   disobeyed.'

too intense one's own party might also emerge tainted. The expense and the danger led both parties to arrange 'saw-offs,' a quite illegal practice whereby the two parties mutually agreed to withdraw or not to submit petitions. The widespread use of 'saw-offs' is illustrated in J.W. Dafoe's biography of Laurier's minister of the interior, Clifford Sifton. After the 1900 election, both parties met and agreed to drop all pending election petitions. Sifton for the Grits and Hugh John Macdonald for the Tories were responsible for enforcing this arrangement in the Canadian west. In most constituencies there were no problems, but only the stern intervention of the local Liberal candidate, Walter Scott, enabled Sifton to squelch a petition against the Conservative candidate in West Assiniboia. Sifton's note of appreciation to Scott reveals the motives behind the 'saw-off' as well as the high priority placed upon party discipline:

It may seem peculiar politics to take so much trouble to secure a man like [Nicholas F.] Davin in his seat, but the effort is not at all wasted when the honour of the government is at stake, and when the confining of the party to some kind of discipline is at stake. There are occasions when the members of the government have to take great responsibility and have to depend upon their friends to see them through, otherwise a party would go to pieces and the tail would be wagging the dog, with the result that the dog would grow mad and probably die of hydrophobia.[41]

Although politicians were wary, election petitions were nevertheless a common feature of Canadian political life, particularly in the early post-Confederation period. Because their number may serve as a rough guide to the scale of corruption, a close examination of their frequency has been undertaken. Table 1.1 indicates both the extraordinary prevalence of petitions and an irregular pattern which is undoubtedly the result of 'saw-offs.' There is little consistency in the petitions: appeals were equally frequent from rural and urban ridings, old and new provinces.[42] What is clear, however, is that when the parties neglected to 'saw-off' there was sufficient cause to protest over one-third of the seats of the House of Commons. One can therefore certainly conclude that electoral corruption was a major feature of Canadian politics before the First World War.

41 Dafoe, *Clifford Sifton*, 197.
42 The success of the petitions varied greatly. Many judges simply delayed the cases until another election was held which voided the petition. There were several ridings which repeatedly had petitions lodged after an election, but there is no clear breakdown as there may have been in Britain. See William Gwyn, *Democracy and the Cost of Politics in Britain* (London, 1962), 64-70; and Hanham, *Elections and Party Management*, 262 ff.

TABLE 1.1

Election petitions in Canada in general elections, 1867-1911

Election	Petitions	Total seats	Election	Petitions	Total seats
1867	21	181	1891*	80	215
1872	55	200	1896	31	213
1874*	65	206	1900	21	214
1878	43	206	1904	27	214
1882	47	211	1908†	12	221
1887	25	215	1911	9	221

*The 1874 election petitions were a test of the new act; 49 members were unseated through petitions. In 1891, 40 members were unseated.
†The 1908 election was hailed by both Borden and Laurier as the 'cleanest' ever fought. See Borden, *Memoirs*, I, 103-4.
Source: The figures are compiled from Ward, *Canadian House of Commons*, chap. 14, and from the relevant parliamentary *Journals*.

Nevertheless, legislative corruption is a better known form of corruption to students of Canadian history. The 'great scandals' ranging from the Pacific Scandal of the 1870s to the Rivard Affair of the 1960s were nearly all of this character. Legislative corruption is best defined as the influencing of legislation or administrative regulation through bribery or promise of position by an affected group. The McGreevy Scandal of the 1890s is an excellent example. Thomas McGreevy, a party 'bagman' in the 1880s, arranged that Quebec businesses receiving government contracts or subsidies should remit a portion of their profits to the party coffers. This arrangement was exposed by Israel Tarte, and the result was highly deleterious to Quebec Conservatism. Almost simultaneously, Honoré Mercier's provincial government in Quebec, Liberal in all but name, was dismissed for similar practices. Thus both parties were stained, and, in the future, they were more reluctant to expose the sins of the other.

A listing of incidents of legislative corruption would be very long and quite pointless. There are two more important questions to consider: first, the attitude towards 'conflict of interest,' and, secondly, the needs which legislative corruption fulfilled. The difference between modern notions of public and private interests and those of a century ago is well illustrated by Sir Allan MacNab's famous declaration in 1853: 'Railways are my politics.' The meaning is clear: MacNab's private interests were also his public ones, and his splendid mansion, Dundurn Castle, is solid testimony to the lucrativeness of such an attitude. As the nineteenth century progressed the willingness of politicians to be as candid as MacNab had been in the 1850s decreased, but some politicians continued to be identified as the representatives of special interests. Thus Sir Alexander Tilloch Galt, a Father of Confederation, was regarded as the lobbyist for certain railway companies with which he was associated. The financier Rodolphe Forget, a Conservative MP after 1904, while simultaneously president or director of twenty-nine companies, did not even consider disqualifying himself if one of his numerous enterprises was affected by a proposal under debate. Indeed, Forget believed that his direct interest made him especially qualified to speak on the matter.[43] Another member, John Charlton, a southwestern Ontario lumberman strongly in favour of reciprocity and, on occasion, commercial union, was even known as 'the member from Michigan.'

Galt, Forget, and Charlton were all connected with economic concerns highly dependent upon government regulation or support. Political participation gained for these men protection and advantage in their private affairs. They saw no moral stigma attached to such activities; quite the contrary, they believed their role was a natural and valuable one given Canada's overwhelming need for development. Perhaps they were correct. Legislative corruption may have accelerated Canadian economic growth by eliminating bureaucratic tangles and by making the state a much more accessible source of investment capital than the limited Canadian banking system.[44] On a smaller scale, too, a political 'insider's' knowledge could gain the underpaid member a few extra dollars which would enable him to remain in political life. Even Alexander Mackenzie, a paragon of virtue to generations of Canadian students, has been recently discovered 'boodling' with railway funds.[45] Mackenzie, of course, did not publicize this activity, but the norms of political conduct of the time would not have led to severe censuring of such behaviour by politicians. In Charlesworth's words, this was just another 'merry trick' the politician played.

Would men like Galt, Forget, Charlton, and many others have participated in politics without such tangible inducements? Evidence suggests that they would

---

43 Forget was president of the Richelieu and Ontario Navigation Company, Canadian Car Foundry Company, Quebec Railway, Light, Heat and Power Company, Eastern Canadian Steel and Iron Works, and the Quebec and Saguenay Railway. This last concern was rescued from insolvency by the Borden government of which Forget was a member. The Borden Diary indicates a direct relationship. BP, Borden Diary, 1912 and 1913, *passim*. On Forget's activities see H. Morgan, *Canadian Men and Women of the Time* (Toronto, 1912), 410-11.

44 On this subject generally, see Joseph Nye, 'Corruption and Political Development: A Cost-Benefit Analysis,' *American Political Science Review*, XLI (June 1967), 417-27.

45 Pierre Berton, *The National Dream* (Toronto, 1970), 240-8. Mackenzie died a man of modest means. According to his colleague, Cartwright, political exigencies kept him constantly in debt. *Reminiscences*, 49.

not. In pre-war Canada, business, both commercial and industrial, offered such abundant opportunity, prestige, and other rewards that it attracted the most talented of the age. Laurier believed this and a study of any *Who's Who* for the period confirms it.[46] Lacking a national military, intellectual, or traditional élite, the young Canadian state desperately needed the support of the powerful entrepreneurial class, which might otherwise have shunned politics. As Edward Porritt observed: 'in Canada, there are no long traditions of service to the state. Social distinction does not go in the fullest measure to men who are serving the state, except, perhaps, in the highest offices.'[47] What Samuel Huntington has written about developing countries applies also to turn-of-the-century Canada: 'The new millionaires buy themselves seats in the Senate or the House of Lords and thereby become participants in the political system rather than alienated opponents of it, which might have been the case if this opportunity to corrupt the system were denied them.'[48] Corruption in the form of direct and immediate economic benefit was, to a talented and important class, a necessary evil, which drew them into an otherwise unattractive political system.

Less pleasing to the businessman, however, was administrative corruption, which he increasingly identified with inefficiency, and which was a form of corruption that primarily benefited the lower and lower-middle classes. The

---

46 Laurier is paraphrased in Arthur Ford, *As the World Wags On* (Toronto, 1950), 126.

47 *Evolution of the Dominion of Canada* (Yonkers, NY, 1920), 505.

48 *Political Order in Changing Societies* (New Haven and London, 1968), 61. An excellent description of the fashion in which the government wooed financial interests to gain their support for a system of regulation is found in an account of the drafting of the Bank Act of 1871 by George Hague, general manager of the Bank of Toronto at the time:

'We [bankers, ministers, and other parliamentarians] sat in one of the committee rooms of the House, and discussed the bill with a considerable sense of responsibility, being well aware not only that our conclusions would affect the whole banking interests of the country, but every other interest, commercial, manufacturing, and industrial, not to speak of the interests of the government itself.

Many of the directors of the banks and several of their presidents were members of Parliament; some in the Senate, some in the House of Commons. These, of course, sat with us from time to time, so that, though not formally constituted as such, we really were, in effect, a joint committee of Parliament and of bankers.

I have always considered that this gave our Banking Act its peculiar value, in that it expressed the matured judgment, sharpened by experience, of the foremost men in banking, commercial, and political life. After all this preliminary work, in which members of both political parties joined, it may be imagined that the bill passed through Parliament with little criticism and no opposition.'

Hague, *Banking and Commerce* (New York, 1908), 365. See also James Cappon, 'The Party System of Government,' *Queen's Quarterly*, XI (April 1904), 434-6.

Canadian method of appointment to public office was, characteristically, a blend of British and American practice. On the one hand, the British tradition that public servants were officers of the Crown meant that a Jacksonian 'spoils system,' which made a virtue of purging the public service after an election, did not emerge in Canada.[49] On the other hand, North American egalitarian assumptions, the pre-Confederation struggle by the popular legislature to gain control of the political executive, and, not least, the intense demands of the Canadian parties for constituency workers combined to make virtually all *new* appointments to public office political ones. In his study of Saskatchewan Liberalism, David Smith concludes that before 1917 'there was no question but that, excluding the very few non-partisan boards, patronage appointment was the rule for filling government jobs ...' Moreover, Smith discovered that 'there was no distinction drawn between federal and provincial Liberal party organizations ... The same people were active in both. Patronage was clearly federal or provincial in origin, but either might be rewarded to individuals whose claim rested on service in the other realm.'[50]

The extent of the pre-war member's patronage is most difficult to estimate since reliable statistics do not exist on the number of government employees during that period,[51] but much evidence suggests that it was great. For example, W.A. Griesbach, a defeated Conservative candidate in Edmonton in 1911, has described the enormous scope of the duties which he, a party leader, had in his constituency.

I was defeated in Edmonton by nine votes only, but quite heavily defeated in the county districts. The party, however, was returned to power at Ottawa, the result of which was that I controlled the patronage of a large part of the province of Alberta. In short, I became the sole representative of the Government in that area. I found it a full-time job. I was, of course, not paid for doing it. I frequently had to reject proposals made to me for the appointment of individuals to public office and had to advise against a course which could only end in graft, and as I saw it the ultimate destruction of the party. Unfortunately,

49 R. MacGregor Dawson's claim that the years from 1867 to the 1920s were the period of a 'spoils system' in Canada is an overstatement. *The Civil Service of Canada* (Toronto, 1929). For a repudiation, see Hodgetts *et al., The Biography of an Institution*, 10-12.
50 *Prairie Liberalism*, 31, 42; see also J.E. Hodgetts, *The Canadian Public Service: A Physiology of Government, 1867-1970* (Toronto, 1973), 52-4.
51 *Civil Service Employees*, the principal source for the pre-1915 period, omits 'outside' employees for many departments. See the discussion in Urquhart and Buckley, eds., *Historical Statistics*, 607-8. They give the figure of 20,016 full-time civil servants in 1912.

I was like the man who had a bear by the tail. I was loathe to carry on but I dare not let go.[52]

Edmonton's system lacked the sophistication in method of patronage distribution in other centres. In Toronto an advisory board composed of the representatives of Conservative members in the Toronto district and chaired by a full-time party agent forwarded recommendations directly to the appropriate minister in Ottawa.[53] Yet, however the decision was made, the responsibility lay ultimately with the member or, as in Griesbach's case, with the recognized representative of the party in the constituency. The party faithful could not be offended but neither could the utterly incompetent or the immoral be appointed. After all, what could be more damaging politically than a drunken postman who lost a constituent's mail? Griesbach tried to circumvent such problems by appointing from the ranks of the militia (which was largely Tory in his area) on the recommendation of the senior officers. Thus the former North West Mounted Police hero strengthened his favourite institution, the militia, while securing what he thought were sure to be competent and incorruptible public servants. We must remember, however, that this was the idiosyncrasy of a defeated candidate, and one which Griesbach himself admits was highly unpopular with party regulars. Alas, few sitting members could indulge such whims, however patriotic the whim might be.

As the importance of governmental activities increased and as the belief grew that a civil service staffed through political appointments was inefficient, attempts were made to circumscribe the ruling party's freedom to appoint. By 1914 most of the higher posts within the civil service of Canada were held by non-political appointees, although the lower ranks were still overwhelmingly filled with party men. The tenacity with which the members in both parties clung to their right to choose public servants indicates the value which the pre-war politicians attached to patronage within a constituency.

Politically appointed public servants, their relatives and friends, normally formed the core of continuing party organization within the constituency. Equally, or perhaps even more, important in the politician's view was control of the local press. There was scarcely a newspaper in Canada which was not

52 *I Remember* (Toronto, 1946), 342.
53 A.R. Birmingham, Ontario party organizer, to A.E. Kemp, 23 Nov. 1911, PAC, Kemp Papers, v. 1, folder 2. Such boards also existed in Quebec: see James Woodward to Sir George Foster, 17 July 1914, BP, v. 28. Most revealing are the patronage files in the Bristol Papers at the Public Archives of Ontario. These are studied in Norman Ward, 'The Bristol Papers: A Note on Patronage,' *Canadian Journal of Economics and Political Science,* XII (Feb. 1946), 78-87.

affiliated in some fashion with either the Liberal or Conservative parties. In some cases, full or partial ownership explained this attachment; in others, lucrative advertising or publishing contracts; in a few, pure habit alone. The last of these seems to apply in the case of the Toronto *Globe* whose editor John S. Willison wrote to Clifford Sifton in 1901 in answer to criticism of the *Globe*'s lack of 'savagery' with Tories:

The *Globe* owes the Liberal politicians nothing. The Liberal politicians do not contribute one dollar to its support. They hold little of its stock. They receive, however, absolutely without fee or reward the service of one of the very best newspapers in Canada. I think I could prove to you that within the last five years between three and four hundred thousand dollars of party money ... has been put into Liberal papers in Canada, and every cent of these investments *The Globe* as a purely commercial property has had to fight. Not only that: newspaper postage has put upon us an additional annual outlay of ten or twelve thousand dollars. In view of all these facts do you not think that our Liberal friends should be a little more charitable in their criticisms of this paper? Personally I resent the assumption of every Liberal politician that I am his hired man, that he has the right to criticize and condemn me ...[54]

Willison later did become a 'hired man' as editor of the *Toronto News* which the Conservative party rescued from bankruptcy in 1915 with a $50,000 grant.[55] Whatever the method, control of a newspaper was of immense value to the politician, particularly since before 1914 the newspaper was the principal instrument

---

54 Cited in A.H.U. Colquhoun, *Press, Politics and People* (Toronto, 1935), 98-9.
55 Frank Cochrane to Willison, 30 Jan. 1915, PAC, Willison Papers, v. 17. The parties frequently owned newspapers entirely. *Le Canada* was controlled completely by Liberal politicians; see 'Liste des Actionnaires du Canada,' PAC, Laurier Papers, v. 726. Individual politicians controlled other publications, such as Clifford Sifton the *Manitoba Free Press* and Robert Rogers its competition, the *Winnipeg Telegram.* The government in power kept advertising lists which showed which newspapers were eligible for government work. These lists were printed and widely distributed. No attempt was made to keep them confidential. Indeed, anyone who chose to scrutinize the spending of various departments could readily discover the favoured papers. Such lists may be found in the Laurier Papers, pp. 92477 and 98840. On the methods by which the parties controlled the press, see 'Who Owns the Press in Canada?' *Printer and Publisher*, XXIII (Feb. 1914), 58-9; Norman Ward, 'The Press and the Patronage: An Exploratory Operation,' in J.H. Aitchison, ed., *The Political Process in Canada: Essays in Honour of R. MacGregor Dawson* (Toronto, 1963), 3-16; and Paul F.W. Rutherford, 'The People's Press: The Emergence of the New Journalism in Canada, 1869-99,' *Canadian Historical Review*, LVI (June 1975), 169-91.

of communication within most, if not all, constituencies. Both parties had central press bureaux which distributed all the news that the party saw fit to print. The results were sometimes ludicrous. In 1913, when Laurier made a major address on the highly contentious naval bill, J.H. Crocket, the editor of the *Fredericton Gleaner* and a close political ally of the Tory minister Douglas Hazen, who had spoken on the same day as Laurier but on some eminently forgettable matter, shocked even the ardent Tory journalist Arthur Ford with his cable: 'Ignore Laurier entirely. Send Hazen verbatim.'[56] This incident alone would seem to confirm the truth of Willison's 1901 charge that the partisanship of the Canadian press was unsurpassed in any other 'civilized country in the world.'[57]

Perhaps Willison's claim is correct, but it does not explain the causes of what he perceived to be an unfortunate anomaly. We can understand the contrasts of Canadian political life which astounded Siegfried and dismayed Willison if we consider that the political system is a component of the social system. As Karl Deutsch has written: 'If political activity fits well into the context of the other functions [of the social system], it will derive strength from them, both for itself and for the social system as a whole.' If it does not it will weaken the system and ultimately destroy itself.[58] Siegfried in 1904 witnessed a social system where political activity no longer fitted so well. It had at one time: in the absence of ideology, tradition, communications, and even formal governmental structure, the locally centred party system, based upon corruption in its many forms, fulfilled important functions which were inadequately performed by 'culturally approved or more conventional structures.'[59] But by 1904 economic change, transportation improvements, urbanization, and industrialization had altered the social system, leading to the emergence of many groups, such as farm associations, religious and suffrage movements, which defined national goals that transcended and, in many cases, repudiated local interests. These groups often became islands within Canadian political society, and, in contrast to a century earlier, these islands, where the touch of party was light, ceased to be primarily geographical and had become social, intellectual, and economic. In this transformation resided the fundamental challenge to the existing party system which Siegfried sensed but did not explain.

A response to this challenge was most difficult for Canadian politicians, for as Canada extended herself towards the west and the north she encountered once

---

56 *As the World Wags On*, 42-3.
57 Cited in Colquhoun, *Press, Politics and People*, 97.
58 *Politics and Government* (Boston, 1970), 133.
59 Merton, *Social Theory and Social Structure*, 134.

again the problems she had faced earlier in the south and the east. Possessing within itself many political cultures at greatly differing stages of development, Canada's pre-war political system inevitably exhibited great tension. An economic historian has argued that a society first confronts 'problems of solidarity' or integration, then, 'those of systemic goal attainment, and finally, those of adaptation.'[60] In the first decades of the twentieth century Canada faced the problems of integration and goal attainment simultaneously. In the northwest integration was of paramount concern, but among the older settlers of Ontario and many of their children then making new homes in the west or in the new cities of the east, political and social movements arose to seek specific national goals. For them, the nation had already become a community which could define and realize common ends. What were these common ends? How would they be expressed? In 1900, Canada's politicians could give few answers.

60 Bert Hoselitz, 'Levels of Economic Performance and Bureaucratic Structures,' in Joseph La Palombara, ed., *Bureaucracy and Political Development* (Princeton, 1963), 188.

2

A party in opposition: the Conservatives 1901–11

How does an opposition party leader organize his party for victory when he is denied all but a few drops of that lifeblood of political existence, patronage? This was the question facing Robert Borden, the new leader of the Conservative party in 1901. The answer was not clear, but Borden's attempts to discover it form an interesting chapter in Canadian political history. Between 1901 and 1911 the Conservatives under Borden became the focus of an uncertain but often creative experiment in transformation. The pressure for such change came from the leader, from a few Conservative members of Parliament sharing his views, and from increasingly powerful groups outside Parliament to whom Borden turned in lieu of organized Conservative support. The resistance to reform arose among the majority of party backbenchers, lower-level party officials, and financial and commercial interests traditionally influential within the Conservative party. The succession of Conservative defeats after 1896 reinforced both factions in their beliefs. To the resisters, Borden's tentative changes bore the responsibility for past failures; to Borden, the party reactionaries had caused the defeats. In 1910 and 1911 these antagonistic viewpoints met in an open clash. This collision, which improbably culminated in a Conservative victory in September 1911, reflected and even perhaps predetermined the political events, alliances, and divisions of the succeeding ten years, particularly the politically complex Union government formed in 1917. To examine the creative pressures exerted within the Conservative party is to study a mirror of the changes throughout Canadian political life.

LEADERSHIP AND POLICY

During the first three decades of Canada's existence the Conservative party was the party of Confederation, the political embodiment of the spirit of 1867. By 1901, however, the party was in opposition and without Macdonald, and lacked such a clear definition. Party differences seemed to be less meaningful and less fundamental. The issue of the survival of Confederation had all but vanished from the political arena; while annexation to the United States and its counterpart, imperial enthusiasm, which had greatly vexed Canadians until recently, now seemed condemned to political death by the mutual consent of both the Liberal and Conservative parties. More than anything else, the ease of the transition from Conservatism to Liberalism in 1896 had produced this widespread sense that party differences had disappeared. The Fielding budget, imperial preference, and Laurier's knighthood further confirmed this belief. While the struggle continued with flourish and fury in the constituencies, national political leaders and commentators hailed the new comity as they groped for an explanation of its emergence.

When the seventy-nine-year-old Sir Charles Tupper led the Tories to a second consecutive defeat in 1900, the 'Cumberland war-horse' knew that he must give way. The Tuppers — Sir Charles and his talented but unpopular son, Sir Charles Hibbert — were reluctant to lose the leadership, but they knew they could prevent the choice of anyone abhorrent to them and, given the absence of a clearly recognized alternative leader, probably nominate the successor. Most of the members of Parliament and senators who gathered in a caucus room on 5 February 1901 to choose the new leader were aware of and accepted the Tuppers' view of the role they would play. After courteously considering some of the party's old warriors, including George E. Foster, J.G. Haggart, and Clarke Wallace, and two unlikely French Canadians — Thomas Chase Casgrain, the prosecutor of Quebec's most recent martyrs, Riel and Mercier, and Boer War supporter Frederick D. Monk — the younger Tupper proposed the name of Robert Borden for the party leadership. Although his principal qualification seems to have been his earlier law partnership with Tupper, the device was nevertheless successful: Borden, a member for only four years, was unanimously chosen leader.[1] The many Tupper enemies were either weary of the fray or, more likely, simply stayed away from a meeting which they could not control.

---

1 This account is taken mainly from the *Montreal Star*, 7 Feb. 1901, and J.C. Hopkins, *The Canadian Annual Review, 1901* (Toronto, 1902), 436. The former account is obviously the product of a 'leak' and differs substantially from the one in Borden's *Memoirs* which minimizes Tupper's role in the selection. See H. Borden, ed., *Robert Laird Borden: His Memoirs* (Toronto, 1938), I, 72-5; also *Toronto World*, 20 July 1905, and R.C. Brown, *Robert Laird Borden: A Biography, 1854-1914* (Toronto, 1975), I, 47-9. The younger Tupper had raised the issue of the leadership with Borden over two months before the meeting, although Borden appears to have forgotten this contact in his *Memoirs*. See Borden to Tupper, 5 Dec. 1900, PABC, C.H. Tupper Papers, 1914-16. Borden's experience included party organization work for Tupper in Nova Scotia: Borden to C.H. Tupper, *ibid.*; and C. Tupper to C.H. Tupper, 15 Aug. 1897, PAC, Charles Tupper Papers, v. 11.

What does the choice of Borden tell us about the character of the Conservative party and of Canadian politics? First, it substantiates the impression of Canadian party politics as predominantly local in orientation. The method of choice of the new leader minimized rather than created public excitement. No thought was given to consultation with Conservatives throughout the Dominion. Indeed, the number of politicians at the leadership caucus suggests that there was not even much interest in the choice among Tory parliamentarians themselves; in fact only 70 of 112 eligible parliamentarians attended. Here surely is further evidence that national party leadership was less important than local party leadership, and that national consciousness in the modern sense of nationally focused politics was yet unformed. Another striking illustration of this is the prominence that Canada's largest English-language daily, the *Montreal Star*, gave to the leadership change – two columns on page six. The *Star* was certainly concerned: its owner, Hugh Graham, regarded himself as the *éminence grise* of the Tory party, but apparently the *Star*'s readers were not thought to be much interested.

Secondly, the selection of Borden and the manner in which it was accomplished betrays the transitional and uncertain state of the party.[2] The great names of the Tory past, the Tuppers, Sir John Thompson, and, most of all, Macdonald, were all absent from the Parliament of 1901 and with them had disappeared the style of leadership and most of the political controversies which they embodied. Even George Foster, who for all his deficiencies was a powerful link with earlier Tory greatness, was not on the Tory front bench because of his election defeat. Borden was, it is true, the choice of the past, but he was scarcely representative of it. That Borden was given 'an absolutely free hand [by the caucus] to do whatever he pleases' means that the Tories recognized that the past could not be recaptured and that the party must come to terms with the success of Sir Wilfrid Laurier and the new political milieu. Borden therefore possessed an opportunity which his predecessors – Tupper, Sir Mackenzie Bowell, Thompson, and Sir John Abbott – never really had: the opportunity to reconstruct the party in his own image.

Borden had more freedom than past leaders but, in his biographer's words, he sensed '... that his work would be slow, demanding, often discouraging. He recognized that it would call for patience and understanding far beyond what he had been called upon to exhibit in his legal career ... The security of the law, of

---

2 It should be noted that there was an agreement never publicly stated that Borden would serve as temporary leader for a year. This was undoubtedly an 'escape clause' in the event that Borden proved entirely unsuitable. Borden, *Memoirs*, I, 73. Laurier also began with a one-year probationary term.

its established precedents, of its traditional procedures, of its professional respect, had no real equivalent in politics.'[3] And there certainly was much discouragement and even embarrassment in Borden's first few years as leader when he could use only what he inherited. During 1903 and 1904, for example, the inexperienced leader became involved in an extraordinary plot with Montreal Conservative interests, the Canadian Pacific Railway, and Hugh Graham, which included bribery of journalists, resignations of Quebec Liberal candidates late in the campaign, and large transfers of funds to the Conservative party in return for certain promises. The plot failed and so did Borden when Laurier triumphed in the 1904 election.[4] Not surprisingly, Borden's initial reaction to the defeat was a decision to return to Halifax where before he entered politics in 1896 he had earned $30,000 annually. His wife disliked politics, and the performance of his 'extremely lazy' caucus frustrated him. The caucus, he told his wife, 'continually neglected' what he considered to be 'matters of moment.'[5] But Borden did not return to Halifax, to the security of the law and his comfortable income. His impulse to flee was halted by a unanimous appeal to his sense of duty by the Conservative caucus, which overrode – not for the last time – the wishes of Borden's wife.[6]

Having decided to remain, Borden began to reorganize his party and to lure new interests and men to the Tory cause, and it was then that policy became important. An opposition party without much patronage had little chance in a party-to-party confrontation. If, however, the opposition could attract significant 'interests' – we call them 'pressure groups' today – their financial and other resources could dramatically alter the political balance. By 1905 there were several groups which had organized their committed followers and, indeed, were performing many of the functions which parties had previously undertaken. They defined national goals and in many cases repudiated local interests, and they existed as alternate forms of socialization to the political party. There were many such groups who shared Borden's dissatisfaction with Laurier Liberalism: 'farm and labour leaders who believed that their followers had received less than a fair share of the new affluence, French-Canadian *nationalistes* fearful for

3 Brown, *Borden*, 51.
4 For fuller details, see my 'Sir Robert Borden, the Conservative Party and Political Change in Canada, 1901-1920,' unpublished PhD thesis, Harvard University, 1973, 72n. Borden himself was possibly corruptly involved in the plot.
5 Brown, *Borden*, 83-6, and Borden to Laura Borden, 5 July 1904, cited in *ibid.*, 87.
6 See Laura Borden to Borden, 11 Feb. 1906, PAC, Borden Papers (BP), v. 327, for evidence of Mrs Borden's dislike of politics, apparently a common trait among Canadian prime ministers' wives.

the future of their society's distinctiveness, feminists demanding political equality, urban reformers concerned about slums and sanitation, prohibitionists zealous to "Banish the Bar," and advocates of "Canadianization" uneasy about the foreign immigrant.' The differences among these groups were great, and Borden knew that any dreams that all reformers might rally to the Tory standard were chimerical. Yet each group in its own way did assert, in the words of Craig Brown and Ramsay Cook, 'the increasing irrelevance of Laurier's kind of liberalism' and thus represented 'the search for a new public philosophy.'[7]

It was to this search and to this mood that Borden's Halifax Platform of 1907 responded. Historians have devoted much attention to the intellectual origins and significance of these Halifax proposals; what concerns us here is their political utility. The platform, Borden wrote, would be 'an effective and honest rallying cry which will appeal to the more progressive spirits and communities.'[8] Like W.S. Gilbert, Borden knew:

That every boy and every gal
That's born into the world alive
Is either a little Liberal,
Or else a little Conservative.

But little boys grew up (until 1917 a politician did not need to worry about little girls). And although usually reluctant to cast off their political birthright, sometimes they did – in fact, Borden himself had.[9] Those who did so were likely to be the most thoughtful, intelligent, and concerned – in short, the 'more progressive spirits and communities.' Thus the planks of the Halifax Platform promising 'civil service reform' and 'clean elections' would appeal to the many Canadians who felt wronged by the strong political machines and who might be willing to become Conservatives. The 'restoration' of public lands to Saskatchewan and Alberta, rural free mail delivery, and a public utilities commission to regulate railways and telephone and telegraph companies would surely win the approval of those western 'farm leaders' who believed their followers had not received their 'fair share.' There were few independents in Canadian politics, but given the extraordinary stability of Liberal and Conservative party support (in the three elections, 1900, 1904, and 1908, the Tory popular vote varied only

---

7 R.C. Brown and Ramsay Cook, *Canada, 1896-1921: A Nation Transformed* (Toronto, 1974), 186.
8 See Brown, *Borden*, 129-35. The quotation is from Borden to R.P. Roblin, 2 Aug. 1907, BP, v. 351.
9 See his *Memoirs*, I, 42.

5 per cent), the independent's choice was all important. Because a very small swing could mean success in the election, the independent or 'floating vote' was most carefully tended.[10] This was the essence of political leadership, and Robert Borden eventually proved to be its master.

There were three major groupings which Borden eventually drew into alliances of varying degrees of formality with the federal Conservative party: the Quebec *nationalistes*, the imperialists and 'progressives' of English Canada, and the Conservative provincial premiers, who of course would have voted Tory federally but who, without Borden's wooing, might not have worked very hard for them. Yet, while these groups may have provided the margin of victory, they did not provide its foundation. This was the part of the Conservative voters and their representatives, the Conservative members of Parliament, and for that reason they deserve our first attention.

RANK AND FILE

Borden regarded his party's rank and file as narrow men of limited talent. Thus he wrote to a friend who had objected to his strong support for a bill providing for an increase in the members' indemnity: 'Those who are opposed to any increase of indemnity have their views altered if they had undergone my own experience in endeavouring to get representative men to enter public life. This is rapidly becoming impossible under present conditions.'[11] What type of men were entering public life? Laurier once described a member's typical career pattern: '... In the average rural riding, the large majority of all ridings, the member had served in township and county councils and possibly been warden. This has brought him close acquaintance with the electorate. He is an honest, faithful conscientious member, but with no outstanding ability.'[12]

An examination of the characteristics of the Conservative members largely verifies Laurier's impressions. Unexciting, unambitious, and always alert to the whims and needs of their constituencies, the Conservative rank and file were an unimpressive lot. But however unimpressive, they *were* the Conservative party to most Canadians and therefore should be studied in some depth. Fortunately, the diligence of contemporary chroniclers, of the Public Archives of Canada, and of

10 Interestingly, the stability of partisan choice remains in those areas of Canada where third parties have made relatively minor inroads, namely the Maritimes and Quebec. See Mildred Schwartz, *Politics and Territory: The Sociology of Regional Persistence in Canada* (Montreal and London, 1974), 148-53. On the importance and character of the floating vote, see V.O. Key, *The Responsible Electorate* (New York, 1966).

11 *Memoirs*, I, 150; see also Borden to Laura Borden, 5 July 1904, cited in Brown, *Borden*, 87.

12 Cited in Arthur Ford, *As the World Wags On* (Toronto, 1950), 126.

Norman Ward, whose 1950 study of representation has remained unsurpassed, has created a strong framework upon which to carry out an analysis.[13] For our purposes here the year 1909 has been selected to examine the Conservative members — Borden had been leader of the party for eight years and within two years was to come to power.

When Borden assumed the leadership, Conservative representation was geographically maldistributed although the Conservative popular vote was relatively high in all provinces. This pattern continued through the next two elections, as can be seen in Table 2.1. The stability and the pattern are striking, as are the inequities of the electoral system. Ontario was the core of the Conservative party, electing more than half of the Tory representation throughout this period. Borden could not capture his home territory, the Maritimes. In the west, the Conservative provincial governments of Manitoba and British Columbia used their prestige and patronage to advance the federal cause; but the Conservatives were distressingly weak in the most rapidly growing provinces, Saskatchewan and Alberta, which, it should be noted, were Liberal creations in 1905. Yet it was Quebec which kept the Conservatives on the opposition benches. Whether Louis Riel's execution, Tory indifference, or Laurier's French-Canadian background were responsible for the death of Conservative Quebec, each succeeding election confirmed that the province was now a Liberal bastion.

Given the predominance of Ontario representation, one would expect that the main racial and religious characteristic of Conservative members would be British Protestant. Still, the degree to which British Protestants did dominate the Tory caucus in 1909 is nevertheless quite astonishing (see Table 2.2). That Borden was bound by the prejudices and perceptions of middle-class English Canada is therefore quite understandable. The well-known witticism that the Church of England is the Tory party at prayer might properly be applied to the Conservative party of Canada in 1909 if one added to the Anglican total the Methodists and the Presbyterians. Canadian Conservatism bore the unmistakable marks of its origins, British and established; but for all its outward similarity, it possessed little of the excellence of its British counterpart — it was, at best, a pale reflection.

---

13 The sources consulted are Henry Morgan, *Canadian Men and Women of the Time* (Toronto, 1912); J.K. Johnston, *The Canadian Directory of Parliament* (Ottawa, 1968); E.J. Chambers, ed., *The Canadian Parliamentary Guide, 1909* (Ottawa, 1909); *ibid., 1910; Fifth Census of Canada*, II (Ottawa, 1913); and Ward, *The Canadian House of Commons: Representation* (Toronto, 1950). On the subject of the reliability of statistics, Ward cites J.F.S. Ross: 'Gaps there are and, it is to be feared, errors; but I am satisfied that they are not so extensive, nor of such a character, as to impair the general accuracy of the conclusions reached.' This admirable warning should also be applied to the data given in this paper.

TABLE 2.1

Conservative support in Canadian general elections, 1900-8

	1900			1904			1908		
	Conservative seats	Total seats	Percentage of vote	Conservative seats	Total seats	Percentage of vote	Conservative seats	Total seats	Percentage of vote
Prince Edward Island	2	5	48.2	3	4	50.9	1	4	49.6
Nova Scotia	5	20	48.3	0	18	44.5	6	18	49.0
New Brunswick	5	14	47.8	6	13	48.8	2	13	46.2
Quebec	8	65	43.5	11	65	43.4	11	65	40.8
Ontario	56	92	49.7	48	86	50.3	48	86	51.4
Manitoba	3	7	48.2	3	10	41.8	8	10	51.5
British Columbia	2	6	40.9	0	7	38.8	5	7	46.8
Northwest Territories	0	4	44.9	3	10	41.5			
Yukon				1	1	58.6	0	1	10.8
Alberta*							3	7	44.4
Saskatchewan*							1	10	36.8
Total	81	213	47.4	75	214	46.9	85	221	47.0

*The provinces of Alberta and Saskatchewan were formed in 1905 from the former Northwest Territories.
Source: M.C. Urquhart and K.H. Buckley, eds., *Historical Statistics of Canada* (Toronto, 1965), section W.

TABLE 2.2

Religious and national backgrounds of Conservative members in 1909

	Number	Percentage of total caucus	Percentage of group in population
Anglican	33	37.9	14.47
Presbyterian	17	19.5	15.48
Methodist	18	20.6	14.98
Roman Catholic	12	13.7	39.31
Baptist	2	2	5.31
Other Protestant	5	5	10.45
British	79	90.8	54.08
French Canadian	6	6.9	28.51
German	2	2.3	5.46
Austro-Hungarian	0	0	1.79
Others	0	0	10.16

Where an individual is of mixed British and French parentage he is included as a French Canadian (for example, Monk). In all other cases the father's nationality has been used to determine the member's nationality.
Source: *The Canadian Parliamentary Guide, 1909*, and Morgan, *Canadian Men and Women of the Time.*

One reason for this weakness was, of course, the absence in Canada of any hereditary aristocracy trained from birth for state service and endowed with ample means. There was a very rapid turnover of members and political inexperience was all too common. Fully 45.9 per cent of the Conservative members in 1909 had been elected first in 1908, an election with an overall turnover of 38.4 per cent. The average parliamentary experience of Conservative members in 1908 was 5.8 years, the median only 4 years. Borden's difficulties stemmed from the fact that there were too many new members who were willing to innovate but lacked prestige and political skill and too many veterans who feared change yet possessed manifold political skills and prestige.[14] The inexperience and the high rate of turnover indicates that the Conservatives were having great difficulty

14 Length of service of Conservative members in 1909:

Years served	Number of members	Years served	Number of members
1	40	9 to 12	1
2 to 4	3	12 to 18	8
4 to 6	21	18 and over	6
6 to 9	8		

The Canadian Parliamentary Guide, 1909. All calculations are my own. The turnover of members in Canada has always been high. See Ward, *ibid.*, 115-17. A high median age is quite common among opposition parties, but is not of course desirable.

in retaining their members. Limited interest in politics, faulty organization, and frustration with the party itself are all possible explanations for this failure. Even more serious in light of the number of new Tory members in 1908 is the information that the median age for Conservative members in 1909 was 51.5 compared to an overall parliamentary median of 50. The Liberals, thirteen years in power, were a younger party than the Conservatives. If little comfort could be derived from these statistics, greater unease undoubtedly arose from the knowledge that, despite Borden's recruitment efforts, nearly all the new members were largely cast in the mould of the old.

The Conservative members of Parliament were, on the whole, men who had entered politics after years of participation in the affairs of their constituency. Typical careers would be those of Richard Blain, MP for Peel in Ontario, G.H. Barnard of Victoria, and Pierre Blondin of Champlain in Quebec. Blain entered federal politics at the age of forty-three after serving on a town council for ten years and as reeve and as warden of the county. Barnard, a lawyer, had been elected for Victoria in 1908 at forty years of age after serving as an alderman and as mayor of Victoria. This pattern transcended cultural boundaries: Blondin, also a lawyer, had been the clerk of the circuit court for Champlain and an alderman in the town of Grand-Mère. Of the 87 Tories elected in 1908, 42 identified themselves as having local political experience (undoubtedly many more neglected to mention it); 23 noted that they were mayors of towns before their election to Parliament.[15]

The occupations of the Conservative members in 1909 reflect the local interest of the candidate:

Lawyers	26	Doctors	10	Journalists	3
Merchants	13	Farmers	10	Others	6
Manufacturers	10	Financiers	6	Unknown	3

Very few had advanced training of any type. If one excludes legal training from university education (but includes lawyers with degrees), twenty-two Conservatives had university degrees, only two of these degrees in science or engineering and ten in medicine. The manufacturers in Tory ranks scarcely fitted Borden's rather romantic conception of that group: they were such men as John Stanfield, the owner of a knitting mill and a notorious political manipulator, or George Taylor, the Conservative whip since the time of Macdonald and 'an Orangeman and proud of it.' The merchants and doctors were mostly from small towns as were the few journalists and publishers, professions which were often fertile sources for political talent but not for the Conservative party in 1909.

15 For an evaluation over time of pre-parliamentary experience, see Ward, *ibid.*, 121-4.

The lawyers predominated, as they always have in Canadian politics where the propinquity of the court room and the political back room has been marked.

What, then, can be said about the Conservative rank and file in 1909? Earl Grey, one of a long series of governors-general who had great contempt for Canadian politicians, thought he had found a perfect descriptive phrase for the Tories: 'the stupid party.' One suspects that Borden, in his more despondent moments, might have agreed. More fundamentally, however, the disappointment of Borden, Grey, and many others lay not with the men but with the representative system which produced them. The weak members were a symptom of a weak party and of an electorate blind to any political world beyond their own constituency. Borden favoured, to use Max Weber's term, but not in Weber's sense, a 'plutocratic recruitment'[16] of those who would 'live exclusively for politics and not off politics,' men who were not merely the tool of 'local notables' but the representatives of the best elements in the nation. Could the representative system of constituencies in a land so broad, spiritually and geographically, as Canada bring forth not delegates but trustees who would subordinate local to national ends? Between the Scylla of plebiscitarian democracy and the Charybdis of political feudalism, Borden sought a clear course.

His course was obscured by lack of information about who voted for the Conservatives; he simply did not possess the sensitive political antennae of Mackenzie King, Laurier, or Macdonald whose wide range of correspondents fed them political details which they quickly assimilated and used. Nor did he have the public opinion surveys which a later generation of politicians have both cherished and feared. While the historian also suffers from this absence, some conclusions about voting behaviour are possible. But before we examine how people voted, we should ask who voted in the elections of 1900, 1904, and 1908.

By 1900 'the notion that the franchise was a trust accompanying property, rather than a right normally accompanying citizenship'[17] had all but disappeared. With the adoption of provincial franchises in 1898 full manhood suffrage obtained in all provinces but Quebec and Nova Scotia. The effects upon the size of the electorate in the various provinces can be seen in Table 2.3. A large percentage of those who could vote did, an indication of partisan loyalty as well as of political interest. In 1900, 77.4 per cent of those on the voters' list voted;

16 'Politics as a Vocation,' in H.H. Gerth and C. Wright Mills, eds., *From Max Weber* (New York, 1958), 85-6. Weber uses the term 'plutocratic recruitment' to refer to the recruitment of those who are economically dependent on politics. Borden accepted this, but he also saw that economic freedom alone was not enough; politicians should be 'detached' in a much wider sense.

17 Ward, *Canadian House of Commons*, 225.

TABLE 2.3

The franchise in 1900

	Constitu-encies in sample	Average electorate	Average population	Average electorate as percentage of average population
Ontario	12	5530	20,420	27.1
Quebec	10	4905	23,262	21.1
Nova Scotia	4	5802	23,382	24.8
New Brunswick	4	5328	19,730	27.3
Prince Edward Island*			20,652	
Manitoba	3	11,282	40,443	27.9
British Columbia	3	5443	24,903	21.9

*Under provincial law the Island had no voters' lists since open voting still applied there.
Source: Ward, *Canadian House of Commons*, 225.

in 1904, 71.6 per cent; and in 1908, 70.3 per cent. In certain provinces the turnouts were astonishingly high (in 1900 in Ontario 85 per cent voted and in Nova Scotia 75 per cent); in other provinces rather low, undoubtedly a product of such factors as distance from polls, bad weather, recent immigration, and lack of interest in the campaign (in 1900 in British Columbia 59 per cent, in Manitoba 64, in Quebec 69, and in New Brunswick 76).[18]

Were these voters inspired to vote for the party or for the candidate? No conclusive answer is possible, but the presence of several double-member constituencies does give some indication that the party was paramount in the decision of most Canadians. The strongest evidence for this is the relatively small difference between the vote of the two candidates running for the same party. Only once between 1904 and 1911 did the margin between the candidates of the same party in the three double-member constituencies vary more than 6 per cent. Similarly, a close analysis of double constituencies in the last decades of the nineteenth century led one analyst to conclude, with André Siegfried, that for most Canadians the party was 'almost a sacred institution, to be foresaken only at the cost of one's reputation and career.'[19]

18 H.A. Scarrow, 'Patterns of Voter Turnout in Canada,' in John Courtney, ed., *Voting in Canada* (Scarborough, 1967), 105, 200; and M.C. Urquhart and K.H. Buckley, eds., *Historical Statistics of Canada* (Toronto, 1965), 616.

19 Douglas Baldwin, 'Political and Social Behaviour in Ontario, 1879-1891: A Quantitative Approach,' unpublished PhD thesis, York University, 1973, 274-5. On the basis of a study of polling districts in Ontario, Baldwin claims (p. 277) that at least 68 per cent of the voters in federal elections between 1882 and 1891 voted for the same party every time. See also Norman Ward, 'Voting in Canadian Two-Member Constituencies,' in Courtney, *Voting in Canada*, 127.

If stability and partisanship were the salient features of Conservative support, what were the foundations of these features? As can be seen in Table 2.1, the Conservatives did exceedingly well in 1908 and 1911 in three of the four provinces which had Conservative governments. In the provinces with Tory governments in 1908, the Tories won 67 per cent of the seats and 54 per cent of the total vote. It is not surprising that Borden considered control of provincial governments the stepping stones to federal victory.

In separate studies Douglas Baldwin and Kenneth M. McLaughlin have examined in considerable detail the basis of party support in the last years of the nineteenth century. Baldwin found that in Ontario Macdonald's Tories received support from all areas, but especially strong support in cities and from Anglicans and Irish Protestants. Interestingly, he discovered that Conservative support among Franco-Ontarians declined considerably between 1879 and 1891. In his analysis of the 1896 election, McLaughlin argues that there is 'no statistical evidence to support the existence of a "Catholic vote." ' He also claims that Protestants similarly refused to place 'religion before the interests of their party.' In Quebec, 1896 witnessed a change as French Canadians sought leadership and stability under a French-Canadian prime minister, but, McLaughlin strongly emphasizes, Conservatism did not collapse in Quebec.[20] The pattern of support described by Baldwin and McLaughlin was Borden's inheritance from Macdonald and Tupper.

The Conservatives continued to do very well in the cities. Of the 85 seats won by them in 1908 fully 46 per cent were urban at a time when only 30 per cent of all seats were urban.[21] The Anglican support seems to have remained as well: in the ten constituencies[22] where Anglicans made up more than 28 per cent of the population the Tories were victors in nine and took almost 55 per cent of the popular vote in the 1908 election (compared to 47 per cent of the overall vote). The Conservatives also garnered fairly strong support in Quebec in the constituencies where English Canadians made up over 40 per cent of the population,[23] taking 49.5 per cent of the vote and three of the seven constituencies. Nevertheless, Conservative weakness in French-Canadian areas continued. They lost all six constituencies outside of Quebec where French Canadians constituted

---

20 Baldwin, *ibid.*, 116, 140, 262. Liberals obtained strong support from Scotch Presbyterians; McLaughlin, 'Race, Religion and Politics: The Election of 1896 in Canada,' unpublished PhD thesis, University of Toronto, 1975, 426-9.

21 These calculations are my own. Sources are the *Canadian Parliamentary Guide, 1909,* and the *Census of Canada, 1911* (Ottawa, 1913).

22 Victoria City, Lanark South, London, Toronto East, Toronto North, Toronto South, Toronto West, York South, Nanaimo, and Brome (they lost the last).

23 Brome, Montreal Ste Anne, Montreal St Antoine, Argenteuil, Huntingdon, Pontiac, and Stanstead.

more than 50 per cent of the population[24] and won only 39.5 per cent of the popular vote in those constituencies. Of the 48 Quebec constituencies where French Canadians totalled more than three-quarters of the population, the Tories won only five in 1908. Their popular vote in the 48, however, was a more respectable 42.75 per cent.[25] Finally, of the twelve constituencies where 'others' outnumbered 'British' and 'French' combined,[26] the Tories won three (all in Manitoba) and 44 per cent of the popular vote.

In general, then, the Conservatives had a broader base than the character of their Commons membership suggests. While weaker in French Canada and non-British areas than elsewhere, the Tories were certainly far from vanquished, and Borden might conceivably expect a significant Conservative revival in Quebec once the Liberals turned to an English-Canadian leader. In fact, one of the most troubling aspects of the Conservative supporters in the Conservative caucus was their failure to represent Conservative support in the nation. In an age before the party convention, those unrepresented could seldom make their presence felt. The danger lay in the possibility that the leader would see the caucus as the microcosm of Conservatism in Canada and fail to notice how certain elements were absent. Borden, fortunately, managed to retain a perspective, and he did this most effectively by bringing others forward to represent and speak for those who remained without a voice in the caucus.

OUTSIDERS AS INSIDERS

Borden's major goal was to defeat the Laurier Liberals; secondary and complementary goals were surmounting the mediocrity of the parliamentary Conservatives and attracting allies for his battles with Laurier. Great politicians achieve the support and freedom Borden desired by appealing beyond Parliament to the electorate. 'Gladstone,' the Duke of Argyll observed, 'exercises such a sway over the constituencies, that the members are afraid to call their souls their own.'[27]

24 Russell, Prescott, Victoria-Madawaska, Restigouche, Kent, and Gloucester.
25 These are Bagot, Beauce, Beauharnois, Bellechasse, Berthier, Chambly and Vercheres, Champlain, Charlevoix, Chicoutimi and Saguenay, Deux-Montagnes, Dorchester, Drummond-Arthabaska, Gaspé, Joliette, Kamouraska, Labelle, Laprairie and Napierville, L'Assomption, Laval, Lévis, L'Islet, Lotbinière, Maskinonge, Mégantic, Montcalm, Montagny, Montmorency, Mont St Jacques, Mont Ste Marie, Nicolet, Portneuf, Quebec Centre, Quebec East, Quebec County, Richelieu, Richmond Wolfe, Rimouski, Rouville, St Hyacinthe, St Jean Iberville, Shefford, Soulanges, Temiscouta, Terrebonne, Trois-Rivières, Vaudreuil, Wright, and Yamaska.
26 Strathcona, Victoria, Comox-Atlin, Dauphin, Lisgar, Selkirk, Lunenburg, Waterloo North, Humboldt, Mackenzie, Saltcoats, and Saskatoon.
27 Quoted in John Vincent, *The Formation of the Liberal Party, 1857-1868* (London, 1966), 227.

The failure of the Halifax Platform campaign in the election of 1908, when the Tories suffered a second defeat under Borden's leadership, proved that such a direct route was closed to Borden. One alternative was to begin at the lowest level and build a well-structured national organization based upon widespread participation. Not surprisingly, newspaper clippings on Chamberlain's famed 'caucus' are plentiful in the Borden Papers. The influence of such experiments is apparent in a 1903 letter from Borden to a North-West Territories convention chairman: 'No cause however good can prevail unless its supporters are thoroughly organized and equipped for battle. Organization is all important. If the people remain inert the Government naturally falls into the hands of professional politicians, men whose chief interest in the country is their own political existence, men accustomed to rely upon the unscrupulous methods of the machine.'[28]

But Borden was no populist content with vague images of 'the people' liberating themselves, and modern political organizational methods were unknown. Political participation would be primarily educative, with a clear sense of direction, and inspired from above – not by 'professional politicians' but by men with vision and detachment and, in Borden's words, a 'moral earnestness.'[29] If this is a contradiction, it is one shared by the most prominent social thinkers of the age who were so intoxicated by the possibilities of the state that they could not enunciate a coherent and cogent course for popular action.[30] Borden, however, was no philosopher, and action for him meant seeking out men who conformed to his idea of what public men should be. Many he found outside of politics, and we shall deal with these later, but others he found involved in political life, notably the Conservative provincial premiers. In his struggle to remake the party Borden used the premiers to overcome the stagnation of the parliamentary party and to create a new organization which undermined the traditional sources of power in the party. It was, therefore, not simply fortuitous that federal Conservatives did very well wherever provincial Tories held sway.

With the exception of James Whitney, history has not treated the Conservative premiers of the early 1900s well. The scandals and inefficiency surrounding the last years in office of Rodmond Roblin and Richard McBride are as lamentable as they are comic. Yet in 1905 these new governments seemed to be popular, progressive administrations which 'guaranteed stability and positive

28 Borden to Chairman, Conservative Convention, Moose Jaw, 17 March 1903, v. 350.
29 'An Ideal of a Continental Relationship,' 23 March 1910, BP, v. 300.
30 See, for example, Christopher Lasch, *The New Radicalism in America* (New York, 1965), especially chap. 5.

growth.'[31] Borden accordingly decided to link his party's fate to that of these provincial parties. After the 1904 defeat which revealed the bankruptcy of the old party organization, Borden turned to Whitney, McBride, and Roblin for assistance in constructing a new organization.

In Ontario, Borden had worked quite closely with Whitney since 1901, and by 1907 this friendship had become an organizational alliance. During Borden's period of hesitation about political life, Whitney had encouraged him to stay on as leader – indeed, Whitney later claimed that Borden 'was mainly influenced in his decision to remain in public life by a letter which I wrote him on the subject.'[32] In May 1907, after consultations with the premier, Borden created an organization to serve both federal and provincial Conservatism in Ontario with A.E. Kemp, the manufacturer, as financial manager and J.S. Carstairs, an historian, as the organizer. Carstairs later pointed out how indistinguishable the federal and provincial parties became in this new organization:

In the eighty-one federal ridings (without counting the five Torontos) which may be properly considered to be my bailiewick [sic] there are 115 Liberal Conservative Riding Associations, which may be classified as follows:

A. Purely Federal Associations 14
B. Mixed Federal Associations; that is, where two Provincial Organizations have been united to form a Federal Association 6
C. Purely Provincial Associations 35
D. Associations that perform all political functions both Federal and Provincial[33] 60

There remained two nominal organizations, but, as Carstairs' figures suggest, actual work was done in unison in most cases. A newspaper jointly owned was planned for Toronto, but for various reasons the enterprise failed.[34] Whitney

31 Martin Robin, 'British Columbia,' in Robin, ed., *Canadian Provincial Politics* (Scarborough, 1972), 46. See Brown, *Borden*, 132.
32 Whitney to H.H. Ross, 13 Sept. 1907, PAO, Whitney Papers.
33 'Memorandum Concerning the Organization in Ontario,' 23 May 1912, PAC, A.E. Kemp Papers. Whitney's hesitations about a joint organization, which are understandable in light of the patronage demands of federal members, are detailed in Catherine Pick Warner, 'Sir James P. Whitney and Sir Robert L. Borden: Relations between a Conservative Leader and His Federal Party Leader, 1905-1914,' unpublished MPhil thesis, University of Toronto, 1967.
34 See Floyd Chalmers, *A Gentleman of the Press* (Toronto, 1969), 166-9. The plan was to buy out the moribund *Mail and Empire*. Colonel J.B. Maclean acted as the Tory negotiator. Maclean to Kemp, 17 Dec. 1912, Kemp Papers, v.9.

advised Borden on federal party policy and thought that the Halifax Platform 'hit the nail pretty fairly on the head.'[35] Because he believed this and because he believed that Borden would introduce into the federal arena the programmes he advanced provincially, Whitney actively campaigned for Borden in the 1908 election.

In the other provinces ruled by the Tories – British Columbia, Manitoba, and, after 1908, New Brunswick – similar attempts at organizational unity were made. Premiers McBride, Roblin, and Douglas Hazen, then at the height of their popularity, joined Whitney on federal platforms in 1908, their presence itself becoming a campaign issue.[36] After 1908 Martin Burrell, McBride's former secretary, became the British Columbia premier's representative in the federal caucus.[37] For his part, Roblin lent his most powerful deputy, Robert Rogers, to the federal Conservatives to act, according to one report, as the Conservative chief organizer. Rogers' reputation was yet unsullied and Borden's confidant Charles Hamilton even told a story of three *Manitoba Free Press* detectives 'who followed Rogers for months – were in his office as confidential clerks etc. – & got nothing.' More probable was Hamilton's other claim that Rogers was 'a greater campaigner and organizer than Sifton.' These remarkable skills became the property of the federal party after 1908. Rogers' precise role in the organization is unclear, but evidence clearly suggests it was a major and effective one.[38] Borden's tactics were similar in provinces where the Conservatives were in opposition. Charles Tanner, the Conservative leader of the opposition in Nova Scotia, noticed the remarkable change in federal-provincial party relations: unlike Sir

35 Whitney to Borden, 11 Sept. 1907, BP, v. 351. It should be added that Whitney expressed uncertainty that Borden had gone far enough in advocating public ownership. Earlier evidence of the close consultation between the two can be found in Borden to Whitney, 11 Jan., Whitney Papers, v. 10; Whitney to Borden, 4 Nov. 1907, and Whitney to R.H. Pope, *ibid.*, v. 12.

36 The British Columbia federal and provincial organizations were completely merged by 1911. 'British Columbia Conservative Association,' PABC, McBride Papers, box 1911. Although Hazen's provincial government did aid the federal party, the organizations remained distinct. A.R. Slipp to O. Crocket, MP, University of New Brunswick, Crocket Papers, box 7. Rogers' extensive federal activity suggests a merger, but I was unable to find any evidence in the Manitoba Archives on this. J.C. Hopkins, *The Canadian Annual Review, 1908* (Toronto, 1909), 160.

37 Interview with Mrs Margaret Macintosh (McBride's daughter), Sidney, BC, Oct. 1970.

38 Hamilton to J.S. Willison, 24 May 1908, v. 37, PAC, Willison Papers. Unfortunately the Borden Papers for 1908 are missing, but evidence of Rogers' large role may be found in Borden to Rogers, 25 and 30 Jan., Rogers to Borden, 6 March 1911, BP, v. 133; see also Hugh Graham to Borden, 18 Feb. 1911, BP, v. 327, which tells of Rogers acting as a Borden emissary to Montreal.

Charles Tupper who had 'candidly acknowledged that he had preferred to see the locals in opposition,' Borden took a genuine interest in the fortunes of the provincial party and expected the provincial party to do the same in return.[39]

The rewards of Borden's actions were soon apparent. On the one hand, the campaigns of Whitney, McBride, and Roblin gained decisive victories for the Conservatives in their respective provinces, the only provinces which the federal Tories won in 1908. Furthermore, a great number of youthful, ambitious, and able provincial Conservatives became involved in federal politics with some, such as Burrell, even being elected. Those who remained outside Parliament continued to take part in organizational work for both the provincial and federal parties. The 'sleeping sickness' which had usually afflicted the Tories after earlier elections was thus warded off.[40] Most important, however, was the increased power which the federal-provincial alliance gave Borden within the parliamentary party itself. With the premiers' help, Borden might yet make the federal party his own.

Unfortunately for Borden, there was no Conservative premier of Quebec; indeed, there were few leading Quebec Conservatives. When Borden assumed the leadership of the party in 1901 he had only eight colleagues from Quebec. Obviously something had to be done about this situation, but Borden — a Protestant, unilingual, Halifax lawyer — knew no remedy. Acting upon tradition rather than considered judgment, he moved quickly to appoint a French-Canadian lieutenant.

Borden's choice for the post first held by the great Sir George-Etienne Cartier was Frederick Monk whose principal goal in political life was, by his own admission, an appointment to the judicial bench.[41] During the next three years Monk fought Borden's attempt to ally with Joseph Israel Tarte, who had resigned from Laurier's cabinet, assailed Borden with demands for special favours, and engaged in fierce internecine warfare with other Quebec Conservatives.[42] By mid-1903 Borden was complaining to his wife that 'Monk spends the most of his time in brooding over imaginary conspiracies which he thinks are being hatched against him ... my work would have been infinitely easier during the present session if he had never entered the Chamber.'[43] Finally in an 'act of treason' in January 1904,

39 Tanner to Borden, 3 Dec. 1909, BP, v. 352.
40 The phrase is from H.B. Ames in 'The Organization of Political Parties in Canada,' American Political Science Association, *Proceedings* (27-30 Dec. 1911), 184.
41 Borden, *Memoirs*, II, 401.
42 Monk to Borden, 18 Nov. 1903, T.C. Casgrain to Borden and Casgrain to Taylor, 20 Feb. 1904, Monk to Borden, 29 Jan. 1904, BP, v. 350; *La Patrie*, 1 March, 1904; Michael Carroll, 'Henri Bourassa and the "Unholy Alliance," ' unpublished MA thesis, Carleton University, 1969.
43 Quoted in Brown, *Borden*, 57.

Monk abdicated with an election close at hand. Never again did Borden appoint a French-Canadian Conservative leader: the post would remain vacant until French-Canadian Conservatives showed sufficient 'maturity' to warrant such special consideration.[44] With only eleven seats in Quebec in 1904 and again in 1908, Borden could afford to act boldly, and he did. He attempted to construct an alliance with one of the most virulent critics of corruption in Canadian and Quebec politics, Henri Bourassa.

Borden had met the most prominent *nationaliste* when they boarded together in their first years at Ottawa.[45] No doubt he was charmed and impressed by the vibrant Bourassa, but there is no evidence that close friendship developed. Certainly Borden would not have approved Bourassa's stand on the Boer War or on imperialism in general, but other features of La Ligue nationaliste canadienne programme — provincial rights, opposition to foreign economic domination, and protection of natural resources — were quite similar to Borden's own views. Bourassa gathered about him a well-educated, articulate, and highly political group of young men who 'became convinced that the root of much of the evil lay in politics. And that meant the Liberals: Gouin at Quebec, Laurier at Ottawa.'[46] Contacts between Conservatives and *nationalistes* were therefore inevitable, and they first occurred informally and at the provincial level.

The provincial Conservatives began, after 1905, to detach themselves from their federal counterparts (who in 1905 were opposing the separate school clauses in the Autonomy Bills) and to seek the support of the *nationalistes*.[47] English-Canadian reformers in Montreal, who were often active Conservatives, began to make common cause with the *nationalistes* against various wrongs. Herbert Ames, a Conservative MP and perhaps Canada's best known urban reformer, was a leader in this regard. Hugh Graham's *Montreal Star* also became a supporter of many of the *nationalistes'* reform policies, and it was through Graham and his editor, Brenton Macnab, that Borden came into contact with Bourassa. In July 1907 Bourassa, through Macnab, indicated to Borden his willingness to work with the Conservatives 'to raise the flag of absolutely honest government over the province.' He was referring to provincial politics, but he did

---

44 Casgrain to Borden, 20 Feb. 1904, BP, v. 350. Monk did become French-Canadian Conservative leader again in 1909, but the position had clear restrictions and was not the same one he left in 1904. 'Memo of Conversation between Messrs. Borden, Monk and Casgrain,' 29 Jan. 1909, BP, v. 351.
45 Bourassa to Borden, 18 Oct. 1935, BP, v. 261.
46 Brown and Cook, *Canada, 1896-1921*, 139.
47 See J.A.A. Lovink, 'The Politics of Quebec Provincial Parties, 1897-1936,' unpublished PhD thesis, Duke University, 1967, 98, 148, 321 ff; and H.B. Neatby, *Laurier and a Liberal Quebec* (Toronto, 1973), 177-81.

promise more: he praised Whitney's Ontario policies, similar to Borden's Halifax Platform, and asked for 'an alliance — not open, but real — with Mr. Ames' and a meeting with Borden.[48]

This meeting apparently did not occur — too little time and too many differences prevented any alliance for the 1908 federal election — but the provincial Conservatives and *nationalistes* together fought the government of Sir Lomer Gouin in the 1908 Quebec election. Borden continued to think of Bourassa as an answer to the Conservatives' Quebec weakness and as an ally against corruption and the politics of the past represented by Laurier Liberalism. Bourassa could bring to Conservatism the most talented young men, proven political deftness, a vital organization which Quebec Conservatism lacked, and utter impatience with political corruption and frivolity. The time-servers and the place-seekers so abundant in Quebec Conservative ranks would lose their place to men committed to a different style and understanding of politics.

One hesitates to employ the term 'progressives' to describe the third major grouping which Borden courted: the word has had too many meanings in American history and, in Canadian history, a too specific one, the name of an agrarian political party. Nevertheless, the contemporary use of the word justifies its application here. Borden, the reader will recall, believed his Halifax Platform would appeal to 'progressive' spirits and communities. Similarly, Bourassa thought Whitney's bold political programme was 'progressive,' and newspapers regularly characterized politicians or their policies as 'progressive.'

What Borden understood by 'progressive' is indicated in several of his public statements. To be sure, he meant that the state should assume a more active role than it had in the past and than Laurier was willing to allow it in the future. More fundamentally, though, Borden — in common with Canadians as diverse as the Manitoba visionary E.A. Partridge and the Toronto imperialist George Denison — was rejecting the kind of politics that was marked by compromise and where decision only occurred at the level of the lowest common denominator. Borden sought a larger vision, one which would go beyond mere consensus and would spurn the 'parish pump' politics of Canadian parliamentary democracy: 'Looking to every man as a citizen to stand for that which makes for the interest of the whole country, and overlooking mere transient, temporary and local considerations, we cannot doubt that the interest of the East is the interest of the West, the interest of Nova Scotia is and always must be the interest of British Columbia.'[49]

48 Macnab to Graham, 9 July, Macnab to Borden, 11 and 18 July 1907, BP, v. 327. See also Brown, *Borden*, 128-9.
49 Speech in BP, v. 79. See also Borden, *Memoirs*, I, 373.

This Borden speech and many others like it clearly reflect 'the sense of power' that so many Canadians exuded at that time. There was, on the one hand, self-confidence and, on the other, frustration with the limits imposed by geography, tradition, and human weakness. No matter what the primary focus of interest — imperialism, government ownership or regulation, or economic development — the progressives were united by a disposition to become politically involved and to see national politics as a means of attaining their individual goals. For an opposition leader they presented great opportunities, but how could one take best advantage of them?

In 1904 when Borden was advocating government construction and ownership of the new Grand Trunk Pacific, the Conservative whip received a letter from Watson Griffin, the publicist for the Canadian Manufacturers' Association, commending Borden's stand and proffering advice: 'Let the Conservatives gain the support of the capitalists who are interested in manufacturing industries and they do not need to fear the railway capitalists in carrying out the Borden policy of public ownership of the national transcontinental railway.'[50] Borden needed little coaxing. Even before Griffin's letter arrived, he had developed close ties with J.W. Flavelle and A.E. Kemp, major figures in Toronto financial and industrial circles. Kemp, Flavelle, B.E. Walker, and Herbert Ames, who was elected to the House of Commons in 1904, were in fact the kind of 'progressives' Borden tried to draw into political life. They were mostly businessmen, but not, Borden believed, men whose vision was restricted to their private interests. They were willing to countenance and indeed to encourage a more active, responsible state; and, at least in Borden's eyes, they would 'make their stand' for the 'whole country.'

Borden, Roger Graham observed, 'admired successful businessmen and was inclined to be heavily influenced by their views ...'[51] And why not, at a time when business attracted men of the greatest capacity and vision? Every age has an avenue of energy which the brightest young men seek out. Perhaps the Empire attracted the most creative young Englishmen in 1900; certainly the Church called the best to its fold in the Middle Ages. But in Canada in 1900, business with its excitement and opportunity was an irresistible siren to a young Max Aitken, R.B. Bennett, or Joseph Flavelle. Even the Marxist and the muckraker gave credit to the vitality and talent of their enemies.[52] Laurier traced the

50 Griffin to George Taylor, Conservative whip, 2 June 1904, BP, v. 350.
51 *Arthur Meighen: The Door of Opportunity* (Toronto, 1960), I, 152.
52 Two examples would be Gustavus Myers, *A History of Canadian Wealth* (London, 1914), and Edward Porritt, *Sixty Years of Protection in Canada, 1846-1907: Where Industry Leans on the Politician* (London, 1908). On business thought, see Michael Bliss, *A Living Profit* (Toronto, 1974).

decline in the calibre of members of Parliament to the attraction of business — no longer were the chief openings for advancement for a young man law and politics: 'Today ... and this is particularly true of Ontario, there are such opportunities in business with large remuneration that politics with its uncertainties has little attraction for young men of ability.'[53] Borden hoped to change this for two reasons. First, politics dealt with the most serious matters affecting national life and must therefore involve the most intelligent in the land. Secondly, Borden realized that mere pursuit of wealth was 'a menace' to the political structure of Canada. Political activity could serve as an educator for businessmen to make them aware of national problems and their own responsibilities as citizens. Moreover, their financial aid could free Borden from the dependence upon Montreal interests, notably the CPR, for party funds.[54] In the religious, philanthropic, and cultural activities of businessmen like Flavelle, B.E. Walker, and Thomas White, Borden saw the first stage of full-scale political participation. In the task of bringing order to the chaos of late nineteenth- and early twentieth-century economic change, he envisaged such men as his strongest and most valuable allies.

Borden, it has been seen, had significant personal and political reasons for developing these relationships with extra-parliamentary interests. Indeed, the nature of the pre-war party system, with its patronage, its partisanship, its unrepresentative electoral system, and its stability, meant that the prudent opposition leader had to depend upon such groupings to carry out certain functions which were normally those of the party. Inevitably, Conservative parliamentarians became suspicious of Borden's aims. As Craig Brown has noted, Borden seemed to his caucus 'distant, moody, imperious, sometimes almost scornful of their worth ... he had made policy by memoranda with outsiders; businessmen, journalists, provincial potentates, men who understood little and cared less about the demands, the whims, and the welfare of the parliamentary party.'[55] That this was often necessary few members appreciated. They correctly saw that Borden's larger aims could threaten them even as they brought ultimate victory to the party. Such was the paradox that underlay both the turmoil within Conservative ranks and the triumph of Borden's party in the election of 1911.

53 Laurier's remarks are paraphrased in Ford, *As the World Wags On*, 126.
54 Graham and the CPR, for example, had probably contributed approximately $300,000 to party funds in 1904, that is, well over $1000 per constituency. Charles Hibbert Tupper told Graham that 'Every penny of what we received outside [British Columbia] came from you.' Tupper to Graham, 10 Dec. 1904; also Graham to Borden, 15 July 1904, and 17 May 1907, BP, v. 327. Graham and the CPR expected favours in return, something Borden knew and resented.
55 Brown, *Borden*, 166.

3

The election of 1911

On 27 July 1945 Harold Nicolson wrote in his diary: 'I spend the morning analysing the Election results. It is an amazing statement of public opinion, but I am not yet quite sure what it really means.'[1] Much the same can be said of the historical discussion of the Canadian general election of 1911: no definitive answer has been found to the perplexing question of what that peculiar election 'really means.' W.L. Morton has claimed the election was a 'reaffirmation of national purpose,'[2] but this can only be true if one recognizes that there were several distinct national purposes. Liberal historians have usually referred to the election as the victory of the 'unholy alliance' between Robert Borden and the Quebec *nationalistes*. In *Canada, 1896-1921: A Nation Transformed*, R. Craig Brown and Ramsay Cook have reasserted the significance of the two major issues in that election, the naval question and the reciprocity pact, while pointing to an underlying current of discontent inspired by profound social and economic changes.[3] Our concern, however, is not with the issues themselves, but with the influence these issues had upon political alignments. In this sense the naval and reciprocity issues are important in that they drew the 'independent' vote to the Tory side. Furthermore, because reciprocity offended urban industrial interests and together with the naval issue aroused 'British' feeling in parts of English Canada, these issues tended to reinforce traditional Conservative support.[4] It is

1 *Diaries and Letters, 1945-62*, ed. Nigel Nicolson (London, 1968), 27.
2 *The Kingdom of Canada* (Toronto, 1963), 415.
3 (Toronto, 1974), chap. 9.
4 John Allan, in 'Reciprocity and the Canadian General Election of 1911: A Re-examination of Economic Self-Interest in Voting,' unpublished MA thesis, Queen's University, 1971, has demonstrated that British background correlates with a Conservative vote and that manufacturing, non-agrarian areas had a marked Tory preference. On the issues generally, see R.C. Brown, *Robert Laird Borden: A Biography, 1854-1914*, I (Toronto, 1975) chaps. 8 and 9.

important, then, to concentrate on those who for the first time threw their full support behind the Conservatives.

Three elements were responsible for the Conservative triumph: the close federal-provincial co-operation in British Columbia, Manitoba, Ontario, and, to a lesser extent, New Brunswick; the *nationaliste* campaign against Laurier in Quebec; and the intense participation in the campaign of the new industrialists and imperialists who saw in Liberal policy the harbinger of a 'Little Canada.' These were, of course, the groups which Borden had long courted, and their co-operation in 1911 was not merely fortuitous, although the kind of assistance they rendered could not have been predicted before the emergence of the naval and reciprocity issues. In fact, these groups became the vanguard of the federal Conservative party, 'shock troops' who retained their own identity while assisting the larger force. This was an important innovation, and the overall effect of the Conservative campaign was to nationalize the Canadian party system, to present two collective images of what Canada should be, and to create a political layer made up of provincial premiers and public men previously aloof from active federal politics between the parliamentary party and the political life in the constituency. This represents an abandonment of any major attempt by Borden to revivify Canadian Conservatism through a root-and-branch restructuring of the party and the creation of a broad, hierarchical organization which would inspire widespread local participation in party affairs. This decision to reform the apex rather than the full structure may have been inevitable, but in the long run it was unfortunate, perhaps even disastrous.

PREMIERS, NATIONALISTES, AND 'NEW MEN'

How did the extra-parliamentary forces become so deeply involved, and what impact did their activities have upon the Conservative party? It was, para-doxically, the naval issue, an issue Borden had wanted to avoid because of its divisive character, which brought the new allies to the Tory side. After Borden and his party accepted a compromise resolution on naval defence which did not include a contribution to Britain for naval purposes, a political whirlwind sprang up. Soon many of the most powerful Conservatives in English Canada de-nounced their parliamentarians for so readily agreeing to Laurier's shrewd com-promise and missing the opportunity to show solidarity with the mother country in time of danger. At the same time, Laurier's nemesis and Borden's prospective ally, Henri Bourassa, quickly turned from Sir Lomer Gouin and the granting of timber licences in Quebec to national politics, denouncing the naval bill as a pernicious manœuvre designed to draw Canada into the vortex of European militarism.[5]

Spontaneously, dramatically, and righteously, the naval issue exploded upon a somnolent political scene. Imperialist and anti-imperialist, members of the Round Table and of *La Ligue nationaliste*, fitted their armour, assembled their weapons, and waged fierce public battle. As the historian of American foreign policy, Ernest May, has noted, the 'foreign policy public' tend more than others 'to take unqualified stands and hold opinions dogmatically' despite or perhaps because of their greater wealth and education.[6] In this tendency lay the crux of the Conservatives' problem. Were they to forsake the *nationalistes*, who they were presently courting, or to offend the imperialists, who would perforce remain Conservatives? Secondly, should they take advantage of an intemperate controversy and let events rather than the party leadership dictate the party's direction? Borden was not a Benthamite, confident of the rightness of public choice. His inherent distrust of the irrational and emotional in politics therefore led him to attempt to quell the raging public debate. Yet as 1909 passed into 1910 with the clamour increasing rather than abating, such a hope was clearly futile. At first Borden thought that all his efforts since 1906 were doomed. But his work had not been wasted, for in many ways the reaction of the party and other Canadians to the passions surrounding the naval bill were outgrowths of the work Borden had undertaken.

If the development of the naval issue presented enormous difficulties, it nevertheless offered new opportunities to fulfil major earlier initiatives. Very rapidly, Premiers Roblin, McBride, and Whitney, all vigorous supporters of a contribution to Britain, turned their full energies to assisting the federal Conservative party which alone could meet their demands. Sir James Whitney brought with him from Ontario many potential allies who were strongly opposed to Laurier's naval policy. Sam Hughes pointed out to Borden in March 1910 that B.E. Walker, president of the Bank of Commerce; Joseph Flavelle; W. George, president of the Canadian Manufacturers' Association; E.R. Wood, Thomas White, and G.M. Clark, all prominent Toronto businessmen, were examples of the Liberals and independents in Toronto who were ready to support a strong 'imperial' party committed to progressive national policies in domestic affairs.

5 See, for example, James Whitney to Borden, 24 Nov., A.E. Kemp to Borden, 29 Nov., and R.B. Bennett to Borden, 7 Dec. 1909, PAC, Borden Papers (BP), v. 352. Bourassa's objections to the naval bill may be found in his *Le Projet de loi navale* (Montreal, 1910); and Robert Rumilly, *Henri Bourassa* (Montreal, 1953), chap. 17.

6 *American Imperialism* (New York, 1968), 23.

Even more tantalizing was the rumour that Clifford Sifton, once Laurier's ablest minister, might join a Tory party committed to progressive reform.[7] Here were the type of men Borden had long sought.

While the Conservative premiers and the Toronto businessmen believed that Canada should make a contribution to Britain rather than construct its own 'tin pot navy,' as Rodmond Roblin so derisively termed the product of the Laurier-Borden compromise, French-Canadian Conservatives as well as the *nationalistes* would never accept a contribution and saw the navy as an 'imperialist scheme.' 'With equal sincerity,' Craig Brown has written, Borden's 'French- and English-speaking followers came to opposite conclusions ...'[8] But soon the inevitable questions about sincerity arose, and when Frederick Monk, whose contact with the *nationalistes* was quite close, moved in February 1910 that a plebiscite be held before any naval bill was enacted, the Conservative party's divisions clearly appeared. Borden tried to negotiate with Monk, but negotiations failed. Decisions were postponed; the inevitable discontent erupted; and Borden's leadership was challenged from four quarters: from William Price, W.B. Northrup, and J.D. Reid, who formed a cabal which planned to bring in Richard McBride as temporary leader to pave the way for the immensely wealthy but inexperienced Price; from Thomas Crothers who sought the leadership for himself; from Monk and the French-Canadian Conservatives, who were bitter at the Tory stand on the naval bill and at numerous small offences; and from W.F. Maclean, who simply expanded the peculiar one-man rebellion he had been conducting for many years.[9] Borden was far from blameless. During the naval debate the introverted Tory leader withdrew even further while he considered his future course. Without leadership the party could only drift and divide into factions. Worst of all, a party convention was scheduled for the spring of 1910, a meeting which would magnify the profound split within the party. The situation was impossible: on 6 April 1910 Borden announced he would retire at the session's end.

Premier McBride's name was immediately raised, but he refused at once. Borden's allies rallied quickly to his side. Hugh Clark, an Ontario legislature member, assured Borden 'that every member of the Whitney government and

---

7 Hughes to Borden, 23 March 1910, BP, v. 134. This letter clearly shows that many of the 'Toronto Eighteen' were ready to break with Laurier before reciprocity. See also Hughes to MacArthur, 23 March 1911, *ibid.*, and C.F. Hamilton to J.S. Willison, 8 March 1910, PAC, Willison Papers, v. 37.

8 *Borden*, 163.

9 Borden, *Memoirs*, I, 287-8. Although Borden did not identify Price and Reid, A.E. Blount, Borden's secretary, did. PAC, Blount Papers, v. 2. Crothers is identified as the other unnamed intriguer in S. Hughes to Borden, 24 Nov. 1910, BP, v. 134; and M. Burrell to Borden, 17 Oct. 1932, BP, v. 294. See also Brown, *Borden*, 165-9.

every Conservative member of the Legislature is heart and soul with you.' Roblin urged fortitude and outlined a future course which undoubtedly pleased Borden:

... It would simply break my heart for you to act differently from what I am going to request, [it] is that you figuratively spit upon your hands, take a fresh hold, bear [sic] your muscles, bear [sic] your chest to the wind and not only request, but demand from every man who assumes to be a follower, his allegiance and his willingness to discharge any duty that may be put upon him and to call upon your friends from the Atlantic to the Pacific to rally around you in your patriotic effort to promote such legislation as will foster and develop the moral, social and material life of the people of Canada ... In other words be boss; exercise your power, and then when you have done this, call upon men like myself, McBride, Whitney and Hazen and any others, not only for counsel or advice, which we may or may not be able to give you, but for work and such assistance as will strengthen your hands.

The party factions soon crumbled as they recognized the new power Borden had assembled behind him. When the issue was placed before the caucus on 12 April, Charles Doherty, 'while agreeing that there was dissatisfaction and strong feeling that some change was necessary, moved a resolution of confidence in Borden as leader, coupled with a request for reorganization ...' All stood in support of the motion although some did leave their seats 'with evident reluctance.' The lesson of the incident was clear and not lost upon Borden; future safety lay not in token compromise but boldness.[10]

The party convention was postponed, and Borden asserted his authority by appointing his friends George H. Perley and Herbert B. Ames as whip and organizer respectively. Thomas Crothers, surprisingly enough, was also given an undefined role in the organization, a certain indication of the new confidence felt by Borden.[11] In Roblin's words, Borden 'bared his chest' and defied the old 'party men' who opposed his conception of the party. For the moment,

10 Hugh Clark to Borden, 4 April, Borden to Clark, 6 April, Roblin to Borden, 6 April 1910, BP, v. 352; and Burrell to Borden, 17 Oct. 1932, BP, v. 294. McBride's role is discussed in Brian Smith, 'Sir Richard McBride,' unpublished MA thesis, Queen's University, 1959. At the time, many felt that McBride wanted the leadership but lost it after a disastrous speech to caucus. Smith disagrees, and I am inclined to support him. Burrell's letter to Borden twenty-two years later, when McBride was long in the grave, indicates he did not want the position. Mrs Margaret Macintosh, McBride's daughter, has told me that her father's illness was diagnosed as terminal in 1909 and that he had no thought of leaving British Columbia for the difficult task of federal leader.
11 *Toronto News*, 7 Nov. 1910; Hughes to W. MacArthur, 23 March 1911, BP, v. 134.

intimidation was effective but the grievances lingered. Still, the internal dissension had been overcome without bitter recriminations. In the light of Conservative history, that at least offered grounds for hope.

Hope billowed into optimism in November 1910 with favourable news from a most unexpected source: in a by-election in the constituency of Drummond-Arthabaska in Quebec the anti-government candidate, who had been vigorously supported by Bourassa and the forgotten Monk, unexpectedly triumphed. Although the tone of the campaign by Monk, Bourassa, and their allies had been distinctly anti-imperial and hostile to any type of naval bill, and Borden himself took no sides, English-Canadian Conservatives did not bother to conceal their delight at the results. An overly exuberant William Price told Borden that Laurier would lose Quebec East, his own constituency.[12] Some Tories argued that the response of Quebec to the naval bill could work for the Tory cause elsewhere in a profitable way. The journalist Charles Hamilton, while admitting that the *nationalistes* had 'swallowed up' the Quebec Conservatives, claimed that the Liberals could no longer use the argument that 'Laurier had a solid Quebec behind him and was unbeatable.' Instead they would 'be confronted by the feeling that Laurier has lost his hold on Quebec and that his day as a dispenser of gifts is done.'[13] But the Tories, like Thomas Hardy, were to find that love lives on propinquity but dies on contact.

Reflecting on political parties shortly after the 1911 election, the Conservative member, Herbert Ames, wrote that to overthrow an entrenched government the opposition must often become 'a veritable cave of Adullam, sheltering outlaws of all political factions; and all are welcome, provided they are able and willing to direct telling shafts against the enemy.'[14] The announcement of a reciprocity pact with the United States in January 1911 created a rush to the Conservative cave where the doorman, Robert Borden, was most lenient in

12 Price to Borden, 7 Nov. 1910, BP, v. 351. H. Blair Neatby has pointed out how the ties between the federal and provincial Conservatives in Quebec weakened after 1905, as the provincial Conservatives allied with Bourassa and the *nationalistes*. While dissociating themselves from federal Conservatives, the provincial Tories nevertheless kept fairly close organizational links with the federal party. Borden also approved of the provincial Tories' flirtation with the *nationalistes* and, in fact, used it to his own advantage in 1910. *Laurier and a Liberal Quebec* (Toronto, 1973), 177-81. See also J.A.A. Lovink, 'The Politics of Quebec Provincial Parties, 1897-1936,' unpublished PhD thesis, Duke University, 1967, 98, 148; and Robert Rumilly, *Histoire de la province de Quebec,* XIII (Montreal, n.d.), 144 ff; and Brown and Cook, *Canada, 1896-1921,* 172-3.
13 A Conservative journalist quoted in Brown and Cook, *ibid.,* 173.
14 'The Organization of Political Parties in Canada,' American Political Science Association, *Proceedings* (27-30 Dec. 1911), 184.

allowing entry. From Quebec came Monk who also managed to persuade Bourassa to change his stance on reciprocity from mild approbation to mild disapproval. The agreement on reciprocity contrasted with the continuing division on the naval issue; Borden, nevertheless, now had a pretext for giving Monk free rein in French Canada.[15] Another entrant was Hugh Graham of the *Montreal Star*, who had been outraged by Borden's neglect of Montreal interests and had warned the Tories they would not receive further support. Now Graham decisively rejected reciprocity and rallied behind the imperial cause. Some passed out of the cave: Frederick Haultain, the Saskatchewan Tory leader, supported reciprocity; Harry Corby, the powerful whisky magnate, withdrew from politics; and many provincial western Tories remained uncommitted. When, however, Premiers McBride and Whitney joined Roblin's vigorous public attack on the proposals, the Tory ranks seemed more solid than ever. They were soon to be swollen.

On 20 February, less than a month after W.S. Fielding's dramatic announcement of the reciprocity pact, eighteen Toronto businessmen previously identified with the Liberal party attacked the proposals as a serious blow to Canadian nationality.[16] This group acquired an even more distinguished member on 28 February, when Clifford Sifton announced that Canada was 'putting [its] head into a noose' and that he would fight his former colleagues to prevent it.[17] On 1 March Sifton, Zebulon A. Lash, representing the Toronto group, Lloyd Harris, a prominent manufacturer and Liberal MP, John S. Willison, and Borden met to consider how they might together defeat the government. Borden readily agreed to certain post-election commitments: Quebec and the Roman Catholic Church should be strongly resisted; B.E. Walker, Lash, and Willison should be consulted during the selection of the cabinet; the civil service outside Ottawa should be

15 On reciprocity see Rumilly, *Bourassa*, 402-4; *Le Devoir*, Feb.-March 1911; and, especially, Monk-Bourassa correspondence, 1911, PAC, Monk Papers. In the naval bill dispute there was an element of public dramatics and private compromise. Monk himself claimed that he wanted to remain 'friends' while acting publicly in an independent fashion. Price to Perley, 7 Nov. 1910, BP, v. 352. See also Brown, *Borden*, 170-2, which points out how Borden did grant some concessions to Monk.

16 R.D. Cuff, 'The Toronto Eighteen and the Election of 1911,' *Ontario History*, LVII (Dec. 1965), 169-80. See also W.M. Baker, 'A Case Study of Anti-Americanism in English-speaking Canada: The Election Campaign of 1911,' *Canadian Historical Review*, LI (Dec. 1970), 436-7; and P.D. Stevens, 'Laurier, Aylesworth, and the Decline of the Liberal Party in Ontario,' Canadian Historical Association, *Historical Papers* (1968), 94-113.

17 J.C. Hopkins, *Canadian Annual Review, 1911* (Toronto, 1912), 50-1. Sifton's own account is found in 'Reciprocity,' *Annals of the American Academy of Political and Social Sciences*, XLV (Jan. 1913).

placed under the Civil Service Commission; the Department of Trade and Commerce should be strengthened; outside talent should be introduced into the cabinet 'in order to give confidence to the progressive elements of the country'; and a tariff commission should be appointed to investigate industrial conditions. Borden accepted all these conditions without reservation.[18]

This agreement was concerned with much more than reciprocity; it represented a well-defined progressive programme of government similar to that outlined by Borden in the Halifax Platform in 1907. The opposition to reciprocity created a convenient pretext for the businessmen to leave a Liberal party which lacked imagination and determination. What all shared was an exuberant faith in the potential of Canadian development and a belief that this development should be directed by a technocratic and moral élite, men with the values and skills which they themselves possessed. What they also shared was the Anglo-Saxon nationalist's distrust of French Canada, which, it must be admitted, could take the form of irrational distrust of Laurier. After the 1 March meeting the businessmen felt, quite correctly, that Borden's values were theirs. To Borden, the defections were an extraordinary windfall, the justification of his bold initiatives so despised by many of his parliamentary colleagues. No longer would impractibility and indifference prevent party reform; the force of events would itself dictate a rapid pace.

That the older elements of the party were aware of the deeper significance of the defections was soon apparent: 'the cry went up that [the] negotiations meant the destruction of the Liberal-Conservative party and the ascendancy of Liberal elements.' The conspirators of 1910, notably Reid, Northrup, and Price, and several French Canadians, reappeared and once again nominated McBride for the leadership. In his *Memoirs* Borden stated that he became 'intensely discouraged' and told his wife that his political career was over. He claimed that on 25 March he sent a message to McBride asking him to take over the leadership. Only when some tearful friends beseeched him to reconsider and presented him with a round robin supporting him signed by the overwhelming majority of Tory members did Borden agree to stay on.[19]

This account, while dramatic, is unconvincing, for reasons enumerated elsewhere.[20] Like many other political leaders, Borden used dissatisfaction to crush

---

18 Willison, 'Memo,' n.d. (1911), Willison Papers, v. 105. Cuff, in 'The Toronto Eighteen,' underestimates the broadness of the interests of the Toronto group and focuses almost exclusively on reciprocity. See also G.P. de T. Glazebrook, *Sir Edmund Walker* (London, 1933), 109 ff; Brown and Cook, *Canada, 1896-1921*, 181-2; and Brown, *Borden*, 178-9.
19 Borden, *Memoirs*, I, 309.
20 See my 'Sir Robert Borden, the Conservative Party and Political Change in Canada, 1901-1920,' unpublished PhD thesis, Harvard University, 1973, 112-14.

opposition to his policy. He emerged from the rebellion with his leadership unassailable, and his new political bedfellows publicly unquestioned by the Conservatives. Perhaps influenced by the farcical quality of the rebellion, Craig Brown has described the challenge of the 'party regulars' to Borden as 'incredible.'[21] But the discontent, even at a time when power seemed near, is understandable. Let us consider the members' predicament. Borden had given, or apparently intended to give, many of the functions normally carried out by members, including publicity, organization, and party strategy, to bodies or individuals over which the caucus had little control. Given the 'delegate' orientation of most members, it is not at all surprising they interpreted Borden's manœuvres as a threat to their position and to their party, as they perceived that institution. When forced to the test they could only give way, as they did in the early spring of 1910. Nevertheless, future events proved their fears to be at least partially correct.

In the campaign the party members acted as a chorus, providing the solidity evident in the Conservative campaign performance, but the leading performers were undoubtedly the premiers, the *nationalistes*, and a wide range of organizations representing business and imperialist interests.

THE CAMPAIGN OF 1911

In 1910 and 1911 the premiers had shown their loyalty to Borden while many of his colleagues gave him ample reason for distrust. This was, perhaps, one reason why Borden entrusted party organization within their respective provinces to the premiers; the premiers' access to patronage and their army of party workers were certainly others. As always, details of the character of the organizations are almost as scarce as items on the most intimate details of politicians' private lives. There is, however, a fortunate exception, the province of Ontario, about which Borden retained some most interesting papers which enable the historian to sketch the outlines of the campaign.

William Baker has noted that the co-operation between 'the provincial and federal organizations [in Ontario] was quite amazing,' and Robert Cuff has claimed that the Conservatives would have swept Ontario 'no matter what public issue emerged in 1911.'[22] Both statements are somewhat misleading. To speak of co-operation is to suggest two separate federal and provincial organizations which did not in fact exist. There was one organization dominated by provincial politicians. Premier Whitney's vigorous support of the federal party was very

21 *Borden*, 184.
22 Baker, 'A Case Study of Anti-Americanism,' 446; R.D. Cuff, 'The Conservative Party Machine and the Election of 1911 in Ontario,' *Ontario History*, LVII (Sept. 1965), 156.

much a product of the election issues: he was outraged by the naval debate and by the reciprocity proposal which he believed would 'frustrate Canada's hopes of nationhood within the Empire and ... lead to Political Union with the United States.' Moreover, he believed, with some reason, that the Laurier government had ignored the rights of his province, and he was willing to make this serious, inflammatory charge publicly. In short, he had had enough of Laurier and, accordingly, readily heeded Borden's call to 'fight and fight hard.'[23]

Whitney gave men and material generously, and the federal party willingly accepted the largesse — too eagerly in one instance.[24] The overall director of the Conservative campaign in Ontario was Frank Cochrane, minister of mines in Whitney's government, whose office and background gave him immediate access to great financial resources.[25] Assisting Cochrane as campaign secretary was J.S. Carstairs, who had been appointed permanent party organizer by Borden in 1907. The industrialist and former MP Edward Kemp, a candidate in East Toronto, played a major role financially in the campaign, and his grand home 'Castle Frank' was the scene for many garden parties for potential Conservative donors. By June, however, Kemp's failing health and his own campaign in East Toronto forced him to relinquish most of his duties in the provincial organization leaving Cochrane virtually alone as campaign organizer.[26] The task was too much for him on his own, and some work was allocated to two federal members, J.D. Reid and Thomas Crothers, surprising choices in light of their earlier insurgency. The veteran Reid handled eastern Ontario and Crothers western Ontario, while the remainder of the province in which lay most of Ontario's ridings remained under Cochrane's expert care.[27] The power of this organization is suggested by the surprising extent to which the provincial organization was able to influence the constituency parties in the choice of candidates. The

23 Hopkins, *Canadian Annual Review, 1911*, 98; Christopher Armstrong, 'The Politics of Federalism: Ontario' Relations with the Federal Government, 1896-1941,' unpublished PhD thesis, University of Toronto, 1972, 417-18; and Borden to Whitney, 14 Feb. 1911, PAO, Whitney Papers, v. 19.
24 Whitney warned Borden that Carstairs had been recruiting candidates among the provincial members without fully consulting him. Borden replied that he understood that Whitney had agreed to free provincial members for the federal campaign provided that the riding could be carried provincially. Whitney to Borden, 13 April, and Borden to Whitney, 13 April 1911, BP, v. 16.
25 See Scott and Astrid Young, *Silent Frank Cochrane* (Toronto, 1973), 116, 121-4.
26 Kemp to Borden, 6 June and 28 July 1911, BP, v. 16; and Carstairs, 'Memorandum Concerning the Organization in Ontario,' 23 May 1912, PAC, Kemp Papers, v. 3.
27 Reid to Borden, 15 and 19 April, 11 Aug., Kemp to Borden, 25 July 1911, BP, v. 133. Reid's letter of 11 Aug. clearly shows that Cochrane controlled the overall organization.

leaderless Ontario Liberals retreated in the face of this overwhelming assault. By election day only the margin of Conservative victory continued in question.

Such detailed information is lacking for New Brunswick, Manitoba, and British Columbia, but what evidence exists points to similar close co-operation in the western provinces, though not in New Brunswick where a split between the federal and provincial wings of the party prevented a unified campaign.[28] Premier J.D. Hazen himself was most sympathetic to the federal Conservatives but his own precarious position greatly restricted his assistance. No such animosity or restrictions prevented full provincial commitment in British Columbia where Richard McBride, 'the people's Dick,' then at the pinnacle of his career, stumped the province from remote hamlet and lumber camp to Vancouver's city wards. The entire federal campaign was conducted by the great provincial machine which had thoroughly stifled the provincial opposition by 1909.[29] In 1911 McBride envisaged a similar fate for the federal Liberals in his province. In Manitoba Rodmond Roblin and Robert Rogers graced federal Conservative platforms. Provincial issues, such as the boundary question which directed Manitoba ire towards the federal government, were successfully mixed with national issues, such as the naval issue and reciprocity, to form a most potent brew in Manitoba where British blood more than compensated for the economic appeal of reciprocity. Rogers effectively enlisted his army of provincial inspectors and workers, the kept journalists, and the provincial bagmen for the federal cause.[30] By September 1911, Whitney, Roblin, and McBride had successfully transferred their own considerable prestige and, probably more important, their party machines to the federal branch of their party.

There was irony in this co-operation — which did not escape the Liberal press.[31] While Borden's federal Tories campaigned upon an 'end to patronage' platform, Roblin and McBride used lavish patronage for the federal campaign, and readily admitted that Borden's promise to end federal patronage would have no impact upon their provincial machines. Borden knew this but he believed that the progressive policies favoured by these men justified the close alliance. Furthermore, only the assistance of these provincial premiers could counteract the advantages of patronage which the government possessed. The ends — the

---

28 See O. Crocket to S.N. McCully, 27 Sept. 1911, UNB, Crocket Papers, v. 11. Crocket to Borden, 30 May 1911, *ibid.*, v. 7, shows that Quebec member William Price handled New Brunswick for the Tories.
29 Hopkins, *Canadian Annual Review, 1911*, 248-9.
30 *Ibid.*, 240-1; Rogers to Borden, 8 March, 4 and 11 April 1911, BP, v. 133.
31 *Manitoba Free Press*, 11, 16 and 18 Sept. 1911.

overthrow of the Laurier Liberals, the defeat of reciprocity, and the scuttling of the Canadian navy — justified such temporary embarrassments.

Far more embarrassing was the *mariage de convenance* between the *nationalistes* of Quebec and the Conservatives. That such an 'unholy alliance' was intentionally constructed can now no longer be doubted.[32] Borden's role in the establishment of the link, nevertheless, is still unclear. If one may trust the often unreliable Charles Murphy, Henri Bourassa did meet with Borden in May 1911 to plot their campaign. A more reliable source, Conservative organizer William Price, told another Tory organizer that Frederick Monk had made 'a definite alliance with Bourassa and the nationalistes, and this new combination is calling itself an Independent Conservative Party, under the leadership of Monk.' Bourassa himself confessed that his campaign was backed by Conservative money, particularly that of Hugh Graham.[33] Borden, as we have seen, had long regarded Bourassa as a potential ally, but in 1911 the dominance of the naval issue in Quebec made the character of any alliance fundamentally different. At this time, it was Monk who had created the alliance. Borden was certainly often discomfited by Monk's actions, but the Tory leader would never repudiate his awkward new ally: Quebec was left to Monk and Bourassa. In his *Memoirs* Borden describes the election under the title 'Reciprocity' and conspicuously omits any mention of Bourassa and Monk in his discussion of the election. The reticence is understandable, but it does not reflect Borden's view at the time. As O.D. Skelton remarked, the combination was quite a salad: 'Mr. Monk was the oil, Mr. Bourassa the vinegar, and Mr. Borden had to eat the dose.'[34] Political gain made the fare quite palatable.

Much more savoury to Borden's taste was the widespread participation in the campaign of public men previously uninvolved in politics, such as Thomas White and Sir Edmund Walker. Furthermore, the great involvement of Ontario interests lessened the influence of increasingly troublesome links made long ago. Montreal in 1911 was unable to purchase the obedience of the Conservative party by its predominance in financial support.[35] To be sure, the CPR, the Bank of Montreal,

32 See Michael Carroll, 'Henri Bourassa and the "Unholy Alliance," ' unpublished MA thesis, Carleton University, 1969; Rumilly, *Henri Bourassa*; Borden to Graham, 10 Feb. 1911, BP, v. 327; C.H. Cahan to Borden, 1 Oct. 1911, BP, v. 152; and Armand Lavergne to Borden, 8 Oct. 1911, Monk Papers, v. 2.
33 Murphy to Laurier, 20 May 1911, PAC, Laurier Papers, v. 681; and *Le Devoir*, 20, 26, 27, 28, 29, 30 May and 2, 3, 4, 5, 6 June 1913.
34 *Life and Letters of Sir Wilfrid Laurier* (London, 1922), II, 379.
35 Whitney wrote that Borden was not beholden to 'prominent capitalists' and therefore had no political debts. 'Prominent capitalists' was a code term indicating the CPR and the Montreal interests traditionally so potent within Conservative circles. Whitney to Irwin Hilliard, 11 Oct. 1911, Whitney Papers, v. 21.

and other Montreal interests were deeply involved in 'smashing the damn' reciprocity pact, as Sir William Van Horne bluntly put it. But no longer did Borden have to rely solely upon them for financial and organizational leadership. Numerous other independent organizations, well financed and well organized, worked with the Tories to defeat reciprocity. Most prominent among these was the Canadian National League which channelled the anti-reciprocity sentiment expressed in numerous boards of trades into direct political action. Arthur Hawkes was the secretary of this league and Zebulon Lash, the prominent Toronto lawyer, the chairman. Making a virtue of their lack of previous political activity, the leaders of the league flooded the constituencies with literature urging its recipients to throw off the shackles of party — and vote Tory. Hawkes' major contribution was a pamphlet entitled *An Appeal to the British Born* which was sent to 'British born' individuals whose names were obtained from lists submitted by Conservative workers in the constituencies.[36] An Anti-Reciprocity League organized meetings throughout the Dominion at which non-party speakers denounced reciprocity.

Craig Brown has shown how the 'non-partisan' Canadian Manufacturers' Association also became an integral part of the Tory campaign through a 'front' organization, the Canadian Home Market Association. Its job was 'education,' and to this end tens of thousands of dollars were collected. According to Brown, by the end of August 1911 'the CHMA had distributed nearly nine and one-half million copies of its material and was sending out twenty thousand items a day.'[37] Through work with this organization and others like it former Liberals could aid the Tories without having Liberal blood so obviously on their hands. The most prominent Liberal defector, Clifford Sifton, according to J.W. Dafoe, 'was not openly identified with any of these organizations but he was active in them all; and though it is not a matter of record ... he gave the [Conservatives] the benefit of advice, particularly in regard to Ontario, a political terrain which he knew intimately by reason of his intensive study of it prior to the election of 1908.'[38] The entry into politics of many who formerly believed 'that their clean and dainty hands should not be soiled with politics' meant to Borden that, in the words of the Halifax Platform, victory would 'mean more than party triumph.'[39] For once, a Canadian election was more than mere struggle for place; two clear choices faced the electorate. The Conservative identification of the interests of

36 Hawkes to Crocket, 28 Aug. 1911, Crocket Papers, v. 8.
37 *Borden*, 191.
38 *Clifford Sifton in Relation to His Times* (Toronto, 1931), 371.
39 'Canadian Democracy and Some of Its Problems,' 7 Nov. 1910, BP, v. 300; *The Liberal-Conservative Platform as laid down by R.L. Borden, M.P., Opposition Leader, at Halifax, August 28, 1907*, Public Archives Library.

the party with the interests of the nation was best expressed by James Whitney after the result was known: 'leaving all questions of party aside, and having regard to the future of the British Empire ... no event has occurred since the Battle of Waterloo of such tremendous importance to us and the Empire at large.'[40]

'Leaving all questions of party aside,' the phrase is Whitney's; the deed, Borden's. Borden's opposition to reciprocity and to 'Laurierism' only partly explains his neglect of his party. He was, it is clear, discontented with the Conservative rank and file, both inside and outside. Those he admired (Herbert Ames and George Perley, for example) were rare and all too often resented.[41] Hence he turned outside, finding in men like Whitney, White, Walker, Flavelle, and Willison greater compatibility and understanding. The locally oriented party which lacked a permanent bureaucracy and hierarchy meant that any party leader had to seek assistance from interest groups; but Borden, by allowing essential party functions to escape party control and knowledge, carried this to an extreme. Rather than a transfusion of funds, talents, and energy which might have reinvigorated the party, the outsiders, with Borden abetting, sought to graft a new head and heart upon the body of Canadian Conservatism. On 21 September, election day, the experiment was a great success. Afterwards, rejection occurred.

The pattern of Conservative support was at once a tribute to the Conservative-*nationaliste* campaign and an omen of future difficulties (see Table 3.1). The Tories had won an overwhelming victory by capturing only three provinces: Whitney's Ontario, Roblin's Manitoba, and McBride's British Columbia. The wisdom of the organizational alliance with provincial machines seems irrefutable; but what was to happen when these provincial governments, already long in office, began their inevitable decline? Also, the relatively strong showing in Quebec, twenty-seven seats, sixteen more than in 1908, could not obscure the false pretenses under which the seats had been obtained. Even more surprising and much more disappointing was the rapidity with which the businessmen who had thrown their full energies into the test retreated to their boardrooms and political inactivity. But the greatest problem came in the formation of a cabinet: how could these interests so dominant in the campaign be represented when their leaders did not sit in the Centre Block?

40 Whitney to Donald McLellan, 17 Oct. 1911, Whitney Papers, v. 21.
41 To Sam Hughes, they were 'd_____ noodles.' Ames, he claimed, 'would have made a marvellous main floorwalker for some large establishment such as Eaton's' but was otherwise incompetent. Hughes to MacArthur, 23 March 1911, BP, v. 134.

TABLE 3.1

Results of Canadian general election of 1911

	Conservatives-*nationalistes*		Liberals	
	Seats	Percentage of vote	Seats	Percentage of vote
Prince Edward Island	2	51.1	2	48.9
Nova Scotia	9	48.8	9	50.8
New Brunswick	5	49.2	8	50.8
Quebec	27	49.2	38	50.7
Ontario	73	56.2	13	43.1
Manitoba	8	51.9	2	44.8
Saskatchewan	1	39.0	9	59.4
Alberta	1	42.5	6	53.3
British Columbia	7	58.8	0	37.5
Yukon	1	60.8	0	39.2
Total	134		87	

Source: M.C. Urquhart and K.H. Buckley, eds., *Historical Statistics of Canada* (Toronto, 1965), section W.

To one outsider, Borden faced great opportunity and few difficulties in constructing a cabinet. 'Conservatives of Canada,' Sir William Van Horne argued, 'have been long enough out of power to have lost the office-holding habit and there are very few "left overs" to claim anything.' Borden could 'therefore commence with new and sound materials and build an enduring structure and one that will stand as a model for future governments.'[42] This was a serious misreading of the situation. On the one hand, the belief that there were few claims proved utterly fallacious when *nationaliste*, provincial premier, industrialist, and even Orangeman advanced their favourites. On the other hand, the 'new and sound materials' were in surprisingly short supply. Although many talented, progressive individuals took leading parts in the campaign, few had found their way to the government benches. The rank and file was largely cast in the same mould as that of previous Parliaments, and appointment from this group would occasion little public acclaim and would not keep the promises Borden had made. For the leading positions in the new government, Borden characteristically looked beyond Parliament Hill.

42 Van Horne to Borden, 24 Sept. 1911, cited in Roger Graham, 'The Cabinet of 1911,' in Frederick Gibson, ed., *Cabinet Formation and Bicultural Relations* (Ottawa, 1970), 47-8. See also Heath N. Macquarrie, 'The Formation of Borden's First Cabinet,' *Canadian Journal of Economics and Political Science*, XXIII (Feb. 1957), 90-104; and Brown, *Borden*, 197-211.

At once he asked the Conservative provincial premiers to come to Ottawa. Whitney, McBride, and Roblin, who had done so much for the Tories in the campaign, refused; J.D. Hazen, who had done very little, accepted.[43] In response to Borden's call, Whitney and Roblin nominated two masters of the machine, Frank Cochrane and Robert Rogers (they became respectively minister of railways and interior minister), scarcely the type of politician Borden desired, but men whom he had to accept in recognition of the great debt he owed to Whitney and Roblin. McBride's reward was the appointment of his friend and former secretary, Martin Burrell, to the ministry of agriculture. The provincial alliances which had been a great benefit in opposition were already becoming a liability in power.

The independents and Liberals had extracted a promise from Borden that he would consult them on the formation of his cabinet and that he would introduce 'progressive elements' from 'outside' into the new cabinet. Borden, of course, had no hesitation in concurring, but he did have great difficulty in persuading such 'progressive elements' to leave the pleasant and profitable world of business. Finally, with 'utmost difficulty,'[44] George Perley and Thomas White were induced to accept cabinet posts; the former, a ministry without portfolio; the latter, the ministry of finance, a crucial office. White, a former Liberal and a Toronto trust company executive closely linked with Ontario financial circles and with Ontario development, symbolized the type of federal administration Borden and Whitney profoundly desired.[45] As Hugh Graham bitterly recognized, White's position was tangible recognition of a permanent shift of the locus of Conservative financial power to Bay Street from St James Street.[46]

White fulfilled part of the bargain between Borden and the Toronto businessmen, but Borden's agreement to minimize the influence of 'the French and the Church' conflicted with the demands of the Quebec *nationalistes*. They were, of course, fundamentally opposed to the Borden naval policy which would become

43 McBride Diary, 3 Oct. 1911 (in the possession of Mrs M. Macintosh, Sidney, BC); Whitney to McLellan, 17 Oct. 1911, Whitney Papers, v. 21; Borden, *Memoirs*, I, chap. 16; Perley to McBride, 17 Oct. 1911, PABC, McBride Papers, box 1911.
44 Whitney to Irwin Hilliard, 11 Oct. 1911, Whitney Papers, v. 21.
45 Crothers to Whitney, 23 Sept. 1911, *ibid.*, v. 20; Whitney to E.C. Whitney, 20 Oct. 1911, *ibid.*, v. 21. On 1 Aug. 1911 Whitney told Borden (BP, v. 16) that White was entering the campaign. Charles Humphries seems to believe Whitney and White had broken over hydro policy. 'The Sources of Ontario Progressive Conservatism,' Canadian Historical Association, *Annual Report* (1967), 122. But this evidence clearly suggests not.
46 Cahan to Borden, 12 Oct. 1911, BP, v. 152; *Montreal Star*, 14 Oct. 1911.

the first order of business in the new House. Many of the old *bleus* were moderate on the issue, but they retained little influence within the caucus or within the province. Thus, after direct consultations with *nationaliste* leader Armand Lavergne and indirect contact with Bourassa, Borden named Monk as minister of public works, L.P. Pelletier as postmaster-general, and W.B. Nantel as minister of inland revenue. These men were the choice of Bourassa and Lavergne and, as Roger Graham remarked, their appointment amounted to a signal victory for 'the forces of sentiment and power ranged behind Bourassa and Monk.'[47] So alien were the 'forces of sentiment and power' of Quebec to Borden that he was probably unaware of the likely conflict. One might further suggest that Borden hoped that the appointment of Monk and Pelletier to the patronage-rich portfolios of public works and the post office would secure the permanent loyalty of the two ministers. Like many English Canadians, Borden seemed to believe that loyalty was a purchasable commodity in Quebec.[48]

In opposition Borden had proved himself a master of what Herbert Agar, an American historian of party, has termed 'group diplomacy,' the gathering together of economic, racial, and other interests which had never before cooperated. Paradoxically, Borden had succeeded because of the distance, geographically and emotionally, between these groups, and because they were all unrepresented in Parliament. The emergence of significant interests unrepresented in the party system was a symbol of the changes which had occurred during the Laurier era and which had caused considerable discontent. But this discontent bred no common ideology which might have provided focus for the new government. Even the personalities promised troubles. Small chance existed that the egotistical, extravagant, and imperialist McBride could share the same platforms with Armand Lavergne, the fiery *nationaliste*, or even with the dour, righteous Whitney. Yet from their realms, each had been a major contributor to the Tory victory, and, if they were not themselves present in the new Parliament, their representatives were. To work 'group diplomacy' when in power required rare skills in flattery and appeasement as well as the ability to make 'an immense commotion so that a great deal seemed to be happening.'[49] The stolid Borden possessed certain gifts, but these were not among them.

47 'The Cabinet of 1911,' 60.
48 Borden had been informed that Pelletier was widely considered a grafter and himself admits that Monk had told him that his only goal in politics was a judicial appointment. Cahan to Borden, BP, v. 152; Price to Borden, 2 Oct. 1911, BP, v. 6; Borden, *Memoirs*, II, 501. Monk, in fact, was not a 'grafter' but a politician of some integrity.
49 *The Price of Union* (Boston, 1950), 656.

4

A party in power:
the Conservatives 1911–14

Robert Borden's political programme envisaged no fundamental change in the economic and social relationships of Canadian society, but it did conceive a transformation of the political superstructure. The state's role should be expanded in the economic life of the nation not through direct governmental assistance, as had been done so unsuccessfully in the past, but through an expansion of the complementary role of the state. Civil service reform would create a more 'efficient' bureaucracy;[1] technical education would raise the quality of the work-force; control of public utilities would prevent monopolistic pricing policies which might hinder economic growth; and commissions, such as a tariff commission, a public utilities commission, and a railway commission, would free these contentious areas from partisan influence and control. The greater role for the state must be accompanied by a neutralization of the state, ending its association in the public mind with the fight of the political parties. 'The true ideals of Democracy,' Borden claimed, 'are impossible of attainment unless the individual citizen realizes and accepts his duty to the state.'[2] This realization, however, would never occur so long as the state itself seemed the servant of selfish interest.

In direct matters of social reform such as old age pensions, health insurance, and other legislation associated with the modern welfare state, Borden showed remarkably little interest. He placed great faith in the beneficence of industry

1 'Efficiency' was the strongest justification of civil service reform in the view of its advocates. See J.E. Hodgetts et al., *The Biography of an Institution: The Civil Service Commission of Canada, 1908-1967* (Montreal and London, 1972), 16-19.
2 'An Ideal of a Continental Relationship,' 23 March 1910, PAC, Borden Papers (BP), v. 300. See R. Craig Brown and Ramsay Cook, *Canada, 1896-1921: A Nation Transformed* (Toronto, 1974), 189-90.

and its ability to ameliorate social conditions through great increases in national wealth. When a Conservative candidate in the west interpreted the Halifax Platform's reform measures to be socialist in nature, Borden correctly pointed out that such an interpretation 'was not at all in accord with my views nor indeed with the articles of the Halifax platform.'[3] Taking his own career progress from a Grand Pré, Nova Scotia, farm to the prime minister's office as a lesson, Borden often expressed the views of a Canadian Samuel Smiles: 'To waste time is like wasting one's future.'[4] The earnest, the energetic, and the responsible would inevitably triumph over their circumstances. As his biographer notes, 'Borden and his colleagues would try to correct the worst abuses of modern Canada's industrial society; they were not about to overturn it.'[5] Borden's political faith was closest not to that of Disraeli, who sought to purchase stability through working class legislation and romantic, flamboyant leadership, but to that of Gladstone, who sought to infuse politics with strong doses of morality and to reward 'responsibility' with participation in political life. One can well imagine Borden in Gladstone's place urging with great enthusiasm the grant of the franchise to the 'respectable' element of the working class which would 'look not to the interests of classes, but to the public interest.'[6] It was responsibility alone that could justify privilege.

Yet Borden was no Gladstone, endowed with remarkable colleagues, great personal administrative skill, and popular appeal. Nor was Canada Britain, with few geographical and linguistic barriers, with a long political tradition, and, with certain notable exceptions, a common culture. The task in Canada was therefore greater, but the materials notably inferior. Very soon political exigencies of the moment undermined any possibility of the construction of a long-term programme. And like his American contemporary, President William Howard Taft, Borden's progressive legislation was obscured by a failure to explain his larger

3 H. Borden, ed., *Robert Laird Borden: His Memoirs* (Toronto, 1938), I, 199.
4 This quotation comes from Borden's address to the graduating class at Acadia University on 25 May 1932 in which he spoke about the advantages of discipline and 'earnestness.' BP, v. 300.
5 R.C. Brown, *Robert Laird Borden: A Biography, 1854-1914* (Toronto, 1975), I, 217.
6 This extract, from a Gladstone speech on the second reading of the Reform Bill, 1866, is cited in John Vincent, *The Formation of the Liberal Party, 1857-1868* (London, 1966), 217. Vincent's section on Gladstone's concept of leadership and democracy points to many other parallels between the political thought of Borden and Gladstone. Disraeli's political approach and outlook, however, differ fundamentally from Borden's. See Robert Blake's *Disraeli* (London, 1966). While there may have been a 'transatlantic persuasion' of Liberalism, Conservatism had a much less successful crossing. See Robert Kelley, *The Transatlantic Persuasion* (New York, 1969).

purposes and by a fiery political conflict. Historians would eventually write of 'An Attempt at Reform,' not of 'An Age of Reform.'

A PROMISE UNFULFILLED

The details of Borden's 'attempts at reform' have been set out elsewhere.[7] What is important here is the impact of these reforms, successful or not, upon the structure of Conservative party politics. In this area the effect was significant because it was the political system, not the economic or social system, which Borden sought to change. During his years in opposition he had diagnosed Canada's 'political sickness' and found that lack of talented individuals, corruption, and weak organization were the major ills. The antidotes seemed obvious and painless: civil service reform and a more systematic approach to government expenditure. Once in power, however, they proved to be doses too strong to administer as Borden's colleagues began to realize they would affect not only Laurier's Liberals but themselves as well. Indeed, the side-effects of the cure were almost surely a new personality for the party system, and this Conservative members of Parliament could not accept.

That Borden did not end administrative and legislative corruption is clear, but historians have differed greatly on how much he achieved and how hard he tried. Controversy on this subject erupted in 1929 when R. MacGregor Dawson claimed that eleven thousand civil servants resigned or were removed from office in the three years after 1911. An angry Borden denounced Dawson privately and took issue with him publicly in his presidential address to the Canadian Historical Association in 1931. He denied that dismissals on a large scale occurred but admitted that his promised reforms were not implemented. Rather lamely, he pleaded the outbreak of war as an excuse for his procrastination. A more convincing repudiation of Dawson has been provided in *The Biography of an Institution*, a history of the Civil Service Commission. Examining the 363 questions in the House which Dawson used as evidence, the authors found that many of the supposed dismissals were based on rumour alone. Furthermore, of the eleven thousand who allegedly resigned, many left to join the armed services in 1914. Using documents from Borden's papers, Craig Brown has strengthened the case against Dawson. The Conservatives, he argued, did not purge the 'inside service' (civil servants in Ottawa) and with the 'outside service' Borden adopted the same policy as Laurier had in 1896: 'A civil servant could be dismissed [only] for

7 Brown and Cook, *Canada, 1896-1921*, chap. 10; and Brown, *Borden*, chaps. 10-12.

active political partisanship.' In short, the Conservatives carried out no purge but neither did they significantly improve on the past, despite their campaign rhetoric and Borden's good intentions.[8]

Dawson exaggerated, but he was correct in one respect: Borden's proposed reforms did not occur. Why did Borden, whose sincerity is generally accepted, fail so conspicuously to keep his promise of reform? His own answer is unconvincing; the *Report on the Organization of the Public Service* presented by Sir George Murray in 1912 suggests a more cogent one. Borden had appointed Murray, a former British Treasury official, to scrutinize the Canadian public service. The choice is interesting and reflects, incidentally, the influence of the British model upon Borden and others, notably civil service commissioner Adam Shortt.[9] Murray's report, however, emphasized how different the British model was from Canadian practice. It recommended, *inter alia*, that the Civil Service Commission, created by Laurier in 1908, be given responsibility for all recruitment; that civil servants possess greater security in their positions; that temporary appointments be drastically limited; that closer control of public expenditures be exercised; and that ministers 'direct' not 'administer' policy.[10] In sum, Murray's report, if implemented, would have fundamentally altered the relationship between minister and department, minister and member, and member and constituency. A revolution which had taken years in Britain would have swept Canada overnight. What would have happened to the parties? This was a question Murray understandably did not consider, but one that naturally troubled Borden. Could party leaders rely on party spirit to rally the troops without the adrenalin of patronage? Most likely not. More broadly, could the structure of the state easily absorb those functions which a 'purified' party would necessarily abandon? Even vigorous critics of the party system like the academics James Cappon and O.D. Skelton doubted that it could. 'Suppose you could remove' the party system, Cappon asked, 'what would take its place?'

8 Dawson, *The Civil Service of Canada* (London, 1929), 82; Hodgetts *et al., The Biography of an Institution*, 13-14; Brown, *Borden*, 209. Borden wrote to Meighen: 'The more I read Dawson's book the more I am disappointed and even disgusted. Maclean who knew him in Nova Scotia has an extremely poor opinion of Dawson, and while he was delighted with the tone of my letter, he strongly urged that the book and its author were not worth so much attention.' Borden to Meighen, BP, v. 215; and Borden, 'The Problem of an Efficient Civil Service,' Canadian Historical Association, *Report of the Annual Meeting* (1931), 14-16. See also Borden, *Memoirs*, I, 333n, where he relates how he 'saved' the East Block elevator operator.
9 Hodgetts *et al., ibid.*, 28-31.
10 Canada, *Sessional Papers*, 1913, no. 57a.

The unchecked conflict of class interests, provincial interests, religious interests, the free play of racial jealousy and prejudice? At present all these antagonisms are to a great extent modified and controlled by the party system of government into a certain amount of moderation and mutual understanding. What other system could do that work at present? It is a useful training for nations composed of heterogeneous elements; it has really created our national unity, and it produces probably the best and clearest expression of national opinion and will at which we could arrive. And it remains to be seen whether Canada is capable of making it a good deal better than it is at present.[11]

In the absence of ideology, tradition, or even formal government structure itself, the party system with its attendant corruption fulfilled important national needs which might otherwise be ignored. Like so many Canadian politicians, Borden discovered that what seemed rational in opposition was impracticable in power.

Thus very little changed. Borden did succeed in depoliticizing senior administrative posts, especially those on regulatory bodies.[12] This was in accordance with progressive dogma which held that such bodies must exist 'beyond politics'; but Borden's attempt to extend the sway of such 'non-political' agencies through the establishment of a tariff commission fell victim to an obstructionist Liberal Senate. Few politicians lamented the death. Moreover, the Commons Public Accounts Committee, which Borden had suggested could be reorganized to supervise public expenditure more closely, continued in its 'frank and shameless partisanship.' 'The Conservatives,' Norman Ward wrote, '... spent a joyous year or two exposing the former Liberal administration for the loose-jointed and even scrofulous enterprise they alleged it had become, and the Liberals came into their own as soon as the first Auditor General's report relating to Conservative affairs was tabled.'[13] Politicians preferred to proceed along familiar paths, and Borden was no political Moses to lead them towards a new, promised land. Indeed, absorbed with 'larger' issues, especially the naval bill, he appears scarcely to have tried.

He appointed to his cabinet skilled practitioners in the act of patronage such as J.D. Reid, Frank Cochrane, Robert Rogers, and L.P. Pelletier. While he permitted no purge of the civil service, dismissals did occur and patronage absorbed much of the ministers' time, as it had since Confederation. Frederick Monk, for

11 Cappon, 'The Party System of Government,' *Queen's Quarterly*, XI (April 1904), 436; and Skelton, 'Our Foes at Home,' *ibid.*, XXIII (July 1915), 105.
12 These included the chairman of the Board of Railway Commissioners and the chairman of the National Transcontinental Railway Commission. See Brown, *Borden*, 210.
13 *The Public Purse: A Study in Canadian Democracy* (Toronto, 1962), 143-4.

example, told Henri Bourassa that it occupied 'le 9/10 ième de mon temps depuis que je suis entré en fonctions.'[14] Reid had similar complaints, so did Borden; but from others came objections about the insufficiency of patronage. Sam Hughes warned Borden that Tories were 'getting it in the neck' wherever they neglected to throw out the Grits, and the Toronto Advisory Board to which all appointments had to be referred complained that ministers were not always listening to it.[15]

This advisory board, whose activities are illuminated in correspondence in the papers of A.E. Kemp and Tory backbencher Edmund Bristol, was simultaneously in charge of patronage and the party organization.[16] The tasks were inseparable, and failure in one realm inevitably led to failure in the other. Whatever the differences between Toronto and Quebec City, a similar appreciation of politics at the constituency level obtained in the two cities. A Quebec City Tory warned Borden that party support and efficient distribution of patronage were interrelated: 'Nous nous sommes plusieurs fois plaints, que la direction des

14 Monk to Bourassa, 20 Nov. 1911, PAC, Bourassa Papers.
15 A.R. Birmingham to A.E. Kemp, 20 March 1913, PAC, Kemp Papers, v. 3; and BP, Borden Diary, 1912-13.
16 A fascinating letter from Bristol to a constituent reveals how the system worked (PAO, Bristol Papers, v. 4):
   I have your letter of February 6th. The Members of Parliament do not make any appointments off their own bat − in the first place they take the advice of the officers of the Ward Associations in which the candidate for the position lives, and the general organizer of the Party is better aware than anyone of the vacancies that are apt to occur and the possibility of getting a particular position for a particular candidate. There are hundreds of applicants for positions and the whole thing is dealt with just as you would deal with your business. The applicants first go to Mr. Birmingham; they are then considered by a Committee of gentlemen who are supposed to look into their credentials and capabilities in regard to the particular position for which they are fitted, and are reported on. If it is in the Post Office or Customs, there are hundreds of applicants and once they have been passed upon they wait their turn, so that everybody gets a fair show.
   I presume that the gentleman you are interested in lives in Ward 3, and it would not be unreasonable that he should go to the Secretary of the Ward and become acquainted with him and let him know he was alive, a Conservative and a voter and that he wanted a position and the nature of the position he wanted. In due course the recommendation would have gone forward. Where there are hundreds of people wanting positions they have to be dealt with in a reasonable and systematic manner. The Members of Parliament are not permitted to play favorites, much as they might like to on some occasions.
   I am sorry not to have been able to do anything for you, but if the young gentleman you are interested in is not willing to follow the usual path so as to get himself in line for appointment, I can do nothing myself to assist him, which I much regret.

affaires fédérales, au point de vue du patronage, était faite de manière, à annuler complètement notre travail, et même, avant pour résultat trop fréquent de favoriser nos adversaires.'[17] This association of patronage with party organization and spirit was indelibly impressed upon the political consciousness of men like Hughes, Rogers, and Bristol. Its corollary was bitter partisanship and a bureaucracy pervaded by personal and political ties.

As Sir George Murray recognized, the Canadian state was a penny-farthing bicycle in the age of the automobile, and one of the liabilities of this was the enormous demands placed upon the ministers and, in particular, upon the prime minister. Cabinet business, the astonished Murray reported, could even include discussions on the tender for a pump. Such discussions infuriated Borden and the pettiness and squabbling had a predictable effect upon him. The prime minister withdrew almost entirely from party activities and permitted various ministers to build up their own personal fiefdoms whose existence he tried not to notice. The result was little co-ordination, ministerial disagreements, and an infuriating uncertainty for the party rank and file.[18] With the party leader shunning his necessary, if unpleasant, party tasks, the powerful Conservative machine fell into a state of serious disrepair.

To all concerned, from Borden to the Tory worker who expected a position in the Customs House after October 1911, the party system was seen as an increasingly ineffective tool for the acquisition of the desired end. By this time, Borden's belief that the party might be moulded into an instrument of public education had disappeared. The provincial premiers, upon whom Borden had placed great hopes, soon showed that they had provincial ends which they wanted the federal prime minister to serve. Sir James Whitney, for example, bluntly warned Borden: 'now that our friends are in power at Ottawa, we will be compelled to explain to the people why it is that the unfair treatment which we claimed we received from the Laurier Government is continued.' Unless Borden stood firm against Premier Rodmond Roblin's boundary demands, Ontario members of Parliament would be called upon 'to assist.'[19] This was a dire threat

17 Dr N. Dussault to Borden, 21 Aug. 1914, BP, v. 28.
18 For the effects on cabinet solidarity of this empire-building, see Crothers to Borden, 14 Feb. 1914, BP, v. 147.
19 Whitney to Borden, 18 Jan. 1913, PAO, Whitney Papers, v. 24; see also Christopher Armstrong, 'The Politics of Federalism: Ontario's Relations with the Federal Government, 1896-1941,' unpublished PhD thesis, University of Toronto, 1972, 419; and C.P. Warner, 'Sir James P. Whitney and Sir Robert L. Borden: Relations between a Conservative Provincial Premier and his Federal Party Leader, 1905-1914,' unpublished MPhil thesis, University of Toronto, 1967, 124-31.

and Borden obliged. The experience taught him that he had to escape the premiers' grasp. He did, but the price was the end of close federal-provincial co-operation in the party.[20] Simultaneously, however, Borden learned that national aims which he wished to achieve could only be attained through the use of his party. The result was a very limited vision in which the party was not regarded as an organic structure which required careful attention in all areas. Rather, the leader concerned himself with a few seemingly crucial elements, those which could guarantee him success in his immediate legislative programme. Once power had been acquired, Borden appears to have thought that the party should quietly shrink into the background in order that his full energies might be devoted to the service of the state. In short, Borden became an objective observer of his own party, far distant from its subjective concerns.

Borden's aloofness to traditional concerns and the atrophy of the Conservative organization did not, however, cause a collapse of Conservative support, with one significant exception – Quebec. In Ontario, British Columbia, and Manitoba, the provinces which had provided the foundation for victory, Conservative support apparently remained solid, primarily because of Borden's naval policy and Laurier's adamant opposition to it. Whitney, Roblin, and McBride spoke for Conservatives in their respective provinces when they urged Borden to stand fast. Given the power groupings in his party, Borden could do nothing else; but this confounded his efforts to find a policy which French-Canadian Conservatives could support in good conscience.

THE DECLINE OF QUEBEC CONSERVATISM

An unpopular naval policy, organizational decay, and Borden's lack of understanding of French Canada combined to undermine Quebec Conservatism between 1911 and 1914. In the election of 1911 Quebec had given nearly half of its votes to the Conservative-*nationaliste* alliance but internal bargaining within the caucus and the cabinet never reflected this fact. The fault lay partly with an unrepresentative electoral system and partly with Borden himself. Craig Brown has spoken of Borden's 'indifference' to French Canada and of his belief that 'national development' must take precedence over any special claims of French Canada. French Canada, it seemed to Borden, had not yet achieved political maturity and no better evidence of this existed than his view of his own French-Canadian colleagues. They were regarded as a burden that a political leader must

20 For the decline of the Ontario machine, see J.S. Carstairs to Borden, 23 May 1912, Kemp Papers, v. 3.

bear until the 'coming of age' of the province finally took place. For this reason, from the very first days of the Borden government, no French-Canadian minister was represented or even received a sympathetic hearing in the 'inner circle' of the cabinet.[21] What made this situation particularly unfortunate was the impact which the major decisions of the pre-war years were to have upon French Canada.

Borden's troubles were predicted by many observers the moment he took office. What did Borden know of French Canada? How, they asked, could imperialists and *nationalistes* occupy the same parliamentary benches? Nevertheless, Borden believed they must, and initially he sought a compromise that would satisfy both. In his account of the naval crisis Craig Brown has shown how Winston Churchill's 18 March 1912 announcement of a more rapid Dreadnought building programme subverted Borden's early attempts at compromise by bringing to the fore the question of an emergency contribution from Canada to Britain.[22] As in 1910 Bourassa and Monk refused to believe there was an emergency; but Borden wanted to see for himself and accordingly asked Monk to join him on a visit to Britain in June 1912 where both could learn how great the emergency was. Borden apparently placed his hopes for party unity upon Monk falling prey to the 'Thames fever' which had occasionally infected earlier French-Canadian statesmen who strayed too near the seat of imperial grandeur. Monk, however, knew the dangers and refused the invitation. In the end, Louis Philippe Pelletier represented French Canada, although he lacked Monk's reputation in both French and English Canada as well as his close links with *nationaliste* sentiment in Quebec.[23] He was a most unsatisfactory substitute, and his selection was itself an indication of the rapidly declining fortunes of Quebec Conservatism.

Nevertheless, the common assertion that the Conservative naval bill led directly to the party's collapse in Quebec oversimplifies a complex problem.[24] There is strong evidence that other powerful forces were also active in this process. One of the most important was the persistent struggle for control of the party apparatus in Quebec, a struggle complicated by Borden's rather intentional

21 R.C. Brown, 'The Political Ideas of Robert Borden,' in M. Hamelin, ed., *The Political Ideas of the Prime Minister of Canada* (Ottawa, 1969), 97-9; and Borden Diary, 1912.
22 Borden, *Brown*, 235-6. Ironically, on 18 March Borden had made two concessions to *nationaliste* feeling: he had abandoned Laurier's naval programme and had noted his insistence on a voice in imperial councils in return for Canadian naval aid.
23 According to Rumilly, Bourassa and the *nationalistes* were 'intraitables pour Louis Philippe Pelletier.' *Henri Bourassa* (Montreal, 1953), 463.
24 Borden himself suggests this in his *Memoirs*, II, chaps. 17 and 19.

ignorance of the subject. At no time did either Monk or Pelletier, the titular leaders, control the Quebec organization, and patronage was dispensed haphazardly if at all. Charles G. Power, a politically alert Liberal in Quebec City, recalled the bitter battles among Sir Rodolphe Forget, Pelletier, and Sir William Price. This delighted Power; it appalled Borden. Price, who had been defeated in 1911, apparently tried to retain organizational dominance. When elected members opposed him he reported through an intermediary that he was tired of the constant opposition which he encountered and that he was thoroughly sick of the whole thing. Unless mollified he would 'throw up the whole thing.' Price was appeased, but Borden called in, astonishingly enough, Sir Charles Fitzpatrick, a former Liberal minister of justice and now chief justice of Canada, to sort out Quebec City and area problems. He had some success, and blessings in the form of grain terminals soon flowed.[25] Nevertheless, relief was temporary, and it did not obscure Borden's failure to work through his own parliamentary colleagues. More distressingly, it reveals Borden's apparent need to have a personal buffer between himself and the French-Canadian Conservatives.

This personal barrier to understanding exacerbated political differences when Borden returned from Britain in September 1912 determined to pass a naval bill which would grant Britain $35 million for the 'largest and strongest ships of war which science can build or money supply.'[26] Monk knew that a difficult decision faced him, and in the 4 September Le Devoir Bourassa delivered a public ultimatum to him:

Ceux qui connaissent comme nous le désintéressement personnel de M. Monk, qui ont entendu les accents indignés avec lesquels il a dénoncé si souvent les politiciens qui se collent au pouvoir aux dépens de leurs principes et de leurs engagements, ne doutent pas un instant qu'il fera accepter par ses collègues les principes et les idées qu'il a préconisés depuis son discours de Lachine, en novembre 1909, jusqu'au 21 septembre 1911 — ou qu'il démissionera.

A 17 September meeting of council on the naval issue revealed the wide gulf between the two points of view in the cabinet. Monk did agree that the imperial naval situation was 'grave,' but he demanded a plebiscite before any support was

---

25 *A Party Politician: The Memoirs of Chubby Power*, ed. Norman Ward (Toronto, 1966); Casgrain to Borden, 14 April, Pentland to Casgrain, 23 April 1913, BP, v. 28; Brown, *Borden*, 251; Borden Diary, 1912-13, and BP, v. 25. Fitzpatrick's unusual role is probably explained by his close ties to Quebec contractor, M.P. Davis, who relied heavily on government contracts.
26 A.R.M. Lower, *Colony to Nation* (4th ed., Toronto, 1965), 455.

given to Britain. The English-Canadian ministers, with the notable exception of Charles Doherty, strongly opposed a plebiscite which they felt showed 'weakness and indecision.'

On the following day Borden dined with Sir Hugh Graham in Montreal. One hopes the fare pleased Borden; the conversation certainly did not. Graham warned him that the Quebec organization was 'very defective' and close to collapse,[27] and that Monk's resignation would be the *coup de grâce*. Another visitor to eastern Quebec in the same month discovered that 'reorganization ... is needed by a surface view of the situation.'[28] For their part, the *nationalistes* who had helped so much in the campaign were no longer welcomed now that power was in hand. Thus they stood aside waiting for decisions in Ottawa while the Conservatives engaged in an unseemly struggle for spoils. At the very moment when a strong organization was most desperately needed to sustain the party, it was torn by dissension and disintegrating rapidly. Yet the English-Canadian Conservatives persisted in forcing the issue and forbade even an honourable retreat for their French-Canadian colleagues.

That mine of Conservative gossip, Charles Hamilton, expressed the truculent English-Canadian Tory attitude when he suggested to John Willison that Monk's resignation was 'too great luck for any of us to have any right to expect it.' For once Willison showed better political sense by warning Hamilton that Monk was 'the only man in the Government who counts in the French Province.' Prophetically, he added: 'Without Monk the Government must be utterly overwhelmed in Quebec.'[29] Monk, Willison saw, stood above the mire of constituency battles and alone among Conservatives represented a force which would have a broad appeal to the disillusioned Liberals and the independents in Quebec politics.

But in the middle of October the harassed Monk resigned, stating that the passage of the naval bill without a plebiscite was 'at variance' with his election pledges.[30] The sense of personal betrayal felt by Borden subdued any rational attempt to understand Monk's position. He did, it is true, ask the 'Conservative press' to be 'tender' in its treatment of Monk, but this was more the product of

27 Borden Diary, 17 and 18 Sept. 1912.
28 Arthur Ford to Willison, 10 Sept. 1912, PAC, Willison Papers, v. 30.
29 Hamilton to Willison, 6 Oct., Willison to Hamilton, 7 Oct. 1912, Willison Papers, v. 37. Soon after this Willison fired his veteran Ottawa reporter, Hamilton, and a valuable source for future historians was lost. Hamilton's Tory connections secured him a government job and during the war he became a censor, a task which undoubtedly pleased him given his proclivity to gossip.
30 See Borden, *Memoirs*, I, 400-1, for Monk's letter of resignation. The Monk Papers give some indication that a death in his family and bad health were additional reasons for his departure. He was also a poor administrator who did not enjoy his work in Ottawa.

shrewd politics and human sympathy than it was a reflection of an understanding of French-Canadian grievances.[31] Monk's friend, Bourassa, drifted quickly towards irreconcilable separation from the Tories, and a chapter within French-Canadian Conservatism ended without climax, only confusion.

The English-Canadian Conservatives in Quebec could not escape the affliction. Indeed, they were drastically affected by the organizational chaos and were perturbed by many of the decisions of the new Borden government. The Montreal business community was greatly offended by the strong representation in the federal cabinet of Toronto financial and industrial interests traditionally hostile to Montreal. Borden himself had never been completely trusted since he had advocated public ownership of railways and natural resources. Thus, at a time when the French Canadians were alienated by party policy, the English-Canadian Conservatives, who possessed such great social and economic power within the province, were also disaffected. Never had the Tories' lot in Quebec been so dismal.

The cabinet itself reflected the atrophy of Quebec Conservatism. Monk's departure was not balanced by the entry of an equally important politician. When L.T. Maréchal, a pro-navy French-Canadian politician, hesitated to enter the cabinet, Borden turned to the largely unknown Louis Coderre who became secretary of state, a much less significant portfolio than the patronage-rich one of public works which now passed into the eager hands of Robert Rogers.[32] During the by-election in Hochelaga caused by Coderre's appointment, Borden was warned that his presence would be 'not only unnecessary but undesirable.'[33] He heeded the advice, and left the campaign to several of his ministers and members. Along with Coderre, they reminded the constituents what benefits a cabinet minister could bestow upon them. They also frequently noted that Coderre's opponent was a *nationaliste*, not a Liberal. The arguments proved effective, and Coderre won; but the victory was merely a balm that did not cure. Hochelaga was not a typical Quebec constituency — it was 38 per cent English-speaking and included an imperialist bastion, Westmount. Accordingly, the victory tells us little about Conservative strength among French Canadians; it does signify the end of the Conservative-*nationaliste* alliance.[34]

31 Hamilton to Willison, 16 Oct. 1912, Willison Papers, v. 37. Borden Diary, 25 Oct. 1912. In his *Memoirs* (I, 300) Borden merely says that Monk lacked 'courage.' This remark is further substantiation of Borden's belief that French Canada was a burden to national interests.
32 Borden Diary, 25 Oct. and 1 Nov. 1912.
33 Borden to Bonar Law, 3 Dec. 1912, quoted in Brown, *Borden*, 250.
34 *Canadian Parliamentary Guide, 1913*; *Census of Canada, 1911*, v. 2; *Montreal Star*, Dec. 1912; and Brown, *Borden*, 250. In 1913 the Conservatives won a by-election in Chateauguay constituency using similar methods. It, too, had a large English population (27 per cent), and needed a railway (which it received).

What the Conservatives employed in Hochelaga, Borden applied to the French-Canadian Conservative members. He promised favours, he offered pretexts, and some finally gave way. This was enough; and to the resounding applause of his English-Canadian colleagues Borden presented his naval policy which featured a $35 million 'emergency' contribution to Canada's imperilled motherland.[35] In the spirited debate which followed, as 'primeval passions'[36] surged through the Commons chamber, French-Canadian Tories remained silent; Monk stayed away. Robert Rumilly describes what happened when division came on first reading: 'Sept conservateurs canadiens-français ... se sónt séparés de leur parti. Monk absent, toujours malade, il reste douze députés élus sur un programme nationaliste et qui votent pour la contribution Borden. Le *Devoir* les appelle des traîtres, et publie maint extrait de leurs discours de 1910 et 1911.'[37]

The body of the party suffered as its leadership faltered. To the old *bleu* Thomas Chase Casgrain, writing to Borden in autumn 1913, the situation in Quebec had become almost irreparable:

There is nothing doing here; no organization; no stirring up of the masses; no educational campaign; no telling our people what we have done, what we intend doing; nothing to inspire the young men with confidence in the future of the Conservative Party. I am told, and I really believe that it is true, that the young men are discouraged and are gradually dropping away from us. I know that this is not your fault, and it is a great pity to trouble you with these lamentations, but I, like a great many others, do not know to whom we should address ourselves, if not to you.[38]

Yet Borden did nothing; he knew of nothing which could be done. Perhaps Borden, who understood the value of delay, believed time would heal the

35 J.O. Lavallée, L.P. Gauthier, E. Paquet, J.H. Rainville, P.E. Blondin, and A. Sévigny all agreed to support Borden's policy on 27 Nov. 1912. Of the six opponents Borden listed he misspelled two of their names. Borden Diary, 27 Nov. 1912. For a description of the policy, see Brown, *Borden*, 239.
36 Borden Diary, 15 March 1913.
37 *Henri Bourassa*, 473. The seven men were H. Achim, J.A. Barrette, A. Bellemare, H. Boulay, E. Guilbault, P.E. Lamarche, and A.A. Mondou.
38 17 Sept. 1913, BP, v. 28; see also *Le Devoir*, 22 Nov. 1913. Casgrain was one of the last of the old *bleu* element within the Conservative party and unquestionably Borden's favourite among French-Canadian politicians. A member of a large, predominantly English, law firm; a proponent of electoral reform; a supporter of temperance legislation; and the prosecutor of Louis Riel and Honoré Mercier, Casgrain had great popularity with the English-speaking electorate.

wounds, but more knowledgeable observers of Quebec politics felt otherwise.[39] Casgrain's analysis, an epitaph for the vision of October 1911, could not be contradicted.

In the final months of 1913 and in early 1914 many of Borden's correspondents further confirmed the accuracy of Casgrain's charges. The party secretary in the Eastern Townships complained that French Canadians were not allowed to take their part in Conservative activities in the area and were therefore leaving the party.[40] From Montreal similar cries arose, and in Ottawa the Quebec Tories seemed to reflect the organization's troubles. Coderre rapidly proved a failure, politically and administratively. On 30 April 1914 Borden was urged to appoint the unpopular though capable Casgrain to Coderre's position, but Casgrain's probable inability to obtain a seat rendered the suggestion impossible. When, however, Pelletier submitted in May what Borden sarcastically but accurately termed 'his annual resignation,'[41] so barren were the Tory ranks in Quebec that Casgrain was asked to join the cabinet. As soon as the offer was made, Pelletier withdrew his resignation leaving confusion and, the uncharitable might add, incompetence in Ottawa.

In June 1914 George Perley left for England to become acting high commissioner and Borden lost one of the few links between the wealthy English Canadians and the French Canadians, and an interpreter of the aims and difficulties of both groups to Ottawa.[42] Borden could not fill this void and, indeed, appears to have accepted it with equanimity. Even in September 1914, after the outbreak of war had profoundly disturbed the political atmosphere in Quebec, Perley continued to be Borden's principal adviser on the Eastern Townships from the heart of Trafalgar Square! There is no evidence that any French Canadian, apart from Casgrain whose organizational role was small, was ever consulted during that very important summer of 1914.

The 'fall' of the English Liberal party has been compared to that of a man with a terminal illness stepping off a curb and then being hit by a bus, namely

39 Philippe Panneton to Pelletier, 3 Dec., and George Perley to Borden, 15 Oct. 1913, BP, v. 28.
40 The party organizer in the area, L. Shurtleff, was accused of this prejudice. Panneton to Pelletier, 3 Dec. 1913, BP, v. 28. At this time the Eastern Townships' English population was feeling increasingly threatened by the rapid growth of the French population, a fear well expressed in Robert Sellars, *The Tragedy of Quebec* (Huntingdon, Que., 1908).
41 Borden Diary, 29 May 1914. Casgrain to Borden, 28 Aug. 1914, BP, v. 28. Borden had spoken to Casgrain about a post on 11 May but this would have been Coderre's portfolio. Borden Diary, 11 May 1914.
42 Perley to Borden, 8 Sept. 1914, BP, v. 33.

the First World War.[43] This image has considerable merit as a description of the 'fall' of Quebec Conservatism. The same 'bus,' the First World War, struck it at the very time when it was infected with a probably fatal illness. Would the party have collapsed in the absence of war? There can be no definite answer, but it can be said that by August 1914 the buoyant hopes of Quebec Conservatives in 1911 had disappeared and to most observers they seemed totally beyond recovery.

For the collapse of Quebec Conservatism, both the English-Canadian leader and his deputies, and the mediocre French-Canadian members, must share some of the blame. The collapse, once it had begun, had about it an aura of inevitability. A tantalizing question nevertheless remains: what impact would an open Conservative-Bourassa alliance have had if it had been negotiated in 1907 or 1908? Undoubtedly younger and abler men would have bolstered the party, but it is unlikely that these new men could have long endured the atmosphere of the federal Conservative caucus with its numerous, vociferous Orangemen; its strong attachment to the British connection; and its Protestant, Anglo-Saxon *Weltanschauung*. When an alliance was first mooted in 1907 the imperialist flame burnt with relative dimness. After 1911 the fires had been stoked to burn with even greater intensity than during the South African War. Above all, it must be remembered that Borden, not Bourassa, rebuffed the proposed alliance. The Conservative leader realized that the *nationalistes* could aid the Tories in Quebec and that they possessed a more progressive social outlook than the traditional Quebec Conservatives, but he also understood that any open alliance would be repugnant to a great number of Conservatives. Events after 1907 did not belie Borden's judgment at that time.

In any period of intense political excitement and fundamental disagreement, a party must ponder where its greatest strength resides. Thus the hypocrisy of 1911 could not be sustained when public scrutiny grew. The mists surrounding the Conservative party in opposition were soon dispelled when power was achieved. Borden made a choice; the victim of that choice was Quebec Conservatism. Macaulay once described political parties:[44] 'Every political sect has its esoteric and its exoteric school, its abstract doctrines for the initiated, its visible symbols, its imposing forms, its mythological fables for the vulgar. It assists the devotion of those who are unable to raise themselves to the contemplation of pure truth by all devices of superstition. It has its altars and its deified heroes, its relics and its pilgrimages, its canonized martyrs and confessors,

---

43 Trevor Wilson, *The Downfall of the Liberal Party, 1914-1935* (London, 1966), introduction.
44 Cited in Henry Jones Ford, *The Rise and Growth of American Politics* (New York, 1898), 129.

and its legendary miracles.' By August 1914 most of the 'visible symbols,' the 'mythological fables,' the 'altars,' and the 'relics' of Canadian Conservatism were either unknown or anathema to French Canadians.

THE POLITICS OF ONE CANADA

Abraham Lincoln once compared his position to a man being ridden out of town on a rail who commented: 'If it were not for the honor of the thing, I would rather walk.'[45] Borden's diary suggests he often shared the feeling. His first years in office were an exceedingly rough ride as he discovered that his control over his party and the state were both severely limited. He found that Sir George Murray's complaints about the lack of hierarchy and systemization in the civil service could be equally applied to the party. Like many other Canadians, Borden believed that this should not be so and that strong national policies were impossible under these circumstances. Fundamentally, he looked forward to a day when political and private interests could be separated, but he had to work with a system where they were not. Thus, Sir Rodolphe Forget's threats of political vengeance if his railway did not receive a subsidy were intolerable yet they had to be granted.[46] These decisions, Borden thought, should be made on 'business' not political grounds, and it gave him some satisfaction in his own mind that the former were applied when the Grand Trunk and the Canadian Northern pleaded their cases for governmental help. Yet suspicion abounded that political 'pay-offs' inspired the decisions, even among railway men and some Conservatives.[47]

The doubters could not be blamed; precedent was certainly on their side. But times were changing. By 1911 railways were no longer one of few organized interests, confident of getting their way in Ottawa. Now the interests were many: farmers' groups, imperialists, *nationalistes*, temperance reformers, social gospellers, manufacturing associations, and labour organizations, each with a voice, each believing that national political action was necessary to achieve their goals. Through such groups many Canadians became involved in political bargaining at the highest levels and not merely in their own constituencies. In this situation, positive national policies faced barriers beyond the cabinet and caucus. Delay and controversy were inevitable products when groups frustrated in their own aims found satisfaction in blocking others. In this milieu politics became negative, a symptom of the increasing inflexibility — political scientists

45 Cited in Karl Deutsch, *Politics and Government* (Boston, 1970), 243.
46 Borden Diary, Oct. 1912.
47 Brown and Cook, *Canada, 1896-1921*, 200-3.

would say immobility – of the Canadian party system. To break through this political thicket Borden proposed to reinvigorate his party by drawing to it a significant number of the new interest groups through vague promises of a more dynamic national policy. He had some success in opposition, but in power his hopes dissipated when many newcomers found their influence imperceptible, their 'interests' ignored, and the new 'national policy' not what it had seemed to be. Borden's plan thus failed, and the roots of its failure reside as much in Borden's view of democracy and leadership as in the irreconcilability of the competing interests.

'Democracy,' a modern political scientist wrote, 'requires institutions which support conflict and disagreement as well as those which sustain legitimacy and consensus.'[48] The latter need, Borden appreciated; the former, he could not understand. To Borden, politics – 'that solution to the problem of order which chooses conciliation rather than violence and coercion, and chooses it as an effective way by which varying interests can discover that level of compromise best suited to their common interest in survival' – were an unfortunate attribute of modern democracy, but an attribute above which the general interest must, at certain times, take a clear pre-eminence.[49] Dissent and conflict might be necessary ingredients of a party system, but, like a fire in a hearth, they must be well regulated lest they consume the entire structure. Arthur Meighen drew a fine portrait of his former leader's frustrations with the limitations of democracy: 'Waste of time in Parliament or in Council was a burden for him to endure. When he came to a conclusion as to what was in the public interest, he wanted that thing done and was impatient of restraints imposed by the clamourings of what the Press calls "public opinion." '[50]

Once endowed with the mantle of power, Borden, as Meighen testified, accepted that he had an obligation to interpret and to act upon 'the public interest.' To those holding such a belief, opposition, delay, or obstruction whether in caucus, in cabinet, or in the Commons was not merely troublesome but fundamentally unpatriotic. The failure of Borden's peacetime years as leader lies in his inability to understand the role of opposition and to recognize anything positive in compromises. Compromises came grudgingly from him and were abandoned hastily if opportunity arose. Thus, when the French-Canadian members refused to support his naval bill their protests were ignored and, as a

48 Seymour M. Lipset, *Political Man* (Garden City, NY, 1963), 439.
49 The definition of politics is Bernard Crick's in his *In Defence of Politics* (Harmondsworth, 1964), 30. While Crick's definition is, in his own words, 'narrow and laudatory,' it does illustrate well those features of politics to which Borden objected.
50 'Introduction,' Borden, *Memoirs*, I, viii.

group, they were dismissed as 'variable and unstable,' unworthy of further attention. And when Laurier in opposition obstructed the passage of his naval bill, Borden, for the first time in Canadian history, invoked closure, denying Laurier the right to speak.[51] After the Liberal Senate, outraged by the 'gagging' of Laurier, defeated the bill and challenged Borden to submit it for popular approval, he rejected the dare, announced his eventual intention to take over and pay for three British ships then being built, and imputed the basest motives to his opponents.

The suggestion that conflict in politics might itself be creative would have struck Borden, who believed in an objective and definable general interest, as an utter absurdity.[52] Differences in politics were opportunistic masks which concealed a narrow selfish interest that the 'best element' in the land should transcend. During the naval discussions in Britain, Borden claimed that the Canadian delegates 'had borne [themselves] as representatives not of a party but of the whole people.' Yet at home Canadians were divided, unwilling to accept leadership, locked in the narrow confines of their individual interests. Contemptuous of those who rejected a larger vision, Borden expressed his goal as 'one Canada' without an 'East and West in sentiment and ideals.'[53] Between 1911 and 1914, as this prospect receded rapidly from the political horizon, he learned with chagrin the constraints placed upon political leadership in Canada. Unlike Laurier, Borden could not learn how to use them.

51 Borden, *Memoirs*, 414-18; Borden Diary, 16 March 1913.
52 I am using the term 'conflict' in the sense suggested by Gad Horowitz in his *Canadian Labour in Politics* (Toronto, 1968). With Horowitz, creative politics are based on class divisions. It is wrong to assume that Borden thought conflict would not occur.
53 Borden, *Memoirs*, I, 373.

5

Party life in wartime

On 4 August 1914 a train slowly edged towards a crowded platform in the cavernous Ottawa station. On that platform there was a peculiar blend of apprehension, curiosity, and enthusiasm as the crowd awaited Sir Wilfrid Laurier, Canada's prime minister between 1896 and 1911 and still Liberal leader. All knew that Laurier's statement on the almost inevitable European war would be made when he stepped from that train. Few knew what the war would mean; none knew what Laurier would say. The English-Canadian Liberals, probably the majority of the throng, were particularly expectant. They had bitterly resented the mutterings of the Tories after 1911 that Laurier was a greybeard, sapped of the vigour and courage of his youth, and that their leader, terrified of the inroads which nationalism was making among the young of Quebec, was withdrawing into a political cocoon which limited his vision to his native province alone. Now, these Liberals hoped, Laurier would demolish the bitter caricature drawn by the Tory jingoes.[1]

War confronted Canadian Liberalism, with its widespread Quebec support, its vestigial Cobdenism, and its strength among non-British immigrants, with a difficult decision. Laurier knew that when Britain was at war, Canada was also at war; both constitution and sentiment commanded it. But it was equally clear to Laurier that the kind and the extent of participation must be Canada's own decision: this was the Boer war precedent and had been the basis of the Liberal stand during the naval bill debate. Because the nature of the British connection, the Canadian Liberal's greatest dilemma, was at the core of the question, Laurier knew that he must choose his words deliberately. Beginning his statement with

---

1 This account is taken from the *Ottawa Journal*, 5 Aug. 1914. Laurier was returning to Ottawa from his summer home in Arthabaska. See also O.D. Skelton, *Life and Letters of Sir Wilfrid Laurier* (London, 1922), II, chap. 18.

the hope that Sir Edward Grey might yet be successful in his attempts to avert war, Laurier observed that if conflict erupted, England and France, together the 'noblest expression' of 'higher civilization,' would share the greatest burdens. He continued: 'The policy of the Liberal party under such painful circumstances is well known. I have often declared that if the Mother Country were ever in danger, or if danger ever threatened, Canada would render assistance to the fullest extent of her power. In view of the critical nature of the situation I have cancelled all my meetings. Pending such great questions, there should be a truce to party strife.' To the *nationalistes*' question 'what do we owe to England?' Laurier gave a rather surprising answer: 'assistance to the fullest extent of [Canada's] power.'[2]

War soon followed and Laurier maintained his stand. In a special session of Parliament on 18 August he elaborated upon his position without altering it: 'Speaking for those who sit around me, speaking for the wide constituency which we represent in this House, I hasten to say that to all these measures [of war] we are prepared to give immediate assent. If in what has been done or in what remains to be done there may be anything which in our judgment should not be done or should be differently done, we raise no question, we take no exception, we offer no criticism, and we shall offer no criticism so long as there is danger at the front.'[3] Laurier's statement was unequivocal and extraordinary. He had changed the ground rules of Canadian politics by promising a Canadian *Burgfrieden* during which the Liberal party would support all war measures 'so long as there is danger at the front.' The Conservatives naturally believed that he had given the government a virtual *carte blanche* to prosecute the war. It certainly did not require a strict construction to derive this interpretation from

2 Quoted in J.C. Hopkins, *Canada at War* (Toronto, 1919), 33. 'Que devons-nous à l'Angleterre?' was the title of a famous Bourassa study of Canada's constitutional and political position published in 1915. The question had been implied in Bourassa's writings since 1899 and the South African War. Laurier, it is true, considered that the war was primarily Britain's war, but this did not arise as a justification for a limited Canadian war effort. Canada's effort was to be a full one, to the fullest extent of her power. Laurier's words in 1914 are remarkably similar to those of J.W. Dafoe, a Liberal nationalist who was to break decisively with Laurier in 1917 over conscription: 'If Great Britain is involved in war either by her own decision that the circumstances leave no option, or through the aggression of an outside party, it is quite certain that Canada will come to her assistance with all the power at her disposal.' *Manitoba Free Press*, 3 Aug. 1914. Skelton, however, attempts to argue that Laurier's position was unchanging and always a 'middle ground' while Dafoe became an extremist. *Laurier*, II, chaps. 18 and 19.
3 Quoted in Skelton, *ibid.*, 432-4.

Laurier's words, and where such great opportunity existed the Tories were definitely not strict constructionists.[4]

Reasons for Laurier's tone and words are now easily discovered,[5] but in August 1914 the remarks astonished the Conservatives. The war had erupted when the frustrated Tory party, angered by Liberal obstruction and fearful of the political impact of a severe winter depression, was seriously considering a general election.[6] Since the war was immediately interpreted by the Tories as a justification of their attitude towards the naval question and as proof of the moral bankruptcy of the Liberals, an election was even more appealing after the war began. Revenge for the Liberal defeat of the naval bill in the Senate would be just and sweet; but Laurier's speeches in August 1914, by their high-minded appeal to a greater interest beyond party and politics, had undercut the Tory hopes. As Sir John Willison, one of the most bitter critics of the Liberals' attitude in the naval debate, expressed it, 'the prospect of a party conflict while Canadian soldiers were dying in Europe was intolerable to thousands of patriotic Conservatives.'[7] With Laurier's public pledge that no questions would be raised and no criticism would be offered, an election seemed both unnecessary and dangerous for the Conservatives.[8] The result was no election and an obscuring of national differences: Canada, it seemed, marched into war as a united nation.

The Canadian novelist Ralph Connor — a Presbyterian clergyman and a chaplain in the First World War — described his memory of the first days of war in his 1917 novel, *The Major*: 'The Board of Trade; the Canadian Club, that free forum of national public opinion; the great courts of the various religious bodies; the great fraternal societies and whatsoever organization had a voice, all pledged unqualified, unlimited, unhesitating support to the Government in its resolve to make war.'[9] Whatever the literary merit of such a description, its historical

---

4 See PAC, Borden Papers (BP), Borden Diary, 19 Aug. 1914. Borden believed Laurier had 'committed himself thoroughly to support' the government.

5 Skelton, *Laurier*, II, chap. 18; Sir John Willison, *Sir Wilfrid Laurier* (Toronto, 1927), 435; and PAC, King Papers, King Diary, Aug. 1914.

6 Evidence of consideration of an election in July may be found in BP, v. 33; see especially G.H. Perley to Borden, 6 July 1914. In a speech on 3 May 1915, Robert Rogers stated that the government had intended to call an election in Aug. 1914. *Montreal Star*, 4 May 1915. See also R.C. Brown, *Robert Laird Borden: A Biography, 1854-1914* (Toronto, 1975), I, 253-7; and E. Bristol to Borden, 2 July 1914, PAO, Bristol Papers, v. 2.

7 *Laurier*, 439.

8 See, for example, Arthur Ford's assessment of the great dangers in Ford to Willison, 28 Sept. 1914, PAC, Willison Papers, v. 30.

9 (Toronto, 1917), 333; Ralph Connor was the *nom de plume* of Dr Charles W. Gordon.

validity is highly suspect. Canada's response, in contrast to Borden's and Laurier's, was not in unison, not even in mixed parts, but one whose quality reflected the great diversity of the nation itself. Even Laurier's parliamentary Liberal colleagues frequently differed with him on the war issue. Sir Robert Borden noted in his diary on 19 August that Laurier had told him 'in confidence' that he was having difficulties with 'some of his followers.' Both conspired to keep silent in order to create a false sense of unity and enthusiasm.

But it was not only in the caucus that Liberals indicated that they did not share Laurier's perception of the war. Rodolphe Lemieux, a former minister, placed clear limits upon Canada's role in a European war: 'What is to be done by Canada if the Motherland is involved, as seems quite possible? Canada being an integral part of the British Empire, is certainly at war when the Empire is at war. The reason is that the British flag is our flag, and because it protects our rights, our liberties and everything that is dear and sacred in this free land. We should rally as one man to the defence, first of our coasts and then of the great Empire to which we belong.'[10] This is a distinction that is most definitely a difference. Lemieux's speech, unlike his leader's, has a pragmatic air, a recognition that there can indeed be priorities and limits in wartime. Elizabeth Armstrong in her study of Quebec attitudes towards the war has called this attitude Quebec's 'traditional doctrine': an implied agreement of loyalty to Britain in exchange for defence of the French Canadians' religion and language.[11] The metaphor springs from the marketplace not from the altar.

That this was the metaphor employed by the majority of French Canadians can no longer be doubted.[12] The *Montreal Star* in early August 1914 polled many Canadians on whether immediate aid should be given to Britain. The replies are most interesting: outside of Quebec, the support was overwhelming, unanimous, and often couched in emotional rhetoric. In Quebec, although the proposal was supported by the large majority of respondents, there was much less enthusiasm and very little emotion. Participation was usually justified by the argument that it was Canada itself that would be protected by aid to Britain. Some, including the influential Liberal senators Louis Lavergne and L.G. Power, thought the *Star*'s question 'premature' and were evasive in their replies. Liberal

10 Cited in J.C. Hopkins, *Canadian Annual Review, 1914* (Toronto, 1915), 141.
11 *The Crisis of Quebec, 1914-1918* (New York, 1937), 59-60.
12 Several studies confirm this, notably *ibid.*; Mason Wade, *The French-Canadians: 1760-1945* (Toronto, 1955), II; Robert Rumilly, *Histoire de la province de Quebec* (Montreal, n.d.), XXI; and René Durocher, 'Henri Bourassa, les évêques et la guerre de 1914-1918,' Canadian Historical Association, *Historical Papers* (1971), 248-75.

member Lucien Pacaud boldly asserted that Canada should look after herself first. A few French-Canadian respondents echoed Laurier, but they did so without possessing the responsibility which gave Laurier's words their great meaning. What is important about the *Star*'s poll of French-Canadian public officials is the clear, almost definable, limits which these officials placed upon Canada's activities in the war, limits which found no expression in the responses of their English-Canadian compatriots or in the speeches of French Canada's most prominent politician, Sir Wilfrid Laurier.

To go beyond the politicians of Quebec to the general public is to move from the overly garrulous to the normally inarticulate. Fortunately, Armstrong's study of the rural and small press of Quebec has found much evidence on the attitude of what might be termed the 'general public.' In rural Quebec, she was impressed by the intensity of feeling that Canada should be Canada's main concern in the war.[13] This belief's foundation was the *habitant*'s traditional suspicion of foreign involvement of any type. The war, too, was emotionally distant in rural Quebec: after the initial spate of articles at the time of the war's outbreak, articles on the war became fewer and fewer and completely disappeared from some issues. Interestingly, the war received greater coverage in Conservative papers than in Liberal papers but both justified the war in terms of the defence of Canada. Scant traces of Laurier's appreciation of the conflict appeared in rural Quebec.

In the major Quebec newspapers a similar lack of enthusiasm for the war was discernible. Some French-Canadian papers such as *La Patrie* did engage in the patriotic fulminations which imperialists deemed appropriate to the occasion, but most, while recognizing the importance of the war in editorials and by such devices as intertwined British and French flags on the cover, were more restrained, particularly when compared to their English-language counterparts in Quebec itself. *Le Devoir*, the semi-official voice of Quebec nationalism, was at first non-committal, a most uncharacteristic posture for that most sententious journal, but one which is explained by the absence of its editor, Henri Bourassa, in Europe. Finally, two weeks after his return, *Le Devoir* on 8 September joined the chorus supporting the war, but in notably muted tones. Although Bourassa professed to find 'no direct reason to intervene' and no immediate Canadian interest in the war, he nevertheless argued that Canada's national duty ('le devoir national') required her to contribute to the allied cause. Much later Bourassa admitted that the belated editorial was 'un des rare articles que j'aie écrit avec

---

13 *The Crisis of Quebec*, 63.

répugnance.'[14] In September 1914, however, this was unknown to the politicians in Ottawa who undoubtedly greeted Bourassa's lukewarm support of the war with a collective sigh of relief. What seemed important to these federal politicians was the remarkable absence of the open dissent so manifest during the Boer War. Canada had responded in unison in favour of participation in the war. Laurier's image of a Canada with 'one mind and heart'[15] echoed Borden's dream of a united Canada 'where East and West were one in ideals and sentiment.' What impact would this remarkable comity have upon the Canadian party system?

Lord Beaverbrook has written of Britain at the outbreak of war: 'the problem which leapt into the forefront the moment that war was seen to be inevitable was that of coalition ...'[16] In Canada, however, the idea of coalition did not 'leap into the forefront' when war was declared. Its birth was difficult; its adolescence protracted; and its maturity incomplete. Yet, curiously enough, pre-war conditions in Canada contained numerous impulses, perhaps more than in Britain, from which coalition might have arisen: the widespread distrust of party politics; the willingness of the Conservative prime minister to defy traditional party attitudes and his taste for seeking out good men from the ranks of Liberals and independents; and the eminently successful coalition of the 1860s which had been the midwife to the birth of Canada as a nation. Another factor favouring a coalition or 'national' government was the uneven distribution of party representation in Canada. The governing Conservatives had little strength in the Prairie provinces, where the presence of large numbers of recent immigrants of uncertain loyalties created considerable potential difficulties.[17] Even more significant was the weakness of the Conservative party in Quebec. It

---

14 Bourassa seems to have been affected by the strong support for the war of Mgr Paul-N. Bruchési, archbishop of Montreal, as well as the general popularity of the cause. The quotation is cited in Durocher, 'Henri Bourassa,' 252.

15 Laurier employed this emotive phrase in his first parliamentary speech on the war. Like most Canadians he probably expected the war to be short in length. It therefore seemed 'safe' and politically shrewd to employ such terms which he must have known would return to haunt him in any protracted war. See Skelton, *Laurier*, II, 432-4.

16 *Politicians and the War, 1914-1916* (London, 1928, 1932; 1960), 13.

17 Manitoba was of course an exception – the majority of its federal members were Tories as was the provincial government. A full study of this subject may be found in Joseph Boudreau, 'The Enemy Alien Problem in Canada: 1914-1921,' unpublished PhD thesis, University of California at Los Angeles, 1965. An interesting description of how both political leaders tried to avoid discussion of this sensitive topic may be found in Arthur Hawkes, *The Birthright* (Toronto, 1919), 114-20.

is true that the Conservatives were numerically well represented there, but it is equally valid to argue, as the Liberals did, that a large majority of the Tory members from Quebec was most unlikely to be re-elected.[18] Edmund Bristol had written to Sir Robert Borden on 2 July 1914 that the 'line-up' for the next election was 'apparently ... between the English and French.' The naval debate, he candidly admitted, had virtually sealed the Quebec Tories' doom.[19] Still, no coalition was created, nor were prominent independent figures brought into the government. What is more surprising is the lack of any suggestion that such a course be taken in 1914. Both the idea and the reality were yet unformed.

The principal reasons why coalition was not considered early in the war were the pledge by Laurier to observe a party truce, the seeming unanimity with which Canada responded to the announcement of war, and the benefits which many Tories expected from war contracts and patronage. Moreover, on the Liberal side, the striking weakness of the Conservatives, which would inevitably be exacerbated by the harsh decisions which war government required, made coalition an unreasonable alternative to the opposition benches. The Conservatives, too, saw little advantage in any link with the Liberals in which the plodding and stiff Borden would necessarily yield to the eloquent and even charismatic Laurier. Robert Rogers and many others viewed the abundant patronage which the war created as too rich a windfall to share with the Grits whose pre-war attitude struck many Tories as thoroughly unpatriotic. Yet all of these were not insuperable obstacles to the entry into the cabinet of some individual Liberals or independents who had reputations as skilled administrators or as stirring orators. There is a simpler explanation. The cabinet was not strengthened because in 1914 the crisis seemed insufficiently grave to warrant such action. The war-loving minister of militia, Sam Hughes, for example, worried lest the Canadians should not reach England before the last shot of the war was fired.[20] In Borden's own diary the sense of a great emotional and physical distance from the war is striking. What else is one to make of the

18 The Conservative difficulties are discussed in Chapter 4. Borden was fully aware of the dangers in Quebec: see, for example, D.O. L'Esperance to Borden, 9 April 1915, BP, v. 28, and other letters in this volume.
19 Bristol Papers, v. 2.
20 Most of the Canadian press, with the notable exception of the *Manitoba Free Press* and the *Montreal Star*, believed the conflict would be a very brief one. An interesting telegram was sent by Sir George Perley from England in March 1915 which stated that Earl Grey thought the war would last eight more months; Sir William Harcourt, eighteen months; and Lord Kitchener, a year. Borden Diary, 18 March 1915. Information from Britain constantly underestimated the endurance of the war.

astonishing entry for 31 July 1914: 'Had delightful evening. Every one anticipates war.'

Thus, when Clifford Sifton warned Borden in August 1914 of the demands which this 'most awful war' would place upon Canada, Borden recorded it in a matter of fact fashion in his diary.[21] Sifton himself recognized that few Canadians shared his views, and thought that if he had been in Canada rather than England when war broke out he too would have shared the equanimity with which Canadians accepted the conflict:

I realize what apparently few people do; that this war is a dreadful business, and only imperative necessity can excuse any participation in it. It is, however, to my mind perfectly clear that the actions of Germany have made war on the part of Great Britain inevitable ... There is a bare possibility that the war may not be long, but personally I have no hope whatever that such will be the case. I should not be surprised if we should be sending war contingents a year from now. Furthermore, if our men sail for the continent and get into the midst of the fight, I do not expect more than one-half of them ever to come back.[22]

This brutal vision was to come later and sporadically to other Canadians. Only in May 1915 when 2468 Canadians fell fighting for 'one small orchard and two muddy ditches'[23] did Borden realize the nature of the conflict. 'This war,' he wrote in his diary on 16 May, 'is the suicide of civilization.'[24] From the chaotic first days when Canadian troops assembled at Valcartier to the later months in the mud and death of Flanders and France the meaning of the war came to other Canadians, as to Borden, as a frightening epiphany.

Coalition, then, seemed neither necessary nor desirable in 1914. But already the limitations of the traditional governmental machinery in dealing with the crisis created the need to consider alternatives. As a result, the party machinery performed many of the tasks of recruitment and socialization which Canadians now expect the state to undertake. In wartime this became increasingly

---

21 *Ibid.*, 29 Aug. 1914. There are no reflections on the nature of the war in the 1914 diary. On early impressions of the war, see O.D. Skelton, 'Parties and Coalition,' *Queen's Quarterly*, XXV (Oct. 1917), 219-20, and R.C. Brown and Ramsay Cook, *Canada, 1896-1921: A Nation Transformed* (Toronto, 1974), 212-14.

22 Cited in J.W. Dafoe, *Clifford Sifton in Relation to His Times* (Toronto, 1931), 386.

23 J. Swettenham, *To Seize the Victory* (Toronto, 1965), 94.

24 Compare also Borden's speeches, 'Address' (5 Dec. 1914), in *Addresses Delivered before the Canadian Club of Toronto* (Toronto, 1915), 81-90; and 'The Empire at War' (16 Sept. 1915), in *Addresses Delivered before the Canadian Club of Ottawa* (Ottawa, 1916), 20-31.

intolerable not only to Liberals but to many others as well. Thus, when the inability of the pre-war governmental structure to cope with the demands of war was perceived, the changes proposed in Canadian government quite naturally involved fundamental changes in the Canadian party system.[25] It was in this debate on the character of wartime government that the idea of a 'Union' or 'National' government slowly took form.

Ironically, as awareness of the war's meaning intensified, the spirit of party unity dissipated, and for this the Tories must receive much blame. In those early days of war, Borden responded to Laurier's offer of co-operation with a promise to remove the party from interference with the war effort: in purchasing materials, public tender would apply; in making appointments, ability would supplant loyalty.[26] The promises were not kept, as Sam Hughes' Militia Department became a lavish patron for hundreds of Tory manufacturers, businessmen, and job-seekers. Judging from the fascinating correspondence of Toronto MP Edmund Bristol, Hughes' department was not alone. Bristol, a perpetually impecunious lawyer-speculator, had intended to leave politics in July 1914, but the 'guns of August' renewed his political interest, his patriotism, and his personal profit. He had often acted as a middleman before (in June 1914 he had earned $225 for placing a businessman's case before Robert Rogers),[27] but the war made this a full-time task. Already on 29 August 1914 Bristol was complaining to his old friend Hughes that Toronto was not receiving enough contracts. Borden's pledge obviously influenced him not a whit. Moreover, its influence upon others was questionable for Bristol told the Toronto Tory organizer, A.R. Birmingham, on 9 October that 'the patronage of the Department of Militia and Defence was being administered' by a committee of three: 'Doc' Reid, Sir George Foster, with 'Bob' Rogers, as the chairman. To these guardians of the party faith and treasury, and to Hughes himself, Bristol made his pleas. Firm after firm was recommended for the patronage list, but sometimes things went awry. Discovering a Grit hat company had some government work, Bristol gently reminded General Sam of the rules: 'I know you would not willingly give business to Grits and do not suppose you would allow orders to go to firms other than those on the patronage list.'[28]

---

25 See J.A. Corry, 'The Growth of Governmental Activities, 1914-1918,' Canadian Historical Association, *Report* (1940), 63-73; and David E. Smith, 'Emergency Government in Canada,' *Canadian Historical Review*, L (Dec. 1969), 429-48.
26 Full details may be found in Norman Ward, *The Public Purse: A Study in Canadian Democracy* (Toronto, 1962), 149-51.
27 Bristol to Charles Millar, 19 June 1914, Bristol Papers, box 2.
28 Bristol to Hughes, 21 Dec. 1914, *ibid.*, box 4.

To Borden, Bristol played the patriot, urging a fuller war effort, denouncing the shirkers. On 30 November 1914, for example, he implored his leader to commit Canada more fully to the conflict. This end could be better achieved, he told the prime minister, if a large munitions plant were to be built in Toronto, the heart of British feeling in Canada.[29] Never had patriotism and profit so tenaciously and successfully intermingled. This, however, was not Borden's interpretation. Appalled by the rumours, frustrated by the ineffectuality of his direction, and harassed by the press and the Liberals, Borden in April 1915 announced the establishment of a 'non-political' War Purchasing Commission and the dismissal from the caucus of two Tory members who had transgressed the wide boundaries of fair political and business practice.[30] Sir George Foster offered sad regrets to Bristol: 'There will be, as you well understand, many disappointments under the new arrangements and probably some dissatisfaction but the general good is what, after all, must dominate.' In fact, Bristol had a few more months before the 'general good' fully extended its sway over his activities. In July 1915, for example, he approached the acting minister of militia, James Lougheed, about a war contract for the North Shore Supply Company in which he owned some shares. Bristol later reported the encounter to a company officer: 'He smiled sweetly on me and asked me if I wanted to have the patronage for the North Shore of Lake Superior as well as the City of Toronto and then he told me he would do what he could in the matter.' North Shore got its contract.[31]

Throughout 1915 Bristol was rarely in Ottawa. Very often he was in New York scouring the American economic capital for companies who might have goods to sell and who therefore needed an effective agent in Ottawa.[32] But by mid-1915 the relationship among party affiliation, personal profit, and war needs had become increasingly covert. Evidence appeared that Canadian and British soldiers might bear the ultimate cost of faulty supplies or late orders.[33] This was a charge the traditional system could not sustain, and a scapegoat was

29 Bristol to Borden, 30 Nov. 1914, *ibid.* Later Bristol demanded that nickel not be exported to the United States in an unrefined state and then carried from American ports to other destinations, including Germany. It should be refined in Canada and shipped from Canadian ports in Canadian ships. Bristol was a director of and solicitor for Canada Steamship Lines. *Ibid.*, v. 4 and 5.
30 *Can. H. of C. Debates*, 15 April 1915, pp. 2613-17.
31 Foster to Bristol, 22 April 1915, Bristol Papers, v. 4; Bristol to Roy Wolvis, 7 July 1915, *ibid.*, v. 2.
32 MacArthur Perks and Co., General Contractors, NY, to Ottawa office of same firm, 12 Oct. 1915; and Bristol to David Carnegie, 5 Oct. 1915, *ibid.*, v. 2.
33 See Brown and Cook, *Canada, 1896-1921*, 234-6.

found: John Wesley Allison, a crony of Hughes, who (like Bristol) had negotiated munitions contracts for personal profit. In the future, not even discretion would be sufficient; the Allison case proved that. His activities halted, Bristol left for 'war work' in Britain in May 1916. It would be over a year before he returned to a transformed political world.

The party truce exploded under the impact of these revelations, and most of the casualties were on the Tory side. By late 1915 the protracted brutality of the war had ended any hope of political profit from the conflict. Indeed, the difficulties of war administration, the indifference of Quebec, and the rapidly declining fortunes of the provincial Conservatives who had assisted so greatly in 1911 led to growing fears of imminent political catastrophe. The provincial situation was particularly worrisome. In 1911 there had been five Conservative and four Liberal provincial administrations with 280 Conservative and 187 Liberal members. By the end of 1916 there were seven Liberal governments and 336 Liberal members and only two Tory governments (Ontario and Prince Edward Island) and only 180 Tory seats.[34] The change in Conservative outlook from a soaring optimism in August 1914, when it seemed that the war had justified Tory pre-war policies, to the dark days of 1916, when the prospect of an election created profound Conservative anguish, is illustrated in the wartime careers of two Conservative ministers, Sam Hughes and Robert Rogers. Both attained the pinnacle of their influence in the first six months of the war – Hughes as minister of militia and Rogers as 'minister of elections.' Both regarded the war as a distinctly Conservative enterprise to be fought with and for the party. A conflict of interest between the needs of the party and the needs of the state was inconceivable to them. By 1916, however, their own continued presence in the cabinet had become inconceivable to many Canadians, including many of their own colleagues.

Sir Sam Hughes' meteoric rise and fall in a two-year period must rank as one of the most extraordinary events of the war. In the early days of the war, the press, Liberal and Conservative, treated him as the first Canadian hero. He was a larger-than-life figure, a mass of comical but productive energy, mixed with strong doses of the 'sturdy Canadianism' which Canadian Liberals were wont to admire. Whether denouncing the pompous Duke of Connaught, Canada's governor-general, or claiming, perhaps with some justification, greater military

---

34 Calculations are found in Skelton, *Laurier*, II, 492. Sir James Whitney of Ontario died in 1914 and his death marked the end of the close personal and political co-operation between federal and provincial Conservatism in Ontario. Sir Richard McBride was dying in London while his successor W.J. Bowser led the once powerful BC Tories to defeat in 1916, the same year as the fall of the Manitoba Conservatives.

competency than the British generals, Hughes was to Canada what Lord Kitchener became to Britain after his death: the personification of the war effort.[35] Even those who ordinarily distrusted pomposity were deceived. Clifford Sifton wrote on 21 September 1914: 'Hughes has laboured with tremendous energy, much technical skill and good organizing and executive capacity. Single-minded to turn out the best force possible, he has stood off the grafters and jobbers to the best of his ability, and he is turning out an army in record time ... I know the inside and I know he has done wonders.'[36] For once, Sifton was not on 'the inside.'

Hughes' early triumphs were a tribute not only to the alacrity with which Canadians − or at least British-born Canadians − responded to the call to arms but also to the scope of political party organization in Canada. When war came, Hughes immediately mobilized the army of Conservative party workers, agents, and friends to aid him in the struggle. If shells were needed, why not trust a friend such as Allison, Conservative and Methodist like Hughes himself?

Another to whom party and country beckoned was a young Vancouver Conservative lawyer, Harold Daly, who came to Ottawa − leaving behind over $100,000 in debts which by his own admission were never repaid − to serve as a 'staff officer' to Hughes. His duties brought with them 'a tremendous amount of patronage' because the appointment of officers fell within his ambit. Daly described his office and the manner in which he acted: 'I was particularly good to lawyers, because I knew what business I was going into when I got out of the army; but I'm sorry to say that none of the lawyers remembered me after the war was over. I had done a lot for them − fixed up their sons, brothers, and brothers-in-law, none of them gave me any business. However, it was a very interesting job, and I got to feel very important − much more important than I really was, and I think perhaps I was very rude to people.'[37]

Like Daly, Hughes also forgot that power often consumes its possessor. Very soon, shocking revelations about the disgraceful conditions of the Valcartier camp and the misuse of patronage appeared in the press.[38] To many Canadians the reports were too outrageous to be believed, particularly when the charges were directed against the same minister whom the press had exalted a few months earlier. The prime minister was in a difficult position. He too had joined

35 On Hughes' peculiar spell, see Swettenham, *To Seize the Victory*, 3-5; C.F. Winter, *The Hon. Sam Hughes* (Toronto, 1931); and B.B. Cooke, 'Major-General Sam Hughes, Minister of Militia and Defence,' *Canadian Magazine* (Sept. 1915), 388-94.
36 Cited in Dafoe, *Clifford Sifton*, 387.
37 'Memoirs,' PAC, Daly Papers.
38 Swettenham, *To Seize the Victory*, 37; and A.F. Duguid, *Official History of the Canadian Forces in the Great War, 1914-1919* (Ottawa, 1938), 88.

in the early panegyrics to Hughes and repudiation was difficult personally as well as politically. Even worse, Hughes had never been orally instructed that peace-time rules for contracts and patronage should not apply in wartime, and that the war was more than a massive Conservative rally. Borden himself noted in his diary that 'Hughes [treated] scandals affecting his Department very casually & does not seem to realize the situation.'[39] Yet Borden, who did understand 'the situation' by 1915, if not in the autumn of 1914, did very little to draw atten-tion to the altered circumstances; and until his last days as minister Hughes never appreciated the impropriety of his actions. In fact, Borden had known of Hughes' close connection with the contractor Allison as early as October 1914, at which time the latter was boasting about the 'wonderful profits' Hughes' favour had earned him. Borden was also aware of Hughes' 'unbridled tongue' and of his extremely careless administration. Despite this, he continued to regard him as a valuable colleague.[40]

What finally caused Hughes' fall in 1916 was the deepening impact of the war during that year. Suddenly the management of the war effort became too serious a matter to entrust to the erratic and controversial Sir Sam, who began to appear a very old and even tragic figure. 'The leading journals and newspaper editorials in English Canada had linked the issue of civil service reform to the necessity of expediting the war effort, for without reformed government it remained questionable how an "efficient and ungodly" German juggernaut could be successfully brought to its knees.'[41] Rightly or wrongly, inefficiency was firmly identified with patronage. Hughes' colleagues, who were beleaguered by work, the press, and the opposition, sensed the new temper of public opinion and made him an object of their wrath and a scapegoat for their own frailties. Sir George Foster began the attack by bursting out in council in a 'violent tirade' against Hughes and by denouncing patronage in the House of Commons. Borden was infuriated by these eruptions which were, to say the least, hypocritical:

39 Borden Diary, 8 April 1915. In defence of patronage during the war, Borden later said: 'In Canada, as in Great Britain, the imperative purpose of the Government was to throw the full power of each nation into the conflict ... Thus a meticulous adherence to Civil Service enactments and regulations was not the main purpose of the administration in either country.' 'Problem of an Efficient Civil Service,' *Report of the Annual Meeting of the Canadian Historical Association* (1931), 15.
40 Borden Diary, 21 Oct. 1914; 4 and 25 Jan. and 8 April 1915. On 17 Aug. 1915 Borden wrote that Hughes had earned a new honour which was proposed for him. See also Ward, *The Public Purse*, 151. Ward also finds it significant that Borden would not 'take up' the matter of militia expenditure directly with Hughes.
41 J.E. Hodgetts *et al.*, *The Biography of an Institution: The Civil Service Commission of Canada, 1908-1967* (Montreal and London, 1972), 45.

'Foster has no more political sense than a turnip ... His speech about patronage was eloquent mouthing; in every day practice no one is keener about petty patronage than he is.'[42] But the veteran Foster knew that Hughes' era had passed and that his methods and style had become inappropriate and politically suicidal in Canada in 1916.

Why, then, did Hughes endure so long? As early as 3 April 1916 Borden knew that Hughes could no longer remain in the cabinet, but, although there were others eager for the prestigious militia portfolio, Hughes stayed for many more months. The explanation probably lies in Borden's sense of duty, which compelled him to stand by a colleague who had stood by him during his own difficulties in 1910 and 1911, and in his characteristic indecisiveness. In November 1916 Borden could tolerate no more. Hughes' position was taken by Edward Kemp, a minister who promised to bring the efficient methods he had applied to business to the management of the Canadian war effort.

Robert Rogers, unlike Sam Hughes, was not charged with departmental neglect, nor was his portfolio, public works, closely connected to the Canadian war effort; but the 'Hon. Bob' nevertheless became a special target for Liberal attack. Rogers' past in politics came back to haunt him when his involvement in a scandal over the construction of the Manitoba legislature became a symbolic public issue.[43] This, however, did not anger the Liberals and independents so much as Rogers' blatant refusal to recognize the restrictions which they felt that the war had imposed upon 'politics as usual.' Rogers refused to accept a party truce and had used the abundant patronage which the war created to revivify the listless Conservative organization.[44] To Rogers, the war had justified Conservative policy and meant a thorough repudiation of the doctrines of Canadian Liberalism. The Conservatives were therefore entitled to a fresh mandate to conduct the war and to reward themselves for their loyalty and pre-war perspicacity. 'Vote Conservative,' urged a pamphlet Rogers prepared for the campaign, 'for Borden backs Britain.'[45] This was, of course, precisely the type of campaign which the Liberals most feared. In a highly controversial speech in Montreal on 3 May 1915 Rogers threw down the gauntlet to his critics and called for an election to 'clear the air.'[46]

42 Borden Diary, 26 Feb. 1916.
43 An account of this is found in Hopkins, *Canada at War*, 67-8.
44 Civil service commissioner Adam Shortt claimed in a Feb. 1915 public address that the government had given out ten thousand patronage appointments since the war began, with Rogers being the one most responsible. See Hodgetts *et al., Biography of an Institution*, 38, and Borden Diary, 12 March 1915.
45 Cited in *Canadian Liberal Monthly* (April 1917), 1.
46 *Montreal Star*, 4 May 1915; see also Dafoe, *Clifford Sifton*, 395.

As one would expect, the speech shocked the Liberals, who were themselves flouting the party truce, but who feared and resented anyone who dared to do the same by suggesting an election. More important, the address also perturbed many Conservatives, such as the highly influential Joseph Flavelle who shared Rogers' low opinion of the Liberals but who warned Borden that he and his 'friends' considered an election 'unthinkable.'[47] Flavelle's private warning to Borden was echoed by a 'long and emotional' appeal against an election from Toronto 'manufacturers and imperialists.'[48] Immediately, the cabinet, which less than two months earlier had been 'all keen for an election,' became, in Borden's words, 'not so strong as before.' Foster and Thomas Chase Casgrain threatened to resign on the issue; Kemp and Thomas White urged the cabinet to heed the ultimatum of their Toronto friends.[49]

Sir Wilfrid Laurier sensed at once the significance of the reaction to Rogers' speech and the opportunity which it afforded. In Toronto on 15 May, not knowing that Borden had already decided to abandon the proposed election, he once again reiterated, in highly charged language, his pledge of August 1914: 'I speak honestly when I say there should be ... a change of government ... but I do not care, for my part, so long as the war lasts to open the portals of office with that bloody key.' In return for no election during wartime, Laurier promised that the Liberals would halt 'all preparations [for an election] and think of nothing but the war.'[50] Laurier had trumped Rogers' ace with the lowest card of his suit.

After this débâcle, Rogers never regained his earlier pre-eminence. His most valuable political asset, his sense of the popular mood, had proven unreliable in wartime. The further revelations of his involvement with the legislature scandal in Manitoba battered an already weakened political giant. Yet he remained in the cabinet, primarily because of his intimate knowledge of Conservative political machinery, a knowledge which Borden, because of his aversion to party work,

47 Flavelle to Borden, 4 May 1915, BP, v. 33. Flavelle entirely supported Rogers' charges against the Liberals claiming that they were parading 'an identification with Great Britain and the Empire in this war wholly at variance with their position during the Naval controversy.' Independent opinion, however, would not support the government if it called an election.
48 The description of the appeal is J.S. Willison's who himself felt no 'enthusiasm for a political contest' but feared 'if an election is delayed until the war is over the Opposition will be reasonably certain of ninety or a hundred constituencies before a word is spoken from the platform.' Willison to Kemp, 5 May 1915, PAC, Kemp Papers, v. 12.
49 Borden Diary, 10 March and 1-5 May 1915. For a good account of the decision to postpone the election, see Roger Graham, *Arthur Meighen: The Door of Opportunity* (Toronto, 1960), I, 90-1.
50 Cited in Skelton, *Laurier*, II, 446.

had never bothered to acquire. In the fashion of mortally wounded political animals, Rogers frantically tried to secure a position which would afford him a refuge; he suggested, for instance, that he be appointed as Canada's first high commissioner to Washington, a proposal whose impractibility was guaranteed by its implausibility. To Borden's secretary, it seemed obvious that Rogers 'had lost his nerve.'[51] More likely, Rogers understood, as Hughes did not, that the war had destroyed the basis of his assumptions about political life in Canada. He had always publicly and privately identified the good of the nation with the good of his party. But in wartime a baffling new standard had been erected which insisted upon the subordination of party ends to what was perceived as the much greater one of the war. When Rogers' colleagues indicated in 1915 that they could no longer permit him to act in his traditional role, he became a lonely figure, a pathetic political anachronism.[52]

By the late summer of 1915 both parties knew they had entered a heavily mined political no man's land. The most nagging concern for the Tories was the exhaustion of the parliamentary term at the very time when the party's fortunes were drastically declining. The only exit from the dilemma would be an election forced by the Liberals and that was only likely if the Liberals refused to extend the term. While Borden was in England in the summer of 1915, the cabinet considered their position. No matter where they looked the prospects were gloomy. Reporting to his chief from Ottawa, A.E. Blount succinctly summarized the reasons for this pessimism:

It is opinion majority of ministers that you should carefully consider advisability holding short session immediately after your return for purpose extension

---

51 Borden Diary, 11, 12, and 14 Sept. 1915.
52 As one might expect, Harold Daly was intimately involved with the election fiasco. On the advice of Meighen, Hughes appointed Daly a captain to 'look after Conservative interests at the front.' Daly claims that 'around the last day of April 1915, I was sitting in the lobby of the Chateau Laurier when Rogers' secretary told me that Rogers wanted to see me in his room. He also said that the Cabinet were meeting there, as Rogers was in bed. I went up & found a number of ministers including Sir Robert Borden.' An election was imminent; Daly must go to England. Unfortunately, he chose the wrong ship. In the middle of May Rogers received this letter from Daly: 'I got here on Sunday instead of Saturday and can't get down to France till Monday. I have no orders from your side yet so will go right ahead with my preliminary work ... I had a narrow escape on the Lusitania and went down with the ship having no life-belt on but managed to get a hold of some wreckage when I came up and was picked out of the water after two hours and a half in it. I am still quite willing to die for the Conservative Party but am glad I didn't drown for it.' Meighen to Rogers, 28 April, Daly to Rogers, 12 May 1915, BP, v. 35; and Daly, 'Memoirs,' Daly Papers, v. 2.

Parliamentary term for at least three years. Liberal Press renewing agitation against general election. Ottawa Free Press advocating coalition. Political situation British Columbia very uncertain, foreign vote Western Canada and in Ontario adverse. British vote Manitoba, Ontario and in Maritime provinces favourable. Quebec very uncertain. Ministers largely of same opinion, but if Liberals refuse extension immediate dissolution would be popular.[53]

When Borden returned, negotiations began with Laurier for the extension of the term. Laurier's shrewdness, and the difficult Conservative position, gave the Liberal leader the upper hand. As Roger Graham has pointed out, he demanded in effect: 'Tell us what you propose to do about the railways and if we like it we may allow you to avoid an election, as you so clearly desire.'[54] Now, too, Laurier offered an extension, not until the end of the war but only for one year; and for the first time he suggested that party conflict be 'minimized' not ended.[55] He had retreated significantly from his stand of August 1914, which had been restated in May 1915 when he disdained 'to open the portals of office' with the 'bloody key' of a wartime election. In the spring of 1915 he had asked Borden for a pledge that no election would take place. The agreement which was finally reached delayed the election for only a year, but this was not a triumph for anyone but rather a refusal to accept the consequences of the war for Canadian political life. A successful verdict in the trenches in 1916 might have made this hesitancy worthwhile, but the Germans once again would not be accommodating.

Both Borden and Laurier probably wished in retrospect that the other had forced an election in 1915. In 1916 the political deadlock worsened as the effect of the war upon Canadian life grew. The railways teetered ever closer to bankruptcy. French Canadians and English Canadians hurled charges at each other over the Ontario schools issue. Harvests went untended; shortages appeared. Worst of all was the apprehension with which Canadians turned to their newspapers to read the names of fellow citizens, neighbours, friends, sons, and brothers who had fallen far away at the Somme or Courcelette, once unknown names which became indelibly etched in the Canadian consciousness. And Canadians knew that Borden's pledge on New Year's Day 1916, that Canada would fight to the last man and the last dollar, meant even greater hardships and even longer casualty lists.

53 Blount to Borden, 21 Aug. 1915, BP, v. 63.
54 *Arthur Meighen*, I, 93.
55 Laurier to Borden, 13 Nov. 1915, cited in Henry Borden, ed., *Robert Laird Borden: His Memoirs* (Toronto, 1938), I, 518-20.

The image of a united nation projected by Laurier when he spoke in the Ottawa station in August 1914 had shattered. Nagging doubts and dissatisfaction with the course of the Canadian war effort lurked everywhere. Joseph Flavelle, now an imperial civil servant administering the munitions industry which had proven unsafe in the politicians' hands, reflected this profound melancholy in a March 1916 letter: 'Parliament has not done well. Its spirit does not reflect the spirit in the country. The Opposition have steadily sought to secure party advantage. The Government has not met their charges in an efficient manner and the whole thing has been pretty foggy.'[56] The nation's political system, and notably its political parties, offered no guidance through this 'fog' in which men like Bristol, Rogers, and Hughes had completely lost their way. The apparent failure of government to cope with its enormous tasks had seemingly justified the pre-war critics of the party system. From the end of 1915 until 1917, fundamental questions were asked about the future of Canadian political institutions, and confidence in these institutions waned at the very moment when faith seemed imperative.

56 Flavelle to W.L. Hichens, 14 March 1916, PAC, Lord Brand Papers, file 6F, microfilm copy.

6

The ideology of service

'The truth of the matter is very simple,' declared Stephen Leacock. 'The *form* of government can avail nothing if the spirit is lacking.'[1] Writing in 1917, Leacock reflected two major themes of modern social thought: the belief that certain forms can be found which impart order to society and that a 'spirit' — a bond of affection, understanding, and mutual endeavour — must infuse a successful society. Sheldon Wolin has shown how 'the nostalgia for the vanished warmth of the simple community' — 'spirit' in Leacock's terminology — and 'the obsession with the possibility of large scale organization' have frequently converged in political philosophy, since the beginnings of modern industrialism.[2] Never is this convergence more marked than in wartime when the creation and maintenance of a massive war machine demands large-scale organization, and the emotion of patriotism feeds upon a real or imagined sense of solidarity. Wartime leaders must be simultaneously the masters of the machine and the embodiment of national purpose; virtue and knowledge become one. In times of stress in a Western nation the image of a Solon, a Cincinnatus, or a Pitt — figures of a moral grandeur and an Olympian skill — is omnipresent. Striding forth at the moment of supreme tension this leader reintegrates a divided community by moral leadership and preserves the national state by his skill.[3]

---

1 'Democracy and Social Progress,' in J.O. Miller, ed., *The New Era in Canada: Essays Dealing with the Upbuilding of the Canadian Commonwealth* (Toronto, 1917), 31.
2 *Politics and Vision* (Boston, 1960), 366.
3 In the modern, bureaucratic, rational state, as Max Weber recognized, the classical political hero could not exist. The procedures of a modern bureaucracy, passionless and lacking bias, dispel the element of mystery and minimize the passion which surrounded the great historical leaders. In this same vein, Robert Michels' study of political parties first published in 1911 showed how the organization itself forces the conformity of its supposed masters, making them self-interested and necessarily conservative. In the face

This emphasis upon spiritual regeneration and 'expert' management was especially prevalent in urban English Canada during the First World War. The reasons for this mood are not obscure. On the one hand, the middle and upper middle classes in English-Canadian cities generally shared a common racial and religious background, British and protestant.[4] Furthermore, many of the leaders in patriotic organizations had come to the city from the countryside and therefore recalled an even more close-knit community which had possessed a sense of solidarity based upon strong affective bonds.[5] On the other hand, while the urban English-Canadian leaders often sprang from almost pre-industrial rural roots, they prided themselves on being 'modern' businessmen or professionals, acquainted with the recondite skills of modern management. Regarding themselves as more knowledgeable and selfless than the politicians of the day, these men agreed with the underlying thrust of Plato's historic question: 'Whom else can you compel to undertake the guardianship of the commonwealth, if not those who, besides understanding best the principles of government, enjoy a nobler life than the politicians and look for rewards of a different kind?'[6] Mere

of this dilemma, Michels later turned far away from democracy and socialism and found his modern equivalent of the classical hero in Benito Mussolini who could break through the limits of democracy and bureaucracy. Weber, 'Politics as a Vocation,' in H.H. Gerth and C. Wright Mills, eds., *From Max Weber* (New York, 1958), 77-128; Michels, *Political Parties* (New York, 1962), especially the introduction by S.M. Lipset; and Reinhard Bendix, *Max Weber: An Intellectual Portrait* (New York, 1960), 430-3.

Like these Europeans, the Canadians discussed in this chapter were similarly obsessed with the importance of leadership and disturbed by the apparent contradictory qualities required for leadership. They too minimized the value and the significance of democracy, often regarding democracy and leadership as fundamentally conflicting, especially during war.

4 The persistence of the predominance of British, Protestant Canadians in the nation's economic and social life was shown in John Porter's, *The Vertical Mosaic: An Analysis of Social Class and Power in Canada* (Toronto, 1965). No similar sociological study is available for the earlier period. See, however, T.W. Acheson, 'The Social Origins of Canadian Industrialism: A Study in the Structure of Entrepreneurship,' unpublished PhD thesis, University of Toronto, 1971.

5 After 1881 a truly massive emigration from the land took place in Ontario. Many went to the west and gave to the urban centres there a distinctly British-Ontario urban middle and upper middle class. See W.R. Young, 'Conscription, Rural Depopulation, and the Farmers of Ontario, 1917-19,' *Canadian Historical Review*, LIII (Sept. 1972), 319-20; and Alan F.J. Artibise, *Winnipeg: A Social History of Urban Growth, 1874-1914* (Montreal, 1975).

6 *The Republic of Plato*, trans. F.M. Cornford (London, 1945), 521. It should be noted that many of these 'selfless patriots' were reaping considerable reward from the war. This is not to suggest, however, that they were insincere.

'politicians' could not be trusted with the momentous tasks facing the Canadian state.

The first consequence of this pervasive emotion was the emergence of an extraordinary number of bodies to serve the needs of those dislocated by war and to persuade Canadians generally of the justice of the moral and material requirements of the war. These organizations, which ranged from the Canadian Patriotic Fund and the Belgian Aid Committee to the Win-the-War League and the Vacant Lot Garden Club, arose first in urban English Canada and, in the view of their organizers, they filled some of the vacuum left by the underdeveloped Canadian state.[7] From these beginnings, such groups proliferated as the war made its impact upon Canada. By the end of 1916 it was surely the exceptional man among middle-class English Canadians who was not involved in one of these groups. Professionals and community leaders were, in fact, likely to be involved in several.

Within the spheres where they acted, these organizations were remarkably successful in engendering deeper commitment to the war. In achieving this end, they broke down traditional party divisions. John Godfrey, an Ontario lawyer and one of the most dextrous architects of these bipartisan voluntary groups, believed the attack upon party was an essential part of the role of such groups. Writing to E.M. Macdonald, a Liberal politician, in February 1917, Godfrey pointed to the 'superb' effort which came about from his welding together both political parties in Peel County, Ontario, to carry on 'all necessary patriotic work.' Moreover, when this technique was extended to the entire Second Military District, voluntary recruitment, the best thermometer of war feeling, soared. To Godfrey the corollary was inescapable: 'This is not the time to play party politics. They should be relegated to the limbo of the utterly unimportant.'[8] Yet by late 1916 all the devotion, sincerity, and energy of these patriotic associations could not raise Canadian enlistments above an embarrassingly low level. Alone, without control of the state, these groups felt the constraint of their English-Canadian origins. Men such as Godfrey therefore embarked upon a major effort, perhaps even a crusade — for they certainly saw themselves as fighting for a divine truth — to gain control of the state, with its massive but unrealized potential. As Hughes, Rogers, and Bristol moved to the sidelines, new men, with different goals and understandings of politics, began to influence decisions. The character of this 'crusade' largely created the philosophical framework for a Union government.

7 On these many voluntary groups, see J.C. Hopkins, *Canada at War* (Toronto, 1919), chap. 13; and R. Craig Brown and Ramsay Cook, *Canada, 1896-1921: A Nation Transformed* (Toronto, 1974), 219-23.
8 Godfrey to Macdonald, 2 Feb., PAC, Laurier Papers, v. 706.

Probably the finest document expressing the mood of those who sought national regeneration was a series of essays published in 1917 with the significant title, *The New Era in Canada*. Edited by the principal of Ridley College, an élite private high school, the book is a monument to the views of prominent English Canadians active in public life but not in politics. The introduction announced the intention 'To awaken the interest of Canadians in problems which confront us ...' and 'To urge that the test of national greatness lies in the willing service to the State by its citizens and to point out, so far as possible, opportunities for service.' The bond of unity which must stand above the 'diversities of opinion and belief' was 'the will to serve.' In the essays which followed the authors, all English Canadians, clearly indicate that they knew they had such a 'will to serve.' The problem in Canada lay in the absence of an appropriate 'national superstructure' which could make use of such service. Pre-war Canada should have created such a structure, but the particularism, the thin communication bands linking the nation, and the partisanship of Canadian politics had stunted its growth. Now, Sir Clifford Sifton declared, 'the greatest opportunity of the ages' was at hand.[9]

Stephen Leacock, the contributor of two essays to the volume, pointed to the impediments blocking Canada's acceptance of this opportunity: 'Thousands, tens of thousands, millions of our men, women and children are engaged in silly and idle services or in production that is for mere luxuries and comforts and that helps nothing in the conduct of the war. They are making pianos, gramophones, motor cars, jewellery, books, pictures, clothes in millions of yards and millions of dollars ...' Such individuals were 'mere drones in the hive' as far as the war was concerned. If such men could be organized and such frivolous labour ended, Leacock asserted, the nation would be multiplied 'as ten to one.' The needs of the state must take precedence over the independence of the individual, particularly while 'the great fight for life and death' was going on in the world without. This subordination of the individual might be expected in the conservative Leacock, but the profound faith in the efficacy of organization held by one who cast an uncommonly cynical eye at modern life surely indicates the almost mystical properties which Leacock and his contemporaries attached to management techniques.[10]

9 'The Foundations of the New Era,' in Miller, ed., *The New Era in Canada*, 37 and 56.
10 'Our National Organization for the War,' *ibid.*, 411-13. Leacock's social conservatism is discussed in an essay by Ramsay Cook, 'Stephen Leacock and the Age of Plutocracy, 1903-1921,' in John S. Moir, ed., *Character and Circumstance: Essays in Honour of Donald Grant Creighton* (Toronto, 1970), 163-81. Leacock's satire, *Arcadian Adventures with the Idle Rich* (London, 1914) is a bitter denunciation of 'drones' in pre-war Canada. Later he strongly supported Bennett's 'New Deal' and its policy of state reform, calling for 'the regulated state, preserving the stimulus of individual reward, but with a fairer set of rules to apply it.' Cited in Carl Berger, *The Sense of Power* (Toronto, 1970), 196.

Others who, unlike Leacock, had accepted the catechism of liberal individualism in pre-war Canada now adopted a different creed, which clearly shifted the locus of rationality and freedom away from the individual. Just as the great individualist Emerson had completely abandoned radical egoism during the American Civil War, so too Canadians, like Clifford Sifton, J.W. Dafoe, and Michael Clark, an Alberta Cobdenite, warned of the essential irrationality of individual action and the beneficent rationality of the state. The individual was lost in the overwhelming magnitude of the war effort and in the complex organic conception of the state which it created.[11]

But the ebbing recruitment figures which coincided with the publication of *The New Era in Canada* proclaimed that the 'will to serve,' so fundamental to an organic political community, was deficient in many areas of Canada. What, then, must be done? A pessimistic Leacock had already set out the alternatives: 'The people, one says, will not subscribe. Then, if not, let us perish; we do not deserve to win the war.'[12] But why must the heroic suffer the fate of the coward? If 'will' could not inspire service, then service could be compelled, and in the process the national state would be irrevocably strengthened. For the hundreds of thousands who had wrapped bandages, tended the wounded, given their lives, or lost their sons, such a national state would symbolize and even sanctify their efforts. For those who had not, it would condemn them to deserved ignominy.

The depth of this emotion is suggested in the careers of three public men – Charles Magrath, Sir John Willison, and Newton W. Rowell – individuals who recorded their own intellectual and political growth in 1916 and 1917. Their development is largely representative of others involved in the national government movement during that period and is therefore worthy of closer study. Magrath was an 'independent' Conservative, Willison a former Liberal become Tory, and Rowell the Ontario Liberal leader, but they were all English

11 Emerson's rapid forsaking of individualism is described in G.M. Fredrickson's *The Inner Civil War* (New York, 1968), 176-80. Clark was an Alberta MP and a British immigrant who closely identified his Liberalism with that of Cobden and Bright. He had no less than four sons at the front in the First World War. The new attitude towards the nature of democracy and liberty was often accompanied by curious vestiges of previous liberal assumptions. Sifton, for example, who led in the move to restrict the franchise and to introduce compulsion, continued to object to certain limitations on freedom of speech. Upon hearing in Dec. 1917 of a man who was sent to jail for statements discouraging recruiting, Sifton wrote: 'This case makes my blood boil. We are supposed to be fighting for liberty but there could be no worse and more outrageous tyranny than this in Germany.' Sifton to Dafoe, 'Saturday 1917' (December), PAC, Dafoe Papers, microfilm copy.

12 'Our National Organization for the War,' 419.

Canadians, 'self-made' men who began their successful careers in Ontario small towns. More importantly, they also shared 'the feeling of common culture and the feeling of common interests'[13] which minimized social and economic differences while subordinating politics and urging the existence of a higher, more fundamental, unity.

Charles A. Magrath was elected to the House of Commons in 1908 as an 'Independent Conservative' from Alberta. An irrigation engineer, who 'knew the plains as Gladstone knew Homer,' Magrath shared the suspicion of party politics so prevalent at the time in western Canada and saw political value in his self-professed and self-defined independence. He never hesitated to express his frequently controversial views on any subject in the House, on public platforms, or in rather pretentious books.[14] His behaviour found little favour among the Hughes and Bristols of the Conservative caucus who regarded him as a member of a most peculiar and often undesirable political species. Still, Magrath did possess obvious ability and his views, when not thoroughly eccentric, were respected. So long as the Tories were in opposition he was a vulture, gracefully swooping down to pick apart a decaying Liberal government; in power, however, he promised to become a gnat, as much an irritant to the Tories as to the Liberals. Such fears were never realized because Magrath lost his seat in 1911. Perhaps this defeat was greeted by many secret toasts by Tory regulars, pleased to be relieved of an unpredictable colleague. Nevertheless, Borden regretted Magrath's loss, and to keep him in public life he appointed him Canadian chairman of the International Joint Commission. The commission absorbed his

13 The phrase is David Potter's description of the psychological bases of nationalism. 'The Historian's Use of Nationalism and Vice-Versa,' *American Historical Review*, LXVII (1961-2), 937. The three individuals being considered were indeed of a common culture, and during the war they felt that they had a common interest which was opposed by identifiable forces in Canada.

Magrath was born in Augusta, Ontario, and went to the west in 1878 at the age of eighteen. Rowell and Willison were both born and grew up in southwestern Ontario. None had university educations.

14 Magrath's knowledge of the west is cited in H. Morgan, *Canadian Men and Women of the Time* (Toronto, 1912), 724. He had once been offered the leadership of the Conservative party of Alberta. He wrote a book entitled *Canada's Growth and Some Problems Affecting It* (Ottawa, 1910) which dealt with immigration and the prospects of Canada, and reflected a strong faith in the future of the country and in 'scientific' techniques in government. British ideals, he argued, must be impressed upon immigrants. The Magrath Papers in the Public Archives of Canada contain numerous memos which I suspect were in the first stage of a biography never completed. Two of his nephews were killed in France in 1916. His only remaining letterbook records the profound impact these deaths had on him (v. 1).

considerable energies until 1914, but when war came Magrath coveted a role more directly involved with the war effort. An imperialist and an advocate of greater state involvement, he saw the war as the supreme test for his ideals. In a Canadian Club address on 6 December 1915 he became one of the first prominent Canadians to promote 'national government' for Canada. He had not been the first: W.F. Maclean, the impecunious Conservative MP and publisher of the *Toronto World*, had called for coalition in the autumn of 1915, but Borden accorded the idea the respect which Maclean's proposals usually received – none.[15] The effect of Magrath's speech may have been the same; we have no record of its political impact. The speech is still important, however, because by May 1917 Magrath's arguments of December 1915 were those of the prime minister of Canada and other supporters of Union government.

Magrath began with the assertion that he 'believed' in the British nation for 'with all our faults we have done more for humanity than any other group.' For this reason, 'some cement' should be applied to the various parts of the Empire to create a 'united people.' For this great Empire and for Canada, the war was a 'do or die' crisis. 'Men, munitions, and money' were insufficient without 'management' – that is, centralization, efficiency, and direction. The prerequisite of management was the absolute 'suppression' of 'political partyism.' While the future of British civilization, the highest expression of human achievement, lay in the balance, the Canadians had been 'expert fiddlers.' Now, perhaps too late, they were 'struggling to quench the flames.' Magrath repeatedly emphasized that the government must have the support of the 'whole people,' that the press must be 'reticent,' and that public organs should 'express the best self to the community.' 'National organization' alone could make Canada's effort a success; only inveterate individualism and selfishness, the offsprings of Canada's pre-war political lassitude, prohibited it. Never had the opportunity for public men been so great, but never had their weaknesses been so apparent.[16]

Several important strains are recognizable in Magrath's thought: the view that political parties are divisive, ultimately frivolous, institutions; the identification of the parties with the existence of a lackadaisical state; and the belief that the activities of the state must be isolated from the activities of parties. In Magrath's

15 Borden Diary, 17 Oct., 1915. There were other supporters of 'national government' such as the *Ottawa Free Press* and, in a vague fashion, the *Manitoba Free Press*.
16 For Magrath's ideas see his 'Each for All and All for Each,' in *Addresses Delivered before the Canadian Club of Toronto, 1915-1916* (Toronto, 1916), 65-76; and 'Some Phases of Public Service,' in *Addresses Delivered before the Canadian Club of Ottawa, 1915-1916* (Ottawa, 1916), 45-49. On his imperialism, see his 'Stray Thoughts about Canada and the Empire,' in *Addresses Delivered before the Canadian Club of Toronto, 1911-1912* (Toronto, 1912), 69-71.

opinion, this isolation must lead to the 'suppression' of political parties. But who would suppress the parties and what form would this suppression take? To the latter question, Magrath would have replied 'management,' the creation of independent agencies to control large areas of society previously untouched by government; the means of the future would recapture the vision of the past of a united community. To the former question, Magrath would have responded that management should be undertaken by those Canadians 'who have acquired the habit of doing things in a big way.'[17] Charles A. Magrath left no doubt that he was such a man and that most of Canada's parliamentarians were not.

Sir John Willison shared Magrath's perception of the extent and nature of the war crisis, though Magrath's denunciation of parties and his cavalier disdain for parliamentary democracy would not have secured Willison's full approval. For Willison in 1916, the Conservative party had become the vehicle through which the war effort should be conducted. Like Magrath, he sensed that the war had forced upon Canada a crucial decision about its nationality, but Laurier's former confidant now believed that only the Conservative party could be trusted to make this decision. Willison therefore became ever more closely identified with the Conservative party.

To Willison, as to most Tories, the war had justified Tory pre-war policies, but by mid-1915 he knew that past justification could not alone keep a Conservative government in office. He warned his friend A.E. Kemp that the Conservatives must secure their position by linking the successful prosecution of the war with the fate of their party. If they did not, the unthinkable would follow: the Conservative party would lose an election and Canada would 'have taken [its] last step in Imperial unity for a quarter of a century and perhaps for all time.'[18] Canada would not be safe in Liberal hands; first, because Sir Wilfrid Laurier had no higher conception of politics than beating the other man, and, secondly, because the character of such 'elements as would carry [Liberalism] to power' was inimical to the national interest.[19]

17 'Some Phases of Public Service,' 49.
18 Willison to Kemp, 6 April 1915, PAC, Kemp Papers, v. 12. See also Willison, 'The War and the Empire,' *Addresses Delivered before the Canadian Club of Ottawa, 1914-1915* (Ottawa, 1915), 157-8. It should be noted that the Conservative party supported Willison's *Toronto News* to the extraordinary extent of $50,000 to $60,000 in 1915. Frank Cochrane to Willison, 30 Jan. 1915, PAC, Willison Papers, v. 17.
19 After Laurier's death Willison expressed his opinion of his erstwhile paragon: 'Sir Wilfrid was unmoral, not deliberately immoral. After forty-five years of age he had no sentiment nor any strong conviction on any subject ... He told me once, I think in 1902, that he was in politics for one reason only – to beat the other man.' Willison to Hugh Clark, 12 March 1919, PAC, Borden Papers (BP), v. 101.

French Canadians and 'foreigners' would be the foundation on which a future Liberal government must rest. Never could the Conservatives, committed to the war and to British ideals, hope to win support from such elements. There were, however, many Liberals of wider vision and of British birth who could understand this most fundamental Liberal weakness, but these same Liberals were repelled by the corruption, the fecklessness, and the inefficiency of the Conservative government. Leadership and efficiency were therefore imperative: Borden must see the urgency of his task. In April 1916 an obviously aroused Willison exhorted Canada's prime minister to exercise leadership:

Of course you cannot know that you are more modest than you ought to be. I think also that you are too kind. This is blunt and almost impudent but I am speaking for a reason. It is hard for a political leader of your characteristics to know how much the country trusts you and how ready it is to respond to any straight appeal from you. In all the noise and clamour of the moment you are the outstanding figure and I do believe the public confidence in your integrity is absolute. I believe that any appeal you may make for support will meet with a response, and that you can afford to be more of an autocrat if that is necessary because I am writing to express confidence and not to suggest criticism of the course you have pursued or to give advice as to the course you should pursue. In short I believe the country will follow where you lead and I want to say that I am not in the least daunted by all the shouting of the last few months.[20]

But of course Willison was 'daunted': otherwise he would not have written. Nor was Willison certain that the country would follow where Borden led. Because a wartime election had become a certainty when Borden and Laurier could not agree on more than a one-year extension of the parliamentary term, the future seemed very bleak indeed. In May 1916 there was a sudden flash of hope when the Liberal ranks split over the Lapointe resolution which called for French education for French children in Ontario. An excited Willison interpreted the result as a severe blow to the federal Liberal party in Ontario and the west and a strong challenge to French-Canadian domination of the party.[21] The Conservative party should court the disaffected. Willison outlined the possibilities to Arthur Meighen, who had forwarded a letter from another Conservative MP urging the disfranchisement of German Canadians: 'Sir Wilfrid

20 Willison to Borden, 10 April, BP, v. 18.
21 *Toronto News*, 13 May 1916. On the Lapointe resolution; see Brown and Cook, *Canada, 1896-1921*, 261.

will have behind him a pretty solid French Vote and a very strong German and Austrian vote with certain other non-English elements. The Government can live *only* by appeal to the English-speaking population. I hope this fact will be recognized and that we will fight boldly for only in boldness is there safety.'[22]

What Willison meant by 'fighting boldly' was soon apparent in the *Toronto News* during the latter half of 1916.[23] The English population, which alone perceived the meaning of the war, was identified as the Canadian nation. The pre-war vision of a nation unified by excellence and leadership was transferred to a particular group, the English Canadians. In Willison's eyes, Quebec and Laurier had fallen into a trance, induced by the seditious teachings of Bourassa. Proof of this lay in the Lapointe resolution. All patriotic Canadians should resist the blandishments of Laurier and yield absolutely nothing in their enthusiasm for the momentous task at hand. Willison was desperate and fearful, embarrassed by what he knew he must do. And yet it had to be done; defeat would come first at home, not in the mud of France.

Willison was sustained in his ambition to break down the federal Liberal party and to transform the Conservative party into the English-Canadian national party by the uncertainty with which many of his Toronto Liberal acquaintances regarded the political future. One of the most notable and the most troubled of these was Newton Wesley Rowell, leader of the Liberal opposition in the Ontario legislature. John Bright had made a 'creed' of Liberalism[24] and Rowell followed this tradition. For Rowell, Liberalism was an ideology in the sense that, through its lenses, facts became linked to ideas and ideas to facts in a fashion that created a coherent world image.[25] Liberalism was the secular complement to his devout Methodism. But with the rapid industrialization and urbanization of Canada after the 1880s, both the secular and sacred world images had become less convincing: facts were less amenable to ideas. Because of this discordance, Methodism in Canada and elsewhere refashioned itself through a new organizing concept, the social gospel, which synthesized the new religion of society with the older religion of the Gospel. In Rowell's view, this was a most successful synthesis. But Canadian Liberalism, or more specifically Laurier Liberalism, had

22 Willison to Meighen, 27 July 1916, Willison Papers, v. 57.
23 Dafoe thought Willison's attempt to 'fire the heather in Ontario' might succeed. Dafoe to C. Sifton, 17 Oct. 1916, PAC, Sifton Papers, v. 204.
24 Asa Briggs, *Victorian People* (London, 1954), chap. 8, 'John Bright and the Creed of Reform.'
25 The definition of ideology used here is drawn from Erik Erikson's *Young Man Luther: A Study in Psychoanalysis and History* (London, 1958), 20. Erikson's definition is particularly apt in the discussion of Rowell because of its emphasis upon the role of ideology in personality.

not undergone the appropriate transformation, though such a change had taken place in the Liberal party of Great Britain after 1906. Liberalism in Canada, Rowell intuitively sensed, had failed to meet the challenge of modern industrial society. Thus, when he assumed the leadership of the Ontario Liberals in late 1911 he moved immediately to recast the image of his party.[26]

As a prominent Toronto lawyer representing George Brown's historic Oxford County constituency, Rowell was well chosen for the task. Harking back to the period when Brown first made Liberalism the party of 'voluble virtue,' Rowell believed that such moral issues as temperance and reform of electoral methods were highly popular, not only among the traditional supporters of such causes but also among the new professionals and managers who were profoundly disturbed by the long-run implications of the social dislocations caused by the rapid growth of Canadian society. He further committed the party to a programme of social reform similar to the British Liberal programme, though more moderate in tone. But compared to the federal Liberal programme, Rowell's election platform of 1914 was certainly 'advanced' in the wide scope which it envisaged for state action.[27]

Rowell's perception of the beneficent role of the state in society was widely shared among prominent federal Ontario Liberals like Mackenzie King, but not by the federal Liberals as a whole or by Laurier in particular. He also found that he could not accept Laurier's indifference to the emotional appeal of imperialism. In the idea of service, the wholesome core beneath the morbid husk of imperialism, Rowell perceived a truly liberal principle.[28] These two questions, imperialism and social reform, troubled Liberals everywhere, but Ontario Liberals were peculiarly troubled by them. They found it hard to justify the role

26 Rowell took the party leadership only six weeks before a provincial election in 1911 which, of course, he lost badly. He was not himself a member of the legislature before this election, and he was 'parachuted' into the leadership by prominent Toronto Liberals closely identified with financial interests and the Methodist Church. See Margaret Prang, *N.W. Rowell: Ontario Nationalist* (Toronto, 1975), chaps. 6 and 7.

27 Rowell himself termed his programme 'advanced.' See C.W. Parker, ed., *Who's Who and Why* (Toronto, 1915-16), VI and VII, 518; and Margaret Prang, 'A Victorian Liberal: N.W. Rowell,' in Ontario Historical Society, *Profiles of a Province* (Toronto, 1967), 134-5.

28 'The Britannic and Germanic Ideals of Empire,' *Addresses Delivered before the Canadian Club of Ottawa, 1914-1915* (Ottawa, 1915), 129-37. Rowell urged 'a community of free nations working and co-operating together in order to attain the highest good for the whole empire.' Although he supported reciprocity in 1911, 'After the Liberal defeat ... Rowell encouraged the non-partisan movement that developed in Ontario in favour of a positive naval policy and supported Borden's Naval Aid Bill ...' Prang, 'A Victorian Liberal,' 130; see also *N.W. Rowell*, 121-5.

of French Canada within the Liberal party, the presence of a fundamentally conservative element within a party of reform. In 1916 the bilingual schools controversy in Ontario forced Rowell to ponder deeply whether he could remain in a Liberal party led by Sir Wilfrid Laurier.

Laurier's approval of the Lapointe resolution astonished Rowell. To him, the resolution broke with the Liberal policy of non-interference with provincial educational affairs, the policy which had brought the Liberals to power in 1896 and which had permitted English Canada to develop the progressive 'national' schools which he deemed so necessary in an industrial society.[29] He accordingly warned the federal leader that it would not be in 'the Mowat tradition' for the federal government to intervene in the controversy. While recognizing that Laurier faced great pressure from Quebec on the issue, Rowell suggested that the 'greatest work' of Laurier's life lay ahead 'in seeking to break the force of the Nationalist movement,' which had forced the confrontation with Ontario. A firm stand on the principles of 1896 would destroy nationalism.[30] Laurier, on the other hand, believed that such a stand would destroy the Liberal party and his own personal reputation in Quebec. There was no plateau upon which these conflicting arguments could meet. Laurier supported the Lapointe resolution; Rowell, Regulation 17.[31]

By his actions in 1916 Rowell explicitly rejected the compromises which Laurier Liberalism demanded. Like most Ontario provincial Liberals, he had never really accepted them. What Rowell and his predecessors as Ontario Liberal leaders had championed was a French Canadian who had openly identified his political beliefs as British Liberalism, who had fought the ultramontane clerisy within its own fortress, who had, in Archbishop Langevin's angry words, thrown only 'miserable crumbs' to the French Canadians and the clergy in the Manitoba schools debate, and who had, while basking in the imperial glow created by his government's unilateral grant of trade preference to the Empire,

---

29 Rowell supported Regulation 17 which restricted the use of French in the schools to the first two years of education. A contemporary article by George M. Wrong notes that during the war the 'bi-lingual question came to be linked in the minds of many people with venomous attacks on Britain, and the assertion that the terrible sacrifices of Canada in the war were unnecessary and mistaken.' 'The Bi-lingual Question,' in Miller, *The New Era in Canada*, 245-6.

30 Rowell to Laurier, 26 April 1916, PAC, Rowell Papers, v. 3. The correspondence is examined in Margaret Prang, 'Clerics, Politicians, and the Bilingual Schools Issue in Ontario, 1910-1917,' in Craig Brown, ed., *Minorities, Schools, and Politics* (Toronto, 1969), 100-7.

31 With the exception of the French-Canadian members of the provincial Liberal caucus, all Liberals supported the Conservative government's action. Prang, *ibid.*, 110.

declared that his proudest moment would be the sight of a 'Canadian of French descent affirming the principles of freedom in the parliament of Great Britain.'[32] After 1900, many English-Canadian Liberals began to suspect that this image of Laurier was merely a mirage.

The alliance of Conservative and *nationaliste* in 1911 permitted the resurrection of the tarnished portrait of Laurier as a beleaguered defender of Liberalism in Quebec against the clericalism and nationalism of that society. After all, Laurier was so civilized, so eloquent, so charming; in truth, so English. But with the Lapointe resolution and the failure of Laurier's oratorical magic to spur enlistment in Quebec, this portrait once more began to crumble. 'Laurier is too old,' they said; 'his vision is failing.' He nevertheless remained the leader of the Liberal party of Canada which Liberals in Ontario and the west were committed to support. He also might be the next prime minister of Canada. In that prospect resided Rowell's dilemma.

In May 1916 Laurier warned Rowell that the line of cleavage between them was 'final and beyond redemption.'[33] Rowell refused to retreat and was sustained in his refusal by the majority of his colleagues and by such influential friends as Joseph Atkinson of the *Toronto Star*.

In the summer of 1916 a journey to the front in France profoundly affected the Ontario Liberal leader. Here, Rowell thought, bombardment and death compelled Canadians to sink the party differences which plagued himself and his party. On his return he asked one audience: 'How could one witness such a scene, much less be a participant in it, and be just the same?' When Rowell asked what he could do, the soldiers had told him: 'Send us more men, men completely trained and properly equipped. We are prepared to give our lives, but that alone is not sufficient.'[34] Rowell, accordingly, devoted his considerable energy and ability to this end.

To his distress he found that the Canadian people would not 'cheerfully respond' to the challenge which he presented. In December, already greatly perturbed by the indifference shown by many Canadians to the flagging war

32 See Laurier, 'Discours sur le libéralisme politique' (Montreal, 1877). The Langevin description may be found in J.W. Dafoe, *Clifford Sifton in Relation to His Times* (Toronto, 1931), 98, and Laurier's London declaration in O.D. Skelton, *Life and Letters of Sir Wilfrid Laurier* (London, 1922), II, 72.

33 Laurier to Rowell, 11 May. This letter and three others from Laurier to Rowell are cited in Skelton, *ibid.*, 475-7; Rowell's replies are not.

34 'Our Canadians at the Front,' *Addresses Delivered before the Canadian Club of Toronto, 1916-1917* (Toronto, 1917), 11-12. For a description of the trip by Rowell's travelling colleague, see Main Johnson Diary, 'European Trip – 1916,' Metropolitan Toronto Central Library (MTCL), Johnson Papers.

effort, Rowell received a letter from his 'old friend' James Macdonell, formerly of National Trust but now in the trenches of France, who warned him that he must face the issue squarely: 'as time goes on and recruiting news from Canada grows if anything worse instead of better, one wonders if after all in the final stage Canada will fall below the high test.' Macdonnell continued:

But if there is not [sufficient reinforcement] and if things go on as they have been going of late, then I see little comfort in the prospect, unless as a nation Canada is able to make its will felt and to make the unworthy ones, if they still exist, understand that in a crisis like this the individual is nothing and the state everything. May it not be true in other parts of the Empire besides England that the Government might find the people prepared for more far-reaching changes than their timorous rulers suspected. Strong men willing to take their reputations in their hands – that is what we want. After all, other men are taking their lives in their hands. It seems to be the decisive hour for Canada. Three years ago Canada was a country with nothing in its immediate past to stir the blood or thrill the imagination. There was no challenge to high self-sacrifice. Since that time all is changed ... If we fail at the last, all may be lost. To put it practically if the Canadian Divisions are not kept up to strength what will be the feeling of the men who have been here towards those who ought to have come but did not?[35]

The war had become for Rowell as for Macdonell the 'highest test' for their nation and for themselves as individuals. An election during this test would be blasphemous, but, astonishingly enough, one was inevitable, and many Liberals, including Laurier, thirsted for it. Though Laurier had proven his incapacity for leadership, Laurier's party would likely be victorious in this election.[36] Soon, their worst fears would be realized: the December 1916 recruiting figures showed that only 5791 men had enlisted, 23,421 less than in January of the same year.[37] The National Service Board reported that roughly 20 per cent of

35 18 Dec. 1916, Rowell Papers, v. 3. Rowell circulated this letter widely among his friends.
36 All Liberals, even disaffected ones, were sure of a Liberal victory based upon solid French-Canadian and 'foreign' support. J.G. Turriff to Sifton, 12 Dec., Dafoe to Sifton, 17 Oct. 1916, Sifton Papers, v. 204; Dafoe to Wrong, 12 Dec. 1916, Dafoe Papers.
37 Cited by Borden, *Can. H. of C. Debates*, 22 Jan. 1917, pp. 25-31. Monthly figures for 1916 were: Jan. – 29,212; Feb.– 26,658; March – 32,705; April – 23,289; May – 15,090; June – 10,795; July – 8675; Aug. – 7267; Sept. – 6357; Oct. – 6033; Nov. – 6548; Dec. – 5791.

Canadian males between eighteen and sixty-five did not return their registration cards. There were, moreover, almost 300,000 males not in essential services, who remained in civilian clothes, and despite the publicity and pressure they showed no inclination to shed them. The national service scheme, an attempt to encourage enlistment by registration, had failed dismally; by implication, so too had the voluntary system of recruiting.[38]

With this knowledge, Rowell wrote to Laurier on 20 January 1917 and recommended 'national government' combined with a policy of 'no election.' Setting out the well-known arguments against a wartime election, he urged that Laurier should enter a 'national government' to scuttle the election. If Borden would not make an offer, Laurier should make the proposal himself.[39] The suggestion was not novel: the *Toronto Star* and the *Manitoba Free Press*, both Liberal newspapers, had also called for a non-partisan war administration in early January.[40] At that time, Laurier had refused to take the idea seriously: 'c'est simplement une chose en l'air, dont personne ne s'occupe sérieusement.' It seemed to Laurier that Toronto, the source of Canada's most dangerous political fantasies, had given birth to yet another. In his opinion, Toronto Liberalism was not to be trusted and Rowell himself was, in Laurier's own words, 'a tory cuckoo hatched in a Liberal nest.'[41] Rowell's letter, following as it did similar appeals by such members of the 'Toronto crowd' as J.W. Flavelle, J.H. Gundy, A.E. Ames, and W.E. Rundle, reeked of conspiracy.[42]

With a bluntness born of exasperation, Laurier replied to Rowell's appeal: 'The situation is simply this that the government has been constantly losing ground, but a good many of those dissatisfied, and perhaps all, do not want to

38 Brown and Cook, *Canada, 1896-1921*, 220.
39 Rowell Papers, v. 3. See Rodolphe Lemieux to Laurier, 23 Jan. 1917, Laurier Papers, v. 705, for the hostile attitude of the Quebec Liberals towards the election postponement.
40 *Star*, 4 Jan. 1917; *Free Press*, 6 Jan. 1917. Joseph Atkinson, the publisher of the *Star*, was a close political and personal friend of Rowell and was largely responsible for his entry into Union government.
41 Laurier to Lemieux, 4 Jan. 1917, Laurier Papers, v. 705. The description of Rowell is from a later letter, but since it summarizes very well Laurier's impression of the Ontario leader, its use seems justified here. Laurier to Walter Scott, 9 Aug. 1918, Public Archives of Saskatchewan (PAS), W.R. Motherwell Papers, M 12, file 109.
42 Flavelle, a close business associate of many Toronto Liberals though himself a Tory, had made a public speech advocating coalition on 16 Dec. 1916. Gundy, Ames, and Rundle had tried to arrange a meeting with Laurier to promote 'national government' in early Jan. George Graham to Laurier, 11 Jan. 1917, Laurier Papers, v. 705. The *Manitoba Free Press* support for coalition was immediately seen by Laurier as an indication of the machinations of Sir Clifford Sifton who had shown in 1911 his close link with the Toronto interests.

entrust the direction of affairs to a leader of French origin. Analyze the situation any way you please and tell me candidly if this is not at the present moment the true and only difficulty.' Rowell, stunned by the candid tone of these remarks, replied negatively to the rhetorical question. And certainly fear of a French-Canadian leader was not 'the true and only' reason for the proposal. But Rowell was too honest to deny that it was a very important one: 'no government which had its chief source of strength in Quebec and which did not include the leaders from [Ontario] could secure the whole-hearted sympathy and co-operation of [Ontario].'[43] Only a coalition would surmount the immense obstacles, and coalition depended on Laurier. Since an election was unacceptable, there was no alternative. on 2 February 1917 Rowell asked in a speech: 'have not the soldiers the right to expect that those who remain at home, leaders and people alike, will make corresponding sacrifices?'[44] Laurier, a leader, would not make the sacrifice which Rowell believed the situation required. He therefore searched for a leader who would.

Magrath, Willison, and Rowell, and many other English Canadians, had passed through the thickets of wartime politics to a common meeting place. Solidarity, not unity, was their overwhelming emotion, and in the idea of service as the basis of a wartime state they had developed an ideology to justify their exercise of power.[45] While they still disagreed on particulars, they none the less shared the belief that the war had to be prosecuted by Canada to 'the last man and the last dollar' and that all barriers which stood in the way of this aim were unworthy of consideration. What cannot be overemphasized is the sense of common experience and common interest held by these prominent English Canadians. While many areas of Canada, such as outlying parishes in Quebec or scattered ethnic communities on the prairies, remained almost untouched by the war, this was not at all true of the geographical and intellectual orbits which

43 Laurier to Rowell, 23 Jan., and Rowell to Laurier, 25 Jan. 1917, Rowell Papers, v. 3.
44 Cited in J.C. Hopkins, *Canadian Annual Review, 1917* (Toronto, 1918), 558.
45 One may cavil with the use of the term 'solidarity' in this instance because of its normal association with Marxism and class analysis, but this would be most unfortunate in that it would deprive us of a descriptive term connoting a higher level of association than mere 'unity.' Writers in 1916 and 1917 often employed the term to describe the mutual dependence which trench warfare bred, and it bore the same mystical sense which it has in Marx's usage. David Apter, following Sorel, has recently expanded the meaning of solidarity by identifying it as a moral system held together by myths in a fashion not unlike that adopted here: 'Solidarity and myth ... supply a moral dimension to political forms. In this sense, the creation of myth, the moral solidarity of the community, and its authority are intimately linked.' *Ideology and Discontent* (New York, 1964), 20.

encompassed the activities of Magrath, Rowell, Willison, and their kind. Thus when the propagandist 'Private Peat' said to the members of the Toronto Empire Club that 'he had no doubt that the majority of those [in the audience] have or had had, sons or relatives over there,' he undoubtedly spoke the truth.[46] The war had become their war, and because they were Canadians it was also, a cabinet document explained, 'Canada's war for reasons of self preservation and self interest, apart from any other considerations.'[47]

To return to Leacock's assertion of the interdependence of 'form' and 'spirit,' it is clear that these prominent English Canadians had defined 'spirit.' The 'ideology of service,' so completely if somewhat disingenuously expressed in *The New Era in Canada*, created a scale to measure the quality of citizenship. Thus Meighen and Willison readily accepted the recommendation of their 1916 correspondent who urged that the franchise be taken from certain groups who had failed to serve. There is an exclusiveness reminiscent of Calvinism: good works (service) are evidence of election (possession of the spirit), and, conversely, election leads to good works. Hence in the 'ideology of service' the willingness to serve becomes the external evidence of the virtue which entitles one to exercise power. The right of an English-Canadian élite, committed to service and imbued with knowledge, to rule the nation can therefore be unembarrassedly asserted. Having articulated a coherent justification for their leadership, men like Magrath, Rowell, and Willison set out to alter the 'forms' of Canadian political life and to make the Canadian state the expression of their conception of the common good. In time, Borden, and eventually his party, came to accept this change.

46 Private Peat was described in his introduction: 'One of the most striking figures brought to light by the war is Private Peat, of the first Canadian Contingent. Wounded – one arm almost useless and one lung affected – Peat returned to Canada, finished as far as fighting went. Almost his first move was to send for the girl he had met and fallen in love with while in the hospital in England. Early in the fall of 1917, Mr. and Mrs. Peat left Edmonton with a total joint capital of $15.00.' Up to the time of the address, Peat had spoken to almost a million people, and published a book – *Private Peat*, of which 200,000 copies were sold. Peat began his address, 'It is good ... to see so many white heads amongst you – we know where the others are.' 'Experiences at the Front,' in Empire Club of Canada, *Addresses Delivered to the Members during the Sessions, 1917-18, and May to December, 1918* (Toronto, 1919), 235.
47 'Memorandum as to Recruiting,' 10 April 1916, PAC, G.E. Foster Papers, v. 41.

7

Conscription

In December 1916 David Lloyd George, the 'Welsh Wizard' who 'in some vague and inspired manner ... represented all those forces of national energy which were determined on a complete victory,' became prime minister of Great Britain.[1] If September 1914 represented the baptism of the British war effort, December 1916 was its confirmation, its sacred rededication to an earlier commitment made almost unknowingly. To Canadians concerned about their nation's flagging resolve, the British change of leader served as both an omen and a model. Would Canada rededicate itself to the war, or would Canada's contribution continue to dwindle until, in a final moment of national agony, it collapsed? Patriotic groups were unwilling to let events take their course, and in December 1916 they began an intensive campaign to shape the future.

One of the leaders of this movement was the Toronto businessman and Sir Robert Borden's long-time confidant, Joseph Flavelle. As chairman of the Imperial Munitions Board he should, properly, have refrained from direct political action, but the war was not a question of politics for Flavelle: 'I return from England deeply impressed with the absence of party spirit, in the conduct of public business in Great Britain. This results not only from the gravity of the issues which have caused men to rise above party, but because the Government is made up of men from both parties.' On 16 December 1916, at the Ottawa Canadian Club, Flavelle, ignoring Borden's strenuous objections, urged the formation of a 'non-partisan' government for Canada, a coalition comprised of the 'best elements' of both parties.[2] Because Borden's close relationship with

1 Lord Beaverbrook, *Politicians and the War, 1914-1916* (London, 1928, 1932; 1960), 408-9.
2 Flavelle to Borden, 13 Dec. 1916, PAC, Borden Papers (BP), v. 63. An account of this incident is found in Henry Borden, ed., *Robert Laird Borden: His Memoirs* (Toronto,

Flavelle was well known and because the Conservative party had been identified with men of his type since 1911, the speech had unusual significance and Borden was forced to respond to the growing agitation of which it was a part.[3]

Borden shared with Flavelle the perception of the war as the paramount concern of the nation, and he had also shown himself to be a leader who was willing to embark upon unconventional political adventures. Yet he distrusted Flavelle's motives, and perhaps correctly — we cannot be certain — he saw in the speech and the 'national government' agitation an implicit threat to his leadership. He knew that national government would likely mean conscription and, inevitably, a dangerous domestic situation. Moreover, Australia's popular rejection of conscription had shown the perils of moving too quickly.[4] In Canada, a nation with much greater heterogeneity, conscription would surely meet even stronger opposition. Thus Borden moved hesitantly, leaving his options open.

In December 1916 for the first time he publicly refused to reiterate his promise that there would be no conscription.[5] Then, in a letter to his former mentor, Sir Charles Hibbert Tupper, at the beginning of the new year, he outlined the great difficulties involved in introducing conscription, but expressed a willingness to consider it if the voluntary system completely broke down:

I do not know that I can say more as to the question of enforced military service than was expressed at our personal interview in Ottawa. We have more than two and a half millions of French Canadians in Canada and I realize that the feeling between them and the English people is intensely bitter at present. The vision of the French Canadian is very limited. He is not well informed and he is in a

1938), II, 617-19. Borden recalls that his finance minister, Thomas White, was most outraged by Flavelle's action. White's anger may have arisen from his knowledge that Flavelle and many of his friends favoured the former Toronto banker for the leadership.

3 O.D. Skelton, in *Life and Letters of Sir Wilfrid Laurier* (London, 1922), interpreted the Toronto speech as part of a Toronto conspiracy to take over the government, an interpretation supported by some evidence. See, for example, G.M. Wrong to C. Sifton, 2 March 1917, PAC, Sifton Papers, v. 206; and J.W. Dafoe to Wrong, 12 Dec. 1916, Dafoe Papers, microfilm copy. When Flavelle read Skelton's account he wrote to him denying that his promotion of 'national government' represented 'the views of a distinctive body of opinion,' but admitting that he reflected and often inspired the political actions of a close group of Toronto friends in 1916 and 1917. Flavelle to Skelton, 5 June 1922, Queen's University Archives, Douglas Library, Flavelle Papers, box 9, folder S-U.

4 Conscription was defeated twice in Australian plebiscites, first in 1916 and again in 1917.

5 Borden and R.B. Bennett, national service director, refused to rule out conscription when meeting a labour delegation. For an account of this meeting, see Martin Robin, *Radical Politics and Canadian Labour, 1880-1930* (Kingston, 1968), 122.

condition of extreme exasperation by reason of fancied wrongs supposed to be inflicted upon his compatriots in other provinces, especially Ontario. It may be necessary to resort to compulsion. I hope not; but if the necessity arises I shall not hesitate to act accordingly.[6]

Borden made clear in another letter that the necessity had not yet arisen and that a coalition would be of more advantage 'in solution of the railway situation,' which was of extreme 'urgency,' than in the conduct of the war.[7] But he knew that a decision could not be long postponed. An invitation to join in 'special and continuous meetings' of the Imperial War Cabinet gave him a few extra months, but with an election virtually a certainty, 1917 loomed as a crucial year.[8]

No event so magnified the potential dangers of a general election as a by-election in the Quebec constituency of Dorchester in January 1917. By-elections had been one of the few casualties of the Canadian party truce:[9] Dorchester was to be an exception because of the unusually bitter personal feelings involved. The Conservative candidate was the newly appointed minister of inland revenue, Albert Sévigny, who had been elected in 1911 as a 'Nationalist-Conservative.' Unlike Frederick Monk, Sévigny had accepted the Conservative naval policy in 1912 and 1913, disavowing by this action his stand on the issue in the 1911 election. Because of this background he was detested by Quebec Liberals and *nationalistes* who thirsted for revenge for what they regarded as the hypocritical Conservative campaign in 1911. The choice of the Dorchester Liberals and the Quebec provincial party was the fiery young Lucien Cannon. Sir Wilfrid Laurier, sensing the dangers inherent in such a contest, saw nothing to gain and much to lose in a Quebec by-election fought on the war issue. Nevertheless, local sentiment and the decisive voice of Premier Sir Lomer Gouin forced the national leader to capitulate. On 16 January, a scant eleven days before the election, a local convention nominated Cannon.[10] Two days later, an 'assemblée contra-dictoire' brought Cannon and Sévigny face to face.

6 Borden to Tupper, 2 Jan. 1917, BP, v. 16.
7 Willison to Borden, 26 Jan., and Borden to Willison, 2 Feb. 1917, BP, v. 78.
8 Walter Long, colonial secretary, to Borden, cited in Borden, *Memoirs*, II, 625. This journey would also allow Borden to learn British opinions on the length of the war, crucial information for a politician.
9 No writs were issued for twenty constituencies which became vacant between March 1915 and July 1917. See A.M. Willms, 'Conscription, 1917: A Brief for the Defence,' *Canadian Historical Review*, XXXVII (Dec. 1956), 339.
10 Laurier wrote to the party organizer: '... ce ne serait pas un gain politique : ce serait simplement un argument de plus dans la campagne sourde qui se fait dans les autres

Cannon immediately denounced Sévigny's support of the Borden government as a betrayal of the principles upon which he had been elected in 1911. More controversially, he claimed that a Sévigny victory would be interpreted by the government as a mandate for sonscription. The latter, in Cannon's view, would 'ruin the country from the point of view of men and wealth and everything else for England.' The frankness of his remarks astonished not only Sévigny but also the English-Canadian Liberal press, which immediately disavowed him and asked Laurier to do the same. But his willingness to raise the fundamental issue of conscription nevertheless won him the support of *Le Nationaliste* and of the vituperative pen of Georges Pelletier of *Le Devoir*.[11] Sévigny, however, had abundant resources with which to meet the attack. He pointed out the patronage which his election in 1911 had brought to the constituency and which his re-election would bring in the future. More significantly, he brought in his two French-Canadian cabinet colleagues, P.E. Blondin and E.L. Patenaude, and argued that only their presence in the cabinet would provide the electors with a guarantee against conscription.[12] This argument was as decisive in Dorchester in 1917 as it was in 1939 in all of Quebec when the federal Liberal cabinet members employed the same plea to defeat Maurice Duplessis.[13] The effect outside Quebec was also remarkably similar. English Canadians tended to interpret the Sévigny win as an indicator of support for the war effort in Quebec, and as a firm rebuke to the *nationalistes*. The possibility that Sévigny's victory resulted from the belief that he would act as a deterrent to a more intensive war effort from within the cabinet was apparently not considered.[14]

provinces contre Québec. Réservons nos forces pour la bataille générale.' Gouin certainly appears to have had the final word in federal as well as provincial party matters; in the case of Dorchester he believed that if the Liberals did not run the *nationalistes* would. Laurier to Philippe Paradis, 8 Jan., Paradis to Laurier, 15 Jan. 1917, PAC, Laurier Papers, v. 705. See also J.C. Hopkins, *The Canadian Annual Review, 1917* (Toronto, 1918), 483.

11 Cannon was cited in the Toronto *Globe*, 20 Jan. 1917; he finally issued a weak retraction. For the reaction among English-Canadian Liberals, see Frank Carrel to Laurier, 20 Jan. 1917, Laurier Papers, v. 705. For Cannon's support see Robert Rumilly, *Henri Bourassa* (Montreal, 1953), 572; and *Le Devoir*, 20 Jan. 1917.

12 An excellent description of the campaign which illustrates this point is Renaud Lavergne, *Histoire de la famille Lavergne*, ed. B.C. Payette (Montreal, 1968), 105-6. Lavergne campaigned for Sévigny in this election and felt he was a traitor when he later supported conscription.

13 See J.L. Granatstein, *The Politics of Survival* (Toronto, 1967), 34-5.

14 See, for example, the *Globe*, Toronto, 30 Jan. 1917; Hopkins, *Canadian Annual Review, 1917*, 482-6; and Elizabeth Armstrong, *The Crisis of Quebec: 1914-1918* (New York, 1937), 159. Dorchester was an overwhelmingly French-speaking constituency with French Canadians numbering 42,983 in an overall population of 44,823. *Sixth Census of Canada, 1921* (Ottawa, 1924), I, 364.

The Dorchester victory came as a breath of fresh air to a federal Conservative party on the brink of suffocation. Borden noted in his diary the 'great excitement' produced by the event. Little did he appreciate the irony of his analysis which saw the victory as leading to 'a better understanding between the two races.'[15] It was, perhaps, the exhilaration caused by Dorchester which inspired him to discuss the formation of a coalition with his cabinet. After a long series of setbacks, the Tories at last could bargain from strength. In the cabinet discussion of 3 February 1917 several ministers expressed themselves 'apparently in favour of' coalition.[16] But Borden's 12 February departure for the Imperial War Conference was approaching too rapidly for fuller consideration of the question. Furthermore, the full effect of national registration was still unknown, and the new year stirred fresh hopes that the war would end.[17] For Liberals and Conservatives, for patriotic agitators and pacifists, Borden's impending journey created an uncomfortable hiatus. All knew that no action could be taken until his return; all hoped that a favourable verdict in the trenches of France would make a decision unnecessary. Not for the last time in 1917, fate was malevolent.

On 14 February Borden embarked for England from Halifax. The days before he left were filled with discussions on the three major problems facing the government: the railway situation, recruitment, and government reorganization. The railway question awaited the report of a commission, and therefore nothing was done. On recruitment, the cabinet decided that the voluntary system should be continued.[18] No decision was made on government reorganization. To those seeking a definite direction, the government offered none.

The three months of Borden's absence from Canada were probably the most significant months of the war. In March the abdication of the Czar astonished Canadians and left Russia's future role in the war uncertain. One month later, in April, Woodrow Wilson, whose Autumn 1916 campaign slogan 'he kept us out of war' had angered so many Canadians, led the 'great peaceful people' of the United States into 'the most terrible and disastrous of all wars.'[19] At that precise

15 BP, Borden Diary, 27 Jan. 1917.
16 *Ibid.*, 3 Feb. 1917.
17 Good news to Canadians in Jan. 1917 was the enlistment of 9194 men and the 'wastage' of only 4396. Hopkins, *Canadian Annual Review, 1917*, 307. Borden himself regarded Germany as 'relatively weaker' in 1917 compared to 1916 and thought the war might well end that year. Borden Diary, 13 Jan. 1917. In this period the German army was on the defensive and the food shortage in Germany was acute. See Arthur Rosenberg, *Imperial Germany* (1928, Boston, 1964), 153-90.
18 Borden Diary, 7-11 Feb. The railway commission, composed of Sir Henry Drayton, W.M. Acworth of Great Britain, and A.H. Smith of the New York Central, reported in April 1917.
19 Arthur S. Link, *Woodrow Wilson and the Progressive Era, 1910-1917* (New York, 1954), 282.

moment in the war, the impact of these two remarkable events was unknown. Ultimately, the resources of America could assure Allied victory, but would there be sufficient time for American soldiers to set foot upon French soil? Lloyd George's determination to launch a great offensive in the spring and summer of 1917 made this question particularly meaningful for Canadians.[20] The Nivelle offensive, as it was termed, required extensive participation by the Canadian troops, who were already facing manpower difficulties. The Canadians nevertheless participated, and the capture of Vimy Ridge in early April was the one notable success of a generally calamitous operation. But the Canadian laurels were blood-red — 3598 Canadians died at Vimy.[21]

The Vimy triumph had an important side-effect; Borden, visiting Britain at the time, shared the praise lavished upon the Canadian soldiers,[22] and the infectious war enthusiasm was too much for the Canadian leader to resist. Suddenly, the preoccupations of Ottawa became as distant emotionally as they were geographically. Thus, he completely ignored the pleas of his secretary, A.E. Blount, who urged him to return to Canada to retrieve a desperate political situation.[23] When a nervous Sir Thomas White, the acting prime minister, cabled to Borden his view that the 'absolute necessity' of the railway problem compelled his presence, an angry Borden replied that no 'distraction' should interfere with Canada's commitment and, by implication, his own activities in London, during 'the most critical and terrible period of the war.'[24]

Having learned the perilous Allied position, Borden cabled to his militia minister, Sir Edward Kemp, on 5 April: 'It is believed that Germany stakes everything on this Summer[']s operations and the demand for men is therefore very urgent. What success are you having in proposal for home defence force and how is recruiting progressing for Expeditionary Force?' Borden had apparently decided that the Americans would be too late; the supreme test would come in 1917 before they arrived. Kemp had also reached such a decision; he replied promptly and pessimistically: '... General feeling large number of recruits will

---

20 Many of Lloyd George's reasons had little to do with military strategy. See P. Guinn, *British Strategy and Politics* (Oxford, 1965), 211-17.

21 J. Swettenham, *To Seize the Victory* (Toronto, 1965), 161.

22 Borden Diary, 10 April 1917. Borden was most disturbed by the failure of *The Times* to comment editorially on the Vimy capture. See also 'Domino' (Augustus Bridle), *The Masques of Ottawa* (Toronto, 1921), 35.

23 Blount to Borden, 28 March 1917, PAC, Blount Papers, v. 1. Blount was troubled by the lack of leadership in the government and by the stridency of public criticism. According to him there was no one in Ottawa 'to take a leading hand.'

24 White to Borden, 27 and 28 March, Borden to White, 30 March, White to Borden, 2 April 1917, BP, v. 31.

eyes of the Bnts.

not be forthcoming under the voluntary system. Publicity campaign for Home defence force also covers necessity for enlistment overseas forces. Hoped it would be productive of results but voluntary enlistment has about reached its limit. Enlistment overseas for March seven thousand and sixty three ... Thirty five thousand will be shipped during April.' Conscription was inevitable.[25]

On 17 May 1917, three days after his return from Europe, Borden announced to the cabinet his intention to introduce conscription in Canada. The discussion revealed the dangers but nevertheless produced agreement. He wrote in his diary: 'All agreed that conscription necessary. Patenaude and Blondin said they [were] prepared to stand by us but that it will kill them politically and the party for 25 years.' The next day Borden announced conscription to the House of Commons. To conscriptionists, the justifications were unassailable. With the Americans adopting a selective draft, Canada would be disgraced if she refused to follow. Her honour and her new voice in the Empire symbolized by her prime minister's participation in the Imperial War Cabinet would perish. To Borden and to hundreds of thousands of others in English Canada, such a prospect was unthinkable.[26]

It seemed that a failure of leadership and the weakness of national institutions had made compulsory military service necessary. Conscription accordingly inspired in its advocates the desire to alter and strengthen these national institutions and the leadership. During the 17 May cabinet discussion, some had raised the 'question of coalition government.' The majority, Borden recorded in his diary, seemed to be in favour although there was 'considerable divergence of opinion' on the matter. Still, nothing was said about coalition when conscription was announced. A few days after the announcement, however, Arthur Ford, the exceedingly well-informed Tory journalist, reported that a movement for coalition had arisen in the Conservative caucus, 'largely among the Ontario members.' These members were urging Borden to form a coalition with what Ford termed the 'patriotic wing' of the Liberal party.[27] Of course, not all Conservatives

25 Borden to Kemp, 5 April, and Kemp to Borden, 10 April 1917, PAC, Kemp Papers, v. 53, file 8; Borden, *Memoirs*, II, 698. Sir George Foster wrote: 'Only compulsory service can meet the situation and though it is full of grave difficulties come it must.' Foster Diary, 7 May 1917. PAC, Foster Papers, v. 1.
26 Even Laurier felt the intense pressure when three of his former Ontario ministers urged that conscription become Liberal policy in order to pre-empt the Tories. Sir Allen Bristol Aylesworth to Laurier, 10 May, and Sir William Mulock to Laurier, 11 May 1917, Laurier Papers, v. 708. Mackenzie King also supported conscription at this time. See R.M. Dawson, *William Lyon Mackenzie King* (Toronto, 1958), 260. Premier W.M. Martin of Saskatchewan also urged that the Liberals should adopt conscription. Martin to Laurier, 17 May 1917, Laurier Papers, v. 708.
27 Ford to Willison, 23 May 1917, PAC, Willison Papers, v. 30.

favoured a coalition, particularly when conscription sprang open a profound fissure in the Liberal party. The movement, however, soon won the support of Borden himself, who had been impressed by the widespread Liberal endorsement of conscription.

On 18 May Edward Brown, the provincial treasurer of Manitoba, had announced his personal and his government's belief in conscription. The following day the Toronto *Globe*, whose readership was largely drawn from Liberal supporters in Ontario, defended 'the compulsory organization of all the military resources of the country.' After Borden's conscription speech, N.W. Rowell publicly and privately declared that there was 'only one course open to Liberals ... to support the principle of the government's proposals.'[28] Public rallies were held throughout English Canada where Liberals nervously shared the same platform with lifelong Tory enemies. Letter after letter from Laurier's oldest political friends in English Canada — W.S. Fielding, George Gibbons, W.E. Rundle, Hartley Dewart, Levi Thomson, and J.H. Sinclair — told the veteran Liberal leader that he must not oppose conscription.[29] Most Liberals, however, knew that Laurier would surely denounce the measure, and would therefore create for them their most difficult dilemma. Frank Carvell, a New Brunswick Liberal often mentioned as Laurier's successor, has left an excellent description of his own confusion at this time: 'There is something within me which abhors the idea of throwing up my hands when others are fighting my battles and not being willing to do everything possible to stand by the men who are doing this for me voluntarily. I do not know where I am going to land. I am going home this afternoon to consult with my constituents, and I may as well tell you frankly, especially with my family, because after all there comes a time in the life of every man when he and his own must do some hard thinking for themselves.'

Carvell's constituents did nothing to resolve his problem: they unanimously supported coalition, but were split along religious lines on conscription. And, indeed, other proponents of conscription found less enthusiasm than they had

---

28 Rowell to A.K. Maclean, 19 May, and Rowell to R. Lemieux, 21 May 1917, PAC, Rowell Papers, v. 3.
29 In a letter to Laurier on 31 May Fielding favoured the acceptance of the bill, but urged that a referendum be taken before the law took effect. This is, perhaps, the origin of Laurier's own proposal for a referendum. See also Bruce Fergusson, *Hon. W.S. Fielding: Mr. Minister of Finance* (Windsor, NS, 1971), 171-3. Dr Fergusson seems to have overlooked the letter cited here. Gibbons to Laurier, 27 May, Rundle to Laurier, 27 May, Dewart to Laurier, 25 May (Dewart later became an opponent of conscription), Thomson to Laurier, 19 May, Sinclair to Laurier, 22 May 1917, Laurier Papers, v. 708 and 709.

expected at the 'grass roots.' George Gibbons told Laurier that western Ontario farmers were hostile to compulsion. The public attacks upon conscription by two well-known agrarian spokesmen, Peter McArthur and W.L. Smith, seemed to confirm this interpretation. The increasingly influential United Farmers of Ontario, while hesitant to openly denounce the Military Service Act, called for a referendum on the subject.[30] The *Weekly Sun*, the most spirited and candid of all Ontario farm organs, showed no such diffidence, and boldly asserted on 23 May that Canada owed her allies no more men. One of the shrewdest observers of Canadian politics, O.D. Skelton of Queen's University, warned Laurier not to be deluded by the widespread press support for conscription, especially in Toronto. 'The voice of Toronto,' Skelton declared, 'is not the voice of God,' nor even of Ontario, nor of the nation as a whole. In the circumstances, the Liberals must not despair, must maintain cool heads, and await the unfolding of events. Never should they help the Tories 'in pulling the chestnuts out of the fire.'[31]

A cabinet meeting on 24 May revealed that the political chestnuts were as hot as Skelton had suggested. Unanimity disappeared when several Conservative ministers blamed Borden for a situation from which there was no apparent escape. In any election, these ministers argued, a combination of the French Canadians, farmers, and 'slackers' would defeat the government.[32] Borden shared these fears more than he admitted; time alone could afford a solution, and to this end he engaged Laurier in a masterful political minuet.

Borden took the lead and proposed on 25 May that the two leaders join with their parties to carry through conscription. There would be an equal number of Liberals and Conservatives in a new government, apart from the position of prime minister.[33] Laurier was equally nimble: while expressing his adamant opposition to conscription, he took refuge in ambiguity and agreed to consider Borden's proposition. He, too, needed time. Probably neither was serious in this political flirtation. Borden knew that Laurier could not accept any coalition for which the price was support of conscription, and Laurier certainly would never have accepted a role as Borden's deputy when an election promised a strong possibility of a Liberal victory. Both, however, were performing for the benefit of others, in particular, the members of their respective parties.

30 Carvell to A.K. Cameron, 1 June 1917, PAC, Cameron Papers, v. 2; Carvell to Laurier, 4 June, Gibbons to Laurier, 27 May 1917, Laurier Papers, v. 709 (Gibbons pointed out that 'articulate opinion' in western Ontario was for conscription); Hopkins, *Canadian Annual Review, 1917*, 340.
31 Skelton to Laurier, 30 May 1917, Laurier Papers, v. 709.
32 Borden Diary, 25 May 1917.
33 Borden, *Memoirs*, II, 720-1.

Conservative dissent from Borden's course arose in two quarters: the French-Canadian Tories and those Conservatives closely associated with Robert Rogers. Borden's adoption of conscription and coalition flabbergasted Rogers. For five years the prime minister had neglected his party; now he proposed to sacrifice it. Rogers knew very well that he would be the first to be cast off if any coalition was formed. Also, the party machine which Rogers had so lovingly constructed would crumble under any coalition government.[34] He moved quickly to assemble allies to block Borden's apparent path, and he found sympathizers among the machine politicians and among those Tories whose inveterate and even phobic hatred of Liberals made them regard coalition as an outrage. Unfortunately for Rogers, this group, which was centred mainly in Ontario and Manitoba, lacked sufficient numbers to withstand the public pressure favouring coalition in their own political bailiwicks. Yet their presence, if not an insuperable barrier to coalition, was certainly a major irritant, and was bound to become a problem whenever a coalition was formed.

The French-Canadian Conservatives raised questions of a different order for Borden. Their constituency meant, of course, that for them support for conscription was tantamount to political suicide; but, on the other hand, opposition to conscription offered no political reward either. The strength of the French-Canadian Conservatives lay, paradoxically, in their weakness. Realizing that the French-Canadian Liberals would never enter a coalition, Borden and the French-Canadian Conservatives knew that the government must retain the support of some French Canadians in order to give the appearance of national representation. Borden, to whom Quebec Conservatism was a curious mixture of the politics of Ruritania and Mahagonny, with the delightful incompetency of the former and the sordid battles for spoils of the latter, had little choice. His best French-Canadian minister, E.L. Patenaude, resigned on 5 June and denounced conscription as a threat to national unity.[35] This left only two French-Canadian ministers: Albert Sévigny, whose Dorchester victory was tarnished by the discovery of some furniture 'borrowed' from the burnt-out Speaker's Chamber in his own home, and P.E. Blondin, the postmaster-general, who

---

34 Rogers reportedly opposed conscription as well as coalition, seeing in the former the death-knell of the Conservative party in Quebec and in non-Anglo-Saxon areas of western Canada. He was already most concerned about the state of the party in these areas. See Rogers to Borden, 10 April 1917, BP, v. 32; Arthur Ford, *As the World Wags On* (Toronto, 1950), 29; and Ford to Willison, 27 May 1917, Willison Papers, v. 30.

35 *Globe*, Toronto, 6 June 1917. For the Quebec Conservative press the conscription issue was especially difficult: to support conscription was to risk the loss of the party subsidy and government advertising; to oppose it meant the loss of subscribers. They therefore tried to straddle a middle position. See Armstrong, *The Crisis of Quebec*, 177.

devoted his energies in 1917 to a largely futile attempt at recruiting a French-Canadian battalion.[36] Both these ministers agreed to remain in the government after considerable argument and, when the Union government was finally formed, they were the sole French-Canadian members of the cabinet.

Laurier's task was a much more difficult one than Borden's, one which required singular political deftness. Indeed, the skill of Laurier was so great that Borden and future historians have frequently failed to note it. Looking back at the Liberal leader's actions in 1917, Borden attributed his hesitation on coalition to weakness and his advanced years. A close examination of his actions does not sustain that interpretation. On closer scrutiny, one finds that Laurier had lost little of his brilliance or his guile, and, in the end, by his evasiveness, his extraordinary ability to manage individuals, and his sure knowledge of the sources of his political strength, he not only survived the political crisis of 1917 but, unlike most aged political leaders, assured the future effectiveness of his political testament.

When Borden spoke to him about coalition on 25 May, Laurier had already decided upon a stance from which he would never waver.[37] W.L. Mackenzie King, a supporter of conscription himself but nevertheless a close adviser and eager student of Laurier in May and June 1917, had outlined the Laurier formula on 15 May, three days before conscription was announced: 'How I hope a general election may be avoided. Were Borden to bring in conscription, as we hear he is likely to, I think that the Liberal Party should extend the life of parliament at least 6 months. It will be a difficult measure to enforce and may cost his party its life. If the Liberals are wise they will put the responsibility on [Borden] and leave him the consequences.'[38] While Laurier disagreed with King on the questions of extension and conscription, he nevertheless concurred with his analysis of the political impact of conscription and with his recommendation for future Liberal policy.

In the conscription crisis, Laurier saw a great opportunity: Laurier Liberalism had been challenged before 1917 by the aggressive Anglo-Saxon reform Liberalism of the western provinces and Ontario. Step by step, these 'new Liberals' had won concessions from the national leader, such as the National Liberal Advisory Committee which was created in 1915 to develop a policy for the party. The 1916 report of that committee had recommended an advanced social programme which included old age pensions, mothers' allowances, unemployment insurance,

36 Hopkins, *Canadian Annual Review, 1917*, 318.
37 Laurier's firm position was outlined in Laurier to Martin, 21 May 1917, Laurier Papers, v. 708.
38 PAC, King Papers, King Diary, 15 May 1917.

and other similar measures.[39] Such a platform, especially when linked with such reform Liberal planks as prohibition and female suffrage, promised to be most unpopular in conservative Quebec and among the non-Anglo-Saxon immigrants who had flooded the country after 1896 and who had generally voted Liberal. Such men, as fanatic in their different way as the Catholic bishops whom Laurier fought in the 1870s, threatened to impose an exclusive mould upon the national Liberal party that would almost certainly seal its fate. The confrontation between 'new' and 'old' Liberalism was widely expected to occur during the search for Laurier's successor. With conscription, it came in the spring of 1917 with the 'new Liberals' not yet in control of the party.

Thus, when Borden offered coalition and Liberals such as J.W. Dafoe, Rowell, and Joseph Atkinson of the *Toronto Star* urged Laurier to accept, Laurier used the carrot and stick to force the combative conscriptionist Liberals on the defensive. He first marshalled his forces, notably the unbroken phalanx of opponents of conscription in Quebec led by Sir Lomer Gouin. Even the rebel Henri Bourassa could rally behind this Liberal standard.[40] Laurier then waited for reinforcements, which came in the form of the hesitation and, in some cases, antagonism expressed towards conscription in rural areas of English Canada, areas, particularly in Ontario and the west, which had long been Liberal party strongholds. Having received encouragement, he told Borden on 6 June that he totally rejected both coalition and conscription.[41] This was the 'stick' which forced conscriptionist Liberals into the open; there was also a 'carrot.'

On 5 June, the day before he met Borden for the final meeting of the negotiations, Laurier tested his proposal for compromise on Mackenzie King, who was used during this period as political litmus paper for determining English-Canadian opinion: Laurier would permit conscriptionist Liberals to run as 'official Liberals' provided that they agreed to a referendum on conscription. King indicated that he found the position quite acceptable; but others, Laurier knew, would not. Those Liberals who rejected a referendum must therefore be driven out of the party and, in going, give up their right to determine the future course of the party and to choose Laurier's successor. For those prominent English-Canadian Liberals like King who stayed with the old leader, their decision was made easier by Laurier's shrewd declaration that the next Liberal leader must be an English Canadian and a Protestant.[42]

39 The committee and its report are covered in Dawson, *Mackenzie King*, 259, 300-3.
40 Bourassa, however, did not do this immediately. See Rumilly, *Henri Bourassa*, chap. 28.
41 Cited in Borden, *Memoirs*, II, 724-5.
42 King Diary, 5 June 1917.

By rejecting Borden's offer, Laurier assured a Liberal Quebec, not only in the next election but for many elections thereafter. By proposing a referendum, Laurier made the decision to defy the Liberal whip more difficult for English Canadians who favoured conscription. The vote on the Military Service Act was not on a black and white issue, but one which involved considerable shades of grey and therefore safety.[43] Laurier forced the English-Canadian Liberals on the defensive in 1917 and for the future. After 1917, any English-Canadian Liberal leader had to be acceptable to Quebec, which more than ever was the heart of the Liberal party of Canada. Most of all, Laurier's negotiation, hesitation, and manipulation broke the powerful impetus behind the conscription-coalition movement, and afforded him the time to assemble a strong political base in Quebec and among non-British elements in Canada. Many Liberals whom Borden had thought might cross the floor of the Commons hesitated. The Conservative leader was thereby forced to move outside Parliament to find Liberal allies for his enterprise, and there the terrain was almost unknown.

43 Rowell recognized the tempting escape which Laurier's offer created and pleaded with George Graham to resist it. Rowell Papers, v. 3, contains the correspondence.

8

The road to coalition

Sir Wilfrid Laurier's political skill in May and June 1917 had almost irreparably delayed the formation of clear positions upon which conscriptionists could bargain. Only in late June did the outlines of any future coalition government emerge and even then merely in shadows. The unalterable opposition to conscription of French Canada, which coalesced behind Laurier, was unquestionable, and his leadership meant that there would be no French-Canadian Liberal, either federal or provincial, in any national government. Instead, Laurier and Sir Lomer Gouin would form a powerful bloc — Henri Bourassa now with them — adamantly hostile to conscription, which they regarded as a manifestation of a plot to undermine French-Canadian influence in the Liberal party in particular and national politics in general.[1] And, if there were to be no French-Canadian Liberals in a coalition government, it was equally apparent after mid-June that few, if any, federal Liberal members of Parliament of English-Canadian background would join one.

Realizing that his efforts to win federal Liberal members were failing, Sir Robert Borden turned to provincial Liberals and prominent Liberals outside active political life who were more distant from Laurier's charm and guile. Already on 8 June Sir John Willison had informed him that Newton Rowell was prepared to join a coalition. Borden quickly responded and offered Rowell a

---

1 On 27 June Bourassa declared: 'Au nom de tous les nationalistes de la première heure, au nom de tous les nationalistes de la deuxième et la troisième heure, au nom de tous les vrais et sincères nationalistes, j'accepte le remède proposé par M. Laurier ...' Robert Rumilly, *Henri Bourassa* (Montreal, 1953), 583. There is some evidence that Borden tried to split the French-Canadian ranks by making a special appeal to Gouin, an action which undoubtedly strengthened the Laurier-Gouin 'common front.' See G.H. Perley to Borden, 6 June 1917, PAC, Borden Papers (BP), v. 77; also Gouin to Laurier, 25 June 1917, PAC, Laurier Papers, v. 710.

position in a cabinet with one-half Liberal membership. Rowell refused to take immediate action, citing his 'important duties' in Ontario and the need for him to work with the conscriptionist federal Ontario Liberals.[2] Rowell nevertheless added that he hoped that 'the discussion & vote on the Military Service bill might clear up the situation & permit action at a later date.' Encouraged by this tone, Borden quickly arranged an interview with the Ontario Liberal leader which took place on 26 June. At this meeting, Borden reiterated his earlier offer and suggested that the implementation of conscription could be delayed six months in order to allow for one final voluntary effort.[3] An enthusiastic Rowell immediately passed on this proposal for delay to Laurier, who refused to consider it. According to Rowell, Laurier declared that even if he were elected with a majority supporting conscription, he would not put the act into effect. Rowell's worst fears were realized: he knew for certain the depth of Laurier's antipathy to compulsory military service and the impossibility of any coalition involving a Liberal party led by Laurier.[4]

Rowell's interview indicated to Borden that Laurier's refusal had not doomed his hopes for a conscriptionist coalition. The means of attaining this goal were not yet obvious, however. The Tory leader recognized, as he told Rowell, that 'it would not meet the situation or materially help it for two or three Liberals personally to enter the Government.'[5] After all, Rowell could have a real effect only in Ontario where the Tories already controlled the vast majority of the seats and where a 'win-the-war' Conservative platform would probably increase the total. Western Canada, however, was a different matter; there, the four provincial governments were in Liberal hands and the majority of federal members were Liberal. And in the west, unlike Ontario, Borden had few personal ties to exploit.

One potential western liaison was Sir Clifford Sifton, the owner of the *Manitoba Free Press*, the leading minister for western Canada in Laurier's cabinet, the brother of the premier of Alberta, and Borden's valued ally in the 1911 reciprocity campaign. Moreover, J.W. Dafoe, the editor of the *Free Press*,

---

2 BP, Borden Diary, 8 and 18 June 1917. 'Confidential Memorandum of Mr. Rowell,' 18 June 1917, PAC, Rowell Papers, v. 3.

3 Borden had asked Perley if such a delay was possible. If it was, he should have a statement prepared by Generals Sir Arthur Currie and Sir Richard Turner and approved by the War Office. Perley approved the procedure on 26 June, the day Borden met Rowell. Borden to Perley, 23 June, Perley to Borden, 26 June 1917, BP, v. 86.

4 This information is contained in a memorandum on Rowell's entry into Union government which was drawn up in 1918. BP, v. 96. Also Rowell to Laurier, 30 June, and Laurier to Rowell, 4 July 1917, Rowell Papers, v. 3.

5 'Confidential Memorandum of Mr. Rowell,' 18 June 1918, *ibid.*

who unlike Sifton had supported reciprocity in 1911, was very close to the powerful Grain Growers' organizations of the Canadian west, as well as to the Norris government in Manitoba which drew its main support from the British-Ontario element in the province and was accordingly most sympathetic to intensifying the war effort. Sifton had continued to advise Borden on matters of public policy after 1911, but in late May 1917, at the height of the early negotiations, Sifton, to the Liberals' undoubted astonishment, was at Laurier's side, not at Borden's. When Dafoe urged support of conscription and coalition, Sifton angrily denounced Borden for playing the 'party game.' To George M. Wrong on 5 June Sifton praised Laurier's decision to refuse Borden's offer as patriotic, claiming that the real aim of coalition was the 'smashing' of the Liberals and not the securing of men. Two days later, however, he cabled to Dafoe: 'Think you should come here first train.'[6] By the end of June, in a sudden but not uncharacteristic *volte-face*, Sifton had become Borden's most important ally in the attempt to create a conscriptionist coalition.[7]

Sifton's influence was soon apparent. On 28 June he telegraphed to Dafoe asking him and James Calder, perhaps the most powerful member of the Saskatchewan government, to come at once to Ottawa. They came, as did A.B. Hudson of the Manitoba government and Arthur Sifton, premier of Alberta.[8] Sifton had shrewdly arranged to have the westerners in Ottawa for the final vote on the Military Service Act which they approved but their party leadership opposed. As he knew, the westerners' impotence within the national party at once became abundantly clear. Soon, they were meeting with Sir Clifford, debating their future course in a party which they knew no longer represented their interest.

While Sifton coaxed the western Liberals, the Conservatives stood by and speculated. Robert Rogers, whose political senses were completely muddled,

---

6 Sifton to Dafoe, 28 May, 5 and 7 June 1917, PAC, Dafoe Papers, microfilm copy; Sifton to Wrong, 5 June 1917, PAC, Sifton Papers, v. 206; see also R.C. Brown and R. Cook, *Canada, 1896-1921: A Nation Transformed* (Toronto, 1974), 269-70.

7 Borden Diary, 21, 26, 27, and 28 June 1917; J.W. Dafoe, *Clifford Sifton in Relation to his Times* (Toronto, 1931), 400-10. Sifton's motives are most uncertain. There is little doubt that he told Laurier that he was opposed to conscription in May. Later, when challenged by Mackenzie King who knew of Sifton's original attitude, he said he had feared that conscription could not 'be enforced and that there would be trouble.' PAC, King Papers, King Diary, 8 Oct. 1917. To be fair, it should be noted that on 21 June Sifton told Borden that he feared the Quebec situation and thought the bill should be held up. Still, the Liberals had sufficient reason to question Sifton's honesty. See O.D. Skelton, *Life and Letters of Sir Wilfrid Laurier* (Toronto, 1921), chap. 19.

8 Sifton to Dafoe, 27, 28, and 30 June 1917, Dafoe Papers.

told Borden that Laurier had called the westerners to the capital, and the cabinet concluded that they were in Ottawa to arrange the Liberal electoral campaign. While Sifton was carefully assembling the conscriptionist Liberal forces, Borden waited, apparently baffled and certainly frustrated.[9]

On 5 July vague prophecies of Liberal disintegration gave way to reality with the vote on second reading of the Military Service Act. Sir George Foster, present in the Commons for that vote, reflected the sense of an historic event having occurred in his diary entry that evening. 'The French vs. English. To such a pass has Laurier's early teachings and practical lessons brought us. The House to a man rose & sang "God Save the King" – *the man* being Oliver who obstinately *sat.*'[10] Sir George intuitively grasped the significance of the voting pattern. Of the fifty-five opponents of the act, forty-five, over 80 per cent, were from Quebec. The remainder, such as the 'obstinate' Frank Oliver, are best described as the 'steady old guard element of Liberalism.'[11] The overwhelming majority of English-Canadian Liberals, twenty-six out of thirty-eight, sided with the government. Only four members west of the Ottawa River, the Liberals Oliver, Charles Murphy, J.P. Molloy, and Edmond Proulx, opposed the act; all except Oliver represented constituencies in which French Canadians were numerous, and in the case of Murphy and Molloy in a majority.[12] Overall, the national pattern of support is most striking:

	For	Against
Maritimes	15	6
Quebec	7	45
Ontario	71	2
Prairies	23	2
British Columbia	6	0

This vote on 5 July marked the political watershed of 1917. Before it, bargaining positions were necessarily vague or even unformed; afterwards, the

9 Borden Diary, 3 and 7 July 1917. The diary suggests that Borden was not fully informed of Sifton's actions. The latter conducted his negotiations throughout the summer and autumn of 1917 with characteristic secrecy. Borden shared this same style, and for that reason, perhaps, he did not find Sifton's methods objectionable.
10 PAC, Foster Papers, v. 1 (italics in original).
11 J.C. Hopkins, *Canadian Annual Review, 1917* (Toronto, 1918), 343.
12 Most of the English Canadians who voted against the bill had served long periods in Parliament. Oliver, for example, was first elected in 1896. Five of the twelve were English-Canadian Liberals from Quebec. *Sixth Census of Canada, 1921* (Ottawa, 1924), I, table 26.

principal agents in the construction of a coalition were readily identifiable and their assumptions fairly well established. Since most members of Parliament probably thought of themselves as 'delegates,' the result was taken as certain evidence of a national majority for conscription. They acted after consulting with the 'leading men' of their constituencies. Even if the broad mass of a constituency did not agree, such was the conception of public opinion that the members expected that their leaders' attitude would soon be that of the majority. Articulate opinion in English Canada supported conscription; in French Canada it opposed conscription. Upon these premises, all the political bargaining preliminary to a coalition was based.

The decisive vote in favour of conscription, Borden's policy, established him as the individual who would exercise the largest influence upon the result of the political bargaining. Yet, to borrow terms first employed by Richard Neustadt to describe the American presidency, Borden was never a 'prime minister-in-boots' striding forward from his July victory towards his triumph in October, but rather a 'prime minister-in-sneakers'[13] persuading and probing others throughout the summer of 1917. At this task he was remarkably successful, a fact well recognized by contemporary commentators who accorded him abundant praise for his 'patience and persistence.'[14] In a sense, however, this praise is misleading since it makes the Union government seem a logical product of inexorable, hidden, and largely impersonal forces, as if Borden had merely to wait out the course of events and to watch a drama unfold. In reality, however, Borden was similar to Pirandello's ubiquitous author simultaneously directing and participating in the action.

Borden's greatest advantage lay in his office and in the early and clear expression of his goal: the full coalition of the Liberal and Conservative parties. Other options were available, such as reshuffling the administration, bringing in prominent businessmen and public figures, or creating an inner 'war cabinet.' All were suggested; all were rejected. This implies that Borden wanted a wide coalition and disapproved of a confrontation on the war issue. His willingness to delay conscription, which was revealed in his June telegram to Sir George Perley, further substantiates this impression. Furthermore, by 1917 the future of the Conservative party had become a minor consideration to the sixty-three-year-old man who led the party. He admitted this to himself in September; others, like Rogers, knew it much earlier. In council, Borden 'frittered away the time'

---

13 'Whitehouse and Whitehall,' *The Public Interest* (Winter 1966), 64.
14 See, for example, J.C. Hopkins, *Canada at War* (Toronto, 1919), 311; and 'Domino' (Augustus Bridle), *The Masques of Ottawa* (Toronto, 1921), 27-38.

anxious to avoid the topic of reconstruction which obsessed him.[15] He spurned the safest course for his party, and therefore could not discuss his plans in council where he knew many were unsympathetic to his aims.

Borden's objectives developed from his interpretation of the future of Canadian politics. This interpretation was set out in reply to a letter from Sir John Willison in July 1917. Reflecting on Canadian political developments, Willison argued that Canadian politics had reached 'the end of an era.' In his reply, Borden agreed and added, significantly, that 'new party alignments, reconstruction of past political formulas and a new political outlook will result from the intensely critical conditions through which our country is passing and from the broader outlook which the overseas Canadians must acquire in this war.'[16] Borden, a long-time critic of Canadian parties who despaired of the possibility of change once he was in office, now believed that the war could be the agency of liberation for Canadian politics. His responsibility was to assure that change, not to defend the integrity of the Conservative party; in other words, he could act as the midwife at the birth of a new, more creative politics. Surely an aspect of this new political outlook would be a strengthened national state; one that could carry out ambitious programmes unhampered by the weakness of the bureaucracy, the immobility of political structures, and the parochialism of members — in short, all those factors which undermined Borden's post-1911 hopes.

At all times, Borden had his party's support because of the boldness of his actions and, ironically, because of the totality of Laurier's opposition. He could therefore act alone, rarely consulting with his colleagues (whose resignations he held pending reconstruction of the cabinet). In Borden's view, caucus and cabinet could no more become directly involved than a man pass final judgment upon himself. Although Borden could use his position as a party leader as a trump, the party itself could learn only the outcome of the match, not the plays that were made. Throughout July he created or employed avenues of action remote from Ottawa; Sifton, the maverick Liberal, was his main agent, the catalyst to bring about the disintegration of the old structure of the Liberal party.[17] They shared few confidences, and Sifton worked independently, informing Borden of only the outlines of his plan. There was never a common

15 Borden Diary, Sept. 1917, and Foster Diary, 23 June 1917; see also Foster's entries on 20 and 27 July. J.D. Reid was advising Borden to simply extend Parliament and hold no session in 1918 on the grounds of war emergency; this course, he claimed, was safest for the party. Reid to Borden, 5 July 1917, BP, v. 77.
16 Willison to Borden, 22 July, Borden to Willison, 24 July 1917, PAC, Willison Papers, v. 8.
17 Their relationship was most frank. See Sifton to Borden, 30 July 1917, BP, v. 78. Borden was denounced for making 'three cardinal mistakes.'

programme, apart from the general one of coalition. They could nevertheless work together because their analyses of politics were essentially the same.

In an essay Sifton wrote in 1917, he too had called for a 'new era' in Canadian politics. Although vague and surprisingly unimaginative in his actual proposals for change, he implored Canadian politicians 'to get out of the ruts of the past forty years' while Canadians still were 'the masters of [their] own destiny.'[18] He was more lucid in a letter to Mrs J.W. Sifton. Parties as they then existed must end. The 'hope for humanity in Canada' resided in 'co-operative movements and associations amongst the people themselves apart from Government interference which will result in amendments to the laws when they are required, but when such are not required will find methods for improving the condition under which people live.' The Canadian west, so alive to fresh ideas and so hostile towards obsolete tradition, must lead the way.[19] It is not surprising, then, that Sifton's energies were directed towards the securing of a strong and progressive western voice in the coalition. In July 1917 he and his colleague Dafoe proposed to use a Winnipeg convention of western Liberals scheduled for early August to identify and solidify this support.

Sifton and Dafoe wanted the convention to issue a firm declaration against Laurier's hostility to conscription and coalition. What they had not expected was the strength of sentiment for Laurier among rank-and-file Liberals in the west. Thus, while they worked through the top level of provincial party leadership to achieve their goal, others loyal to Laurier, notably Frank Oliver, exploited the grievances and the affection for Laurier of the second and third levels of party leadership. Oliver's technique was successful: the convention became, in Dafoe's words, 'a bomb that went off in the hands of its makers.'[20] The convention supported neither conscription nor the principle of coalition; it did endorse the leadership of Sir Wilfrid Laurier.

What caused this embarrassing collapse of Sifton's carefully plotted scenario? Main Johnson, an observer for Toronto conscriptionist Liberals in Winnipeg, pointed out the central weaknesses in Sifton's plan. When he arrived in Winnipeg, Johnson, to his great surprise, found only in the Manitoba delegation 'much active conscriptionist opinion.' Even there the indications of overwhelming

18 'The Foundations of the New Era,' in J.O. Miller, ed., *The New Era in Canada* (Toronto, 1917), 37-57.
19 Sifton to Mrs J.W. Sifton, Sifton Papers, v. 206.
20 Dafoe to A. Bridle, 14 June 1921, Dafoe Papers. An excellent account of the role of Dafoe and Sifton in Canadian politics in 1917 is Ramsay Cook's, 'Dafoe, Laurier, and the Formation of Union Government,' *Canadian Historical Review*, XLII (Sept. 1961), 185-208.

Laurier strength had forced Premier T.C. Norris into a 'publicly impartial attitude.' In the resolutions committee, the premiers or their representatives brought forth their plan, agreed upon earlier, to break with Laurier and to fight the election as a 'Western Group' on a 'Win-the-War' platform. On the floor of the convention these same men remained silent, leaving only 'a few courageous but obscure men unaccustomed to swaying crowds' to advance their conscriptionist point of view. The Liberals of Alberta and Saskatchewan seemed especially concerned about the large 'foreign vote' in their provinces, and they accordingly were most reluctant to promote conscription. Dafoe even sensed a conspiracy; he suggested to Rowell that the western Liberals had made a secret deal with Quebec exchanging Laurier support for a lower tariff policy.[21]

In their more thoughtful moments, both Johnson and Dafoe became aware of more profound grievances expressed by western Liberals. Johnson, for example, noted the intensity of the hatred felt by the westerners towards the Borden government, which they held responsible for the profiteering and the exploitation of the early days of the war. The Borden government, an 'eastern' government, had conducted the war in the interests of the banking, industrial, and transportation monopolies which controlled the economic life of the west from Toronto and Montreal. For this reason, the visit to Winnipeg of Sir Clifford Sifton, the enemy of lower tariffs and a symbol of eastern 'interests,' was especially 'ill-timed' and 'unfortunate.'[22] Thomas Crerar, a friend of Dafoe's, wrote a few days before the convention that 'Sifton in the West is ... as dead as a doornail.' His recent western trip, he added, 'if anything rallied support against the very thing he was pleading for,' that is, conscription. The unpopularity of Sifton with the 'rank and file' was, in Johnson's view, 'unanimous.'[23] Dafoe was later to agree with this judgment and saw the intransigent opposition to conscription and coalition in early August as a continuation of the June 1917 campaign which the Liberal government of Saskatchewan had waged to great effect against 'eastern domination.' In this light, the Winnipeg convention should not be seen as an expression of faith in traditional Liberalism, although that

---

21 Dairy, 'Notes on Winnipeg Convention'; Johnson to Rowell, 9 Aug. 1917, MTCL, Johnson Papers, v. 8. Large delegate meetings were held to rally Laurier support. See F.C. Wade to Laurier, n.d., Laurier Papers, v. 710. Dafoe informed Rowell that a meeting of Prairie premiers on 24 July had decided upon this course. Dafoe to Rowell, 25 July 1917, Rowell Papers, v. 3.

22 Johnson to Rowell, 9 Aug. 1917, Johnson Papers, v. 8.

23 Crerar to Gordon Waldron, 3 Aug. 1917, Queen's University Archives, Crerar Papers, box 36; Johnson to Rowell, 7 Aug. 1917, Johnson Papers, v. 8. Dafoe supported this later in Dafoe to Borden, 29 Sept. 1917, BP, v. 327.

certainly was a factor with some, but as a further episode in the long drawn-out western revolt against the old Canadian party system.[24]

No matter what the interpretation, the convention was a major disappointment to Dafoe, Sifton, and, of course, Borden. Sifton had assured the prime minister that the governments of Alberta, Manitoba, and Saskatchewan would unanimously support a 'coalition war government';[25] his position had therefore been weakened, but it had not been destroyed. Three factors kept him in the bargaining: first, Borden overestimated Sifton's influence in the west and had developed no alternative intermediary who had ties with the western provincial Liberals; secondly, Sifton still fascinated Borden and the Conservative leader tended to minimize western hostility towards him; and, thirdly, the disunity of the Ontario Liberals gave Sifton undue prominence in the negotiations with the Liberals of that province. Thus, Sifton stayed close to Borden.

Ontario Liberalism played a much smaller role in the Union negotiations than anyone had expected. After all, Ontario was the province in which imperialist and war sentiment was most intense and where Liberals had already shown themselves discontented with their federal party in 1911. Many, in fact, attributed the enactment of conscription to the clamour raised by the 'voice of Toronto.'[26] But by early August this voice no longer spoke in unison, or with much effect. The split in Ontario Liberalism was on federal-provincial lines, and it became publicly apparent in late July when the federal members and candidates for Ontario met to discuss the political crisis. On 16 July, four days before this meeting, the twenty-six Liberals who voted for conscription gathered to chart a common course of action. To the disappointment of some conscriptionist Liberals, the 'win-the-war' atmosphere was 'not as strong as it might have been.'[27] Still, not even the anti-conscriptionist Liberals were prepared for the mood of the Ontario meeting which followed.

On the morning of the twentieth, George Graham and Fred Pardee, the sponsors of the gathering, met with the provincial leader N.W. Rowell to outline a pro-conscription platform which they expected the convention to accept. They agreed that national and party interests demanded that Ontario Liberals, federally and provincially, must stand by conscription and that Liberal conscriptionists

---

24 *Ibid.* This is substantiated in a letter from a Saskatchewan politician to Laurier: W.F.A. Turgeon to Laurier, 3 Aug. 1917, Laurier Papers, v. 711. See also Henry Wise Wood to Crerar, 4 Aug. 1917, Crerar Papers, box 36.
25 25 July 1917, BP, v. 78; Borden Diary, 30 July 1917.
26 Skelton to Laurier, 30 May, Laurier to Gouin, 26 June 1917, Laurier Papers, v. 709.
27 Pardee to Rowell, 17 July, Rowell Papers, v. 3; Hopkins, *Canadian Annual Review, 1917,* 565.

should accept coalition if a 'suitable arrangement' could be found.[28] Such a declaration would be a beacon to the faltering conscriptionists of western Canada and the Maritimes, as well as an affirmation of the future importance or even dominance of Ontario Liberalism within the federal party.

At 2:00 pm about forty-five delegates including fourteen federal members gathered in the new headquarters of the Reform Association with W.A. Charlton, MP, in the chair. Immediately, Pardee moved to the attack, demanding that the meeting support conscription and coalition as the only policy which would maintain the unity of the federal and provincial wings of the party. Two other members, Hugh Guthrie and E.W. Nesbitt, followed in the same vein. Then, when it seemed that the direction of the meeting had been established, a sudden reversal occurred. William M. German, a veteran MP from the Niagara Peninsula who had voted for conscription at the second reading, denounced the proposed platform. This new wave became a torrent which swept away coalition-ist sentiment. Delegate after delegate rose to speak against Pardee's motion. J.A. McMillan, MP, summarized the mood: 'I tell you frankly that if we had known some time ago what we know today, several of us would not have voted the way we did.' Conscriptionists straddling the line were thrust by this momentum into acceptance of Laurier's position. One such example was Mackenzie King, who joined the chorus damning Pardee's proposal. E.C. Drury seemed hopelessly adrift: he expressed the hope that coalition and conscription could be ignored and a campaign fought on the issue of 'honesty in government.' By 7:00 pm, when the last speech was made, the convention had rejected coalition, parlia-mentary extension, and immediate conscription, and had upheld Laurier.[29]

This meeting permanently weakened the bargaining position of Ontario Liberals. The careers of Pardee, Graham, and Nesbitt were fundamentally altered; never again would they attain pre-eminence within Ontario Liberalism. Most astonished and most affected by the outcome were the provincial Liberals. Rowell had been one of the first prominent politicians in Canada to call for a

28 King Diary, 20 July 1917; Rowell to Graham, 21 July, Rowell to Dafoe, 21 July 1917, Rowell Papers, v. 3.

29 This account of the meeting is drawn from King Diary, 20 July 1914; a transcript of the meeting which appears authentic but which is found in PAO, Howard Ferguson Papers, box 16; and an account in the *Evening Telegram*, Toronto, 30 Aug. 1917. See also Arthur Ford, *As the World Wags On* (Toronto, 1950), 94-5. In spite of his damna-tions King continued to tell his pro-conscription friends that he still favoured 'con-scription in principle.' For some time he had distrusted Graham and his influence in the Ontario Liberal party, and because of the latter's prominence King was very much an outsider in Ontario Liberal circles. King Diary, 21 July 1917. See also R.M. Dawson, *William Lyon Mackenzie King* (Toronto, 1958), 260, who claims King had decided that 'conscription was doubtless necessary in principle ...'

Union government, and the vote on the second reading in the federal House had appeared to justify this stance. Suddenly, the actions of the federal Ontario Liberals on 20 July subverted Rowell's argument that his policy alone would maintain party solidarity. An irate Rowell felt that the federal Liberal conscriptionists, particularly his confidants Pardee and Graham, had betrayed him. He questioned Graham's sincerity and warned that the failure to carry the meeting jeopardized 'the future of the Liberal Party in Ontario.' Graham replied apologetically but not convincingly: 'Well, we met and there was an avalanche that could not be stemmed. Pardee and myself at the very outset made our position clear and urged what the platform should be.' The unanimous view of the others insisted that 'Sir Wilfrid was the only leader that could possibly be ...' To further justify his position, he added: '... Although such a thing was not hinted, I could not but infer that the candidates felt the road for them would be much easier and the complicated situation relieved if I were to gracefully vanish.'[30] Graham did vanish, but with little grace. His pathetic indecision stamped him forever as one who could not lead and knew not where to follow.

The importance of the meeting of the Ontario candidates cannot be over-emphasized. Its result assured that Canadian Liberalism would be Laurier Liberalism. If the Ontario conscriptionist Liberals had succeeded, the western Liberals might have performed differently in their later convention. Laurier would then have been isolated as the leader of a Quebec party. When the war ended, the conscriptionist Liberals would have formed the core of a different Canadian Liberalism, less conservative, more doctrinaire, much less influenced by Quebec, and more like the Liberalism of George Brown, Edward Blake, and William Lyon Mackenzie than that of Laurier. Of the participants in Canadian politics in 1917, none played for higher stakes than the Ontario Liberals; none lost so much. Without realizing it, the forty-two delegates made one of the rare, fundamental decisions of Canadian political history.

With the Toronto and Winnipeg conventions, the second stage of the coalition negotiations came to an abrupt end. Coming so suddenly after the exhilaration created by the vote on conscription, the shock was particularly intense. Many, notably Ontario Liberals, abandoned hope of a coalition and took little part in the third and final stage which began after the Winnipeg convention of 7 August. Others, refusing to accept that either the western or the Ontario conventions were representative bodies, continued to work for a Union government. Many of this group had previously taken no active part in the earlier bargaining process, but now were able to advance their own claims.

30 Rowell to Graham, 21 July, Graham to Rowell, n.d., Rowell Papers, v. 3.

The most important new element in the bargaining after 7 August was the Conservative caucus. In the first stages the caucus was almost impotent, its powers delegated, not entirely by choice, to Borden. When Borden decided to seek a coalition, a project of Liberal inspiration, the Liberal conscriptionists were in an extremely strong position. But the double failure of the Liberal conscriptionists in Toronto and Winnipeg instilled a new confidence in the Tory caucus. The Conservatives, it seemed, had quelled their partisanship while the Liberals had continued theirs. No longer could the Liberals cast themselves as men of principle not party, a most effective role in Canadian politics in 1917. If the Conservative caucus had been united in opposition to further bargaining, the coalition movement would probably have lapsed forever. But the caucus was split and its energies were divided between playing a part in the coalition negotiations and an internal party struggle which Borden exploited to the advantage of his policy of coalition.

Even during the long period of silence from May to August 1917, the caucus was divided. The largest faction was made up of Tories who supported Borden's initiative for either personal or political reasons. Many of these saw that an alliance with the Liberals could alone save their seats; nor did they want to force the resignation of Borden, which they regarded as an undoubted catastrophe. For these reasons they willingly entrusted their fate to their leader. The second faction was composed of those who disapproved of coalition. The potential leader of this faction was, of course, Robert Rogers, but as we have seen he had been badly scarred by scandals in Manitoba. In the same week of May 1917, when he might have countered Borden's coalitionist tactics, an investigatory commission brought down a report which declared that Rogers and Thomas Kelly, a Manitoba contractor, had entered into 'a fraudulent conspiracy' to provide Conservative campaign funds and to give Kelly a 'kickback' from the provincial treasury.[31] Poor Kelly went to jail; Rogers remained minister of public works. This report nevertheless assured Rogers' inactivity from May to August as the minister struggled to save his political life. In August, however, the situation altered.

Two new factors returned him to prominence. The first was the Winnipeg convention. Rogers revelled in the failure of the Liberal conscriptionists and pointed out that the Liberals were guilty of that same sin, partisanship, which they had so righteously imputed to him. Coalition seemed out of the question. Never had the Conservative party been in such a strong electoral position as it was after the Winnipeg convention. Rogers' second stroke of fortune rescued his

31 Hopkins, *Canadian Annual Review, 1917*, 734.

personal reputation. His erstwhile friend Kelly was released from jail in August, not long after the report in late July of yet another commission, this time appointed by the Tories, which fully exonerated Rogers from the charges made by the earlier, Liberally appointed, commission.[32] Sensing that vindication had come, Rogers consolidated his forces, freed himself of shackles, and sought to control the situation.

On 2 August seventy Conservative members presented the popular Rogers with a memorial congratulating him on the new commission's report and denouncing the old report as an insidious and politically inspired plot.[33] The date and the number of signatures are important. The memorial coincided with the opening of the Winnipeg convention where coalitionist Liberals hoped to assure their dubious colleagues of the Tories' good faith. Such a document could only fan the partisan fires. Secondly, the number of Conservatives who signed the memorial indicated that Rogers had widespread support within the Conservative caucus. The document was a political masterstroke, a signal to Borden that he could no longer count upon a quiescent caucus.

Rogers' analysis of Canadian politics in August was remarkably similar to Borden's. Like Borden, he sensed that coalition would mean the end of the traditional Conservative party. Unlike Borden, Rogers found this unacceptable. Furthermore, he knew that he, the *bête noire* of western Liberals, would be the first casualty of any coalition. He had many weapons with which to fight. First, he pointed out, quite correctly, that the Conservative caucus was not being consulted on a life or death matter. Secondly, he argued that the Liberals had foisted coalition upon the politically naïve Borden in order to gain time to heal the rupture in their own party. Thirdly, he employed his close links with the Montreal business interests which he had developed in his long years as principal party organizer. These interests, backed by the CPR and publicly led by the *Montreal Star* of Sir Hugh Graham (now Lord Atholstan), were infuriated by Borden's railway policy. On 1 August 1917 the Canadian Northern Acquisition Bill had been introduced over the strongest objections and, indeed, threats from the CPR.[34] Many Tory members, who had greatly benefited from the political largesse of the railway company, were terrified by the spectre of a CPR-Liberal alliance. Rogers exploited this fear within the caucus by intimating that the

32 Kelly was released because of 'his advanced age, very bad state of health, large family, two of his sons at the Front, expressed willingness to make restitution, and imprisonment in connection with the offences, continually, since October 1915.' *Ibid.*, 734-5.
33 *Toronto News*, 3 Aug. 1917.
34 See John Eagle, 'Sir Robert Borden, Union Government and Railway Nationalization,' *Journal of Canadian Studies*, X (Nov. 1975), 59-66.

differences between the CPR and the Conservative party could only be overcome by his intervention.

On 3 August, one day after the presentation of the memorial to Rogers, Borden learned from Sir George Foster of an 'intrigue among [Conservative] members' encouraged by Rogers who had called a meeting of the western Conservative members.[35] Simultaneously, Senator Rufus Pope of Quebec, the son of the old Tory railways minister, J.H. Pope, and a popular, coarse 'backroom boy,' directed a tirade against Borden: 'Hon. Mr. Rogers feels that so long as he is a member of your Cabinet that he should at least be spoken to on subjects affecting [matters] that for 25 years he has had to be responsible for. The rank and fyle [sic] of your supporters feel that Bob should not be thrown out into the street.' Pope continued:

The principles and traditions of the Tory Party in war time or peace are sound enough economically & loyal enough at all times to govern any country.

The Radical Gov't of England had to call them in — why? Because they stood for King and Country — not so with a bunch of Grits.

Your supporters are getting nervous. There is not any organization to hold them together in the Country, only individual cohesion.[36]

This argument was undoubtedly appealing both in its simplicity and its familiarity. Rogers, Pope, and their allies proposed to restore pre-war political alignments and to wage an all-out battle in the fashion of 1891 and 1911 on the 'loyalty' issue. To those who doubted that the electorate would respond as it had in those elections, Rogers had an answer. The electorate itself could be reshaped: a political razor in the form of a franchise act could scrape off the foreign vote which would surely have supported Laurier. By this device, Rogers argued, coalition could be abandoned and Conservative ascendancy assured.[37]

With the failure of the Winnipeg convention Rogers' arguments gained new cogency. A highly publicized but fruitless conference called by the governor-general, the Duke of Devonshire, on 9 August, in which CPR president Lord Shaughnessy, Gouin, Laurier, Borden, Sifton, and Foster reiterated their positions, made coalition seem even more a mirage.[38] Borden had gambled and had

---

35 Borden Diary, 3 Aug. 1917.
36 Pope to Borden, 'Aug. 1917,' BP, v. 78.
37 Rogers to Borden, 4 Aug. 1917, BP, v. 219.
38 PAC, Duke of Devonshire Diary, 9 Aug. 1917, microfilm copy; Borden Diary, 9 Aug. 1917; Gouin to Laurier, 4 Aug. 1917, Laurier Papers, v. 711. Sifton had expected this result and had tried to avoid the conference.

lost much. Now he seemed about to be outflanked by those Tories who had always opposed his policy but had been forced to accept it in May. From the ruins of the coalition strategy, Rogers hoped to resurrect the old Tory party with or without Borden as leader.

The suddenness and skill of Rogers' moves were intended to throw Borden off-balance. Surprisingly, they did not, and in his counter-attack the Conservative leader not only saved himself but also his cherished project of a Union government. He returned to the strategy he had employed during the party revolts of 1910 and 1911, but with a significant variation. As before, he threatened the party with his resignation. This time, however, he indicated that he would nominate his successor, who would be a public figure acceptable to the conscriptionist Liberals. Ironically, the price of Borden's disappearance would be coalition. Thus, when he suggested on 10 August to Arthur Meighen and J.D. Reid that Mr Justice Lyman Duff take his place, the two ministers responded with the 'fierce' opposition which Borden must have anticipated: Duff, a Liberal and a political novice, would be 'fatal' for the Conservative party, and Sifton's nomination on 13 August of the seventy-seven-year-old William Meredith would be no less 'disastrous.'[39] The Tory caucus, thoroughly terrified at the prospect of such leaders, implored Borden to remain. Rogers' insurgency rapidly subsided in the clamour for party unity.

On 15 August a defeated Rogers bitterly lashed out at his conqueror. Borden, he charged, was 'tarrying' with Grits who understood neither the needs of Canada nor the nature of the war. This letter was a final, desperate attempt by Rogers to rally the caucus behind him. Borden immediately construed the letter as one of resignation, and in his reply he accepted the resignation while reaffirming his intention to continue his efforts to build a coalition.[40] One of the principal barriers to any coalition, Rogers' presence in the cabinet, was thus removed.

Emerging from the contest with Rogers with a united party committed to his leadership, Borden re-established his commanding position in the coalition negotiations. Sifton, who had believed that a 'neutral leader' was essential, quickly retreated in the face of a militant Tory caucus. By offering to step aside

39 Borden Diary, 10 and 11 Aug., *Toronto News*, 11, 13 Aug. 1917; In his memoirs Borden dates this conversation with Meighen as 9 Aug. Henry Borden, ed., *Robert Laird Borden: His Memoirs* (Toronto, 1938), II, 741. Meredith had been Conservative opposition leader in the 1880s in Ontario, and in 1917 he was chief justice of Ontario. Duff was well known as a Liberal and had been appointed by Laurier to the Supreme Court.
40 Rogers to Borden, 15 Aug., Borden to Rogers, 16 Aug. 1917, BP, v. 79. Foster Diary, Aug. 1917, reports the cabinet reaction.

and to sacrifice his political career at the same time as Liberals in Ontario and the west were seemingly refusing to risk their political lives, Borden had acquired a new paramountcy. Because of this, Sifton knew that Borden must stay, and he was not repelled by the prospect. Obviously impressed by Borden's skill, he wrote to Dafoe: 'I know Borden and he knows me and we can get along and run the machine effectively.' If necessary, Sifton himself would 'go in & fight it out to the finish.'[41] This, however, might not be necessary, for with Rogers gone coalition had become more appealing to western Liberals.

On 20 August Thomas Crerar and Henry Wise Wood, agricultural leaders from Manitoba and Alberta respectively, met with Borden, and on the following day Arthur Sifton, James Calder, and Crerar did the same.[42] Crerar had earlier proposed that Sir George Foster or Sir Charles Hibbert Tupper should replace Borden as prime minister in any coalition, and both Crerar and Wood were profoundly suspicious of Borden's motives. In early August, Wood had warned Crerar that 'The Conservative party is ... making a desperate effort to get the West to betray its interests into their hands.' 'The endorsation of this particular conscription measure,' he added, 'is not vital to anything.'[43] Without knowing it, the westerners played into Borden's hands by permitting him to use his favourite weapon, the threat of resignation, to rally his friends and to disarm his enemies. Accordingly, he declared that he 'would hold up both hands for Crerar's choice, Foster,' a gesture made in despair so frequently in the past. It is difficult to regard this manœuvre seriously; Foster was almost seventy and, as Borden had said, he possessed 'no more political sense than a turnip.'[44] J.D. Reid and other shrewd politicians would surely not have tolerated Foster as leader. Although Reid and other ministers always listened carefully to Foster in council, they did so 'for the purpose of recording their votes in the opposite sense, as they firmly and invariably relied on the unsoundness of [Foster's] judgment.'[45] Foster was none the less well known, and his age had finally brought him respectability with the general public. He was, then, an excellent tool for Borden's purposes.

The westerners returned home to consult with their colleagues and to consider Borden's offer. Borden turned his attention to the Maritimes asking Frank Carvell and Premier George H. Murray of Nova Scotia to join a Union government.

41 Sifton to Dafoe, telegram, 12 Aug., Sifton to Dafoe, 14 Aug. 1917, Dafoe Papers.
42 Borden Diary, 19, 20, 21 Aug. 1917.
43 Wood to Crerar, 4 Aug. 1917, Crerar Papers, box 36.
44 Borden Diary, 26 Feb. 1916.
45 Borden, 'Estimate of Sir George Foster,' 8 Dec. 1933, in *Letters to Limbo*, ed. Henry Borden (Toronto, 1971), 71.

Rowell was contacted once again. Borden was 'hopeful' that the climax of the long political drama was approaching.[46] He did not fully record his opinions at this time, but he probably believed that the westerners would be forced by intense private and public pressure to repudiate the Winnipeg convention and would then tentatively accept coalition, subject to a change of leadership. Borden certainly knew that any Liberal demand that he step down would be rejected by the Tories. After this rejection took place, the westerners, Borden hoped, would decide that their best interests required that they should come in under him.

On 25 August an exuberant Sir John Willison told Borden that Rowell would join a Union government 'with men such as A. Sifton, Calder and Crerar.' On the following day, Calder, Attorney-General A.B. Hudson of Manitoba, Crerar, and Arthur Sifton replied that they were all in favour of a national government if Foster, Duff, Sir Adam Beck, or Sir William Mulock were its leader. The westerners had made a change of leadership the 'essential' condition of their entry, not just one of a number of conditions offered for negotiation.[47] Still, they had agreed to enter. Borden played out his hand. In council on the 27th, he announced that he was willing to stand aside for Foster. This suggestion was, of course, unthinkable — even to Foster who wrote in his diary on 27 August: 'Council would not hear of the elimination of our leader. They are quite right on all grounds. For the sake of efficient work by the Union Government no one is more necessary. For the prestige of Canada in this present stage no one can take his place, and the party which has held the Govt. — has carried on the war, and is pledged to its firm conduct cannot consent to destroy its prestige by acceding to such a whimsical demand.' On the 29th, the 'largest' Conservative caucus Borden had ever seen unanimously and emotionally endorsed his leadership. The effect was beyond expectation. In the words of a press report reproduced in Borden's *Memoirs*, 'the air was thoroughly cleared and the party placed on a sound and solid basis.'[48]

The enthusiasm of the rejection warned the westerners that they must reconsider their stand. Borden himself felt that Calder and Arthur Sifton had not wanted a change of leadership, but had felt obliged to demand one in order to carry their party organization with them.[49] Here again we see the provincial basis

46 Borden Diary, 22 Aug. 1917; F.B. McCurdy to Borden, 29 Aug., Borden to McCurdy, n.d. (30 Aug.), Willison to Borden, 25 Aug., Borden to Ballantyne, 28 Aug., Borden to Willison, 23 Aug. 1917, BP, v. 77.
47 Calder, Crerar, Hudson, and Sifton to Borden, 25 Aug. 1917, BP, v. 77.
48 II, 743-4.
49 Borden to Willison, 31 Aug. 1917, BP, v. 77.

of party organization at this time. Without their organization, the value of Calder and Sifton would be negligible. Borden kept the pressure on the western-ers by conspicuously sounding out other prominent Liberals. Even if he failed, he knew that the government would benefit greatly from his actions of the previous two months, particularly from the seemingly incontrovertible evidence of selflessness represented by his offer to step down.[50] But failure was not yet in Borden's mind; it was time to play the highest trump of all, the power to determine the franchise.

The War-time Elections Act was sprung upon a largely unsuspecting nation in September 1917. It has been claimed that the western Liberals broke off negoti-ations to escape responsibility for the act, but this is unlikely since it is most uncertain whether they knew the scope of the act when negotiations were terminated.[51] Furthermore, Borden appears to have given them some sort of commitment requiring their consent to any franchise measure. When the negotia-tions broke off, one of Borden's agents, R.F. Green, a British Columbia Conservative MP, telegraphed Borden that 'Liberal friends' in Winnipeg considered that he was released 'from any provisional promise made to them respecting franchise.'[52] Foster's entry in his diary on 5 September indicates that the cabinet 'worked' on the franchise bill, completing its outline only one day before it was introduced.[53] Prior knowledge of the nature of the bill on the part of the western Liberals is therefore most doubtful.

The wartime franchise created by the War-time Elections Act[54] fundamentally rearranged the political pieces in western Canada. At a stroke, tens of thousands

50 Borden's continued and growing confidence is shown in a letter to Perley. Most had given up on coalition, but Borden obviously had not: 'Hope to reconstruct Govern-ment immediately after prorogation which will take place about middle September ... I still hope to include prominent Liberals. Believe we have greatly gained in strength dur-ing past two months.' 1 Sept. 1917, BP, v. 78.

51 Joseph Boudreau, 'The Enemy Alien Problem in Canada: 1914-1921,' unpublished PhD thesis, University of California at Los Angeles, 1965, 83. For a full account of the act, see also Roger Graham, *Arthur Meighen: The Door of Opportunity* (Toronto, 1960), I, chaps. 6-8. Not even Sifton knew of the act; see Sifton to Dafoe, 7 Sept. 1917, Sifton Papers, v. 205.

52 Green to Borden, 29 Aug. 1917, BP, v. 78.

53 The entry in his diary on 20 Aug. indicates that the bill was still under consideration then; the later entry reveals that the specific form of the bill was decided just before it was introduced.

54 *Can. Statutes*, 7-8 Geo. V, c. 39. Citizens of enemy alien birth naturalized after 31 March 1902 were disfranchised. Those who had either a son, grandson, or brother on active duty were not affected — nor were Armenians and Syrians. An analysis of the effect of the act will be found in Chapter 10.

of immigrants, most of them in the west, lost their ballots which they had usually marked for the Liberal candidate. At the same time, wives, widows and other female relatives of men overseas were enfranchised, thereby bringing into existence a considerable vote which the framers of the legislation certainly expected to be cast on the government side. An earlier act passed in late August, the Military Voters' Act,[55] had already disqualified conscientious objectors from voting while permitting soldiers who were unable to name a constituency in which they had been previously resident to cast a 'floating vote.' This, of course, would be a heavily weighted ballot since it seemed that it could be bestowed wherever the soldier thought fit.

The western Liberals, who had been unsuccessfully trying to co-ordinate their efforts, saw their bargaining position swept away from under them. Grudgingly, they admitted that Borden could win the majority of western seats with the aid of the new franchise.[56] Yet Borden himself immediately let the Liberals and, for that matter, his own party know that a Union government still remained his goal. When some Conservatives in the caucus rejoiced at the prospect of victory without a coalition, Borden reaffirmed his commitment to the idea.[57] But it might be too late with an election so near.

An exhausted Borden escaped to the Laurentians on 20 September after Parliament had been prorogued. His rest, however, was to be brief. On the afternoon following his departure, an agitated Clifford Sifton called in Jack Reid, Borden's most trusted political lieutenant, and showed him a telegram from Arthur Sifton, Crerar, Hudson, and Calder which requested yet another interview with the prime minister. In a cryptic note, Reid described this interview to Borden:

[Sifton] appeared terribly excited and pleased over this. Said there was no doubt now they were coming in. That this meant election won and then urged me to go at once to where you were. Give the information to you. That I was to get authority from you to go to Winnipeg and negotiate with them and close this up ...

---

55 *Can. Statutes*, 7-8 Geo. V, c. 34.
56 George McCraney (Liberal, Saskatoon) told Borden that the Conservatives would carry forty seats west of the Great Lakes, a gain of twenty-three over 1911. Borden Diary, 12 Sept. 1917. The *Toronto Star*, 6 Sept. 1917, supported this view, arguing that 'partyism, masking itself as patriotism, [was] the motive for these unwise proposals.'
57 Borden, *Memoirs*, II, 746-7. Foster reported that the Conservative mood was 'very confident.' Foster Diary, 16 Sept. 1917; see also Borden Diary for the same day.

I at once demurred and refused. Said I would not let anything interfere with your well-earned holiday. Neither would I communicate with you, that you would be here in 10 days which would be about that date, and even so we would not run after them. The suggestion was from them they were willing to come here on their own initiative and wanted to see you. Let it stand that way.[58]

The following day Reid, having already broken his pledge to Sifton that he would not communicate with Borden, sent another letter which presented what Reid purported to be 'the general party view' of the situation. He emphasized that he believed any government led by Borden would win the election. The belated attempt by the western Liberals to save their own political skins must be carefully considered: 'If you take them in it may irritate men on our side. If you refuse to deal with them we may have the Winnipeg Free Press backing them as Conscription Liberals but refusing to endorse Laurier.' Reid accordingly recommended that Borden take into the government those Liberals who had always indicated their willingness to join – C.C. Ballantyne from Montreal, Hugh Guthrie and S.C. Mewburn from Ontario, and Michael Clark from Alberta. After swearing these men in, Borden should then tell Sifton that Calder, Crerar, Arthur Sifton, and Hudson were unacceptable to the Conservative caucus. Crerar, however, might be considered because of the 'Grain Grower representation.' In short, Reid argued that the new willingness of the westerners to join a Union government arose from the depreciation of their value. For this reason, their request should be rejected.

Reid soon found a strong ally in Arthur Meighen who had accompanied Borden to the Laurentians and had been negotiating for the entry of either Isaac Pitblado or A.J. Andrews. The former was a prominent Winnipeg Liberal lawyer; the latter was an erstwhile Winnipeg mayor and lawyer and a Conservative who, rather interestingly, had once offered a $100 prize to anyone in the world who could point out any radical difference between the Liberal and Conservative parties.[59] This was surely an excellent qualification for membership in a Union government. Nevertheless, neither Andrews nor Pitblado had given a definite

---

58 Reid to Borden, 20 Sept. 1917, BP, v. 15. Reid's notes are invariably hand-written very badly; although I have undoubtedly misread individual words, the sense of the message is correct. In his second letter, on 21 Sept., Reid added that Calder might be admitted to the government rather than J.G. Turriff for Saskatchewan.

59 'Alfred Joseph Andrews,' in H. Morgan, ed., *Canadian Men and Women of the Time* (Toronto, 1912), 25. On these negotiations, see Borden Diary, 20 Sept. 1917; John Haig to Meighen, 21 Sept. 1917, BP, v. 15; and Graham, *Arthur Meighen*, I, 161-75.

reply to Meighen's queries. The choice betrays Meighen's aim. Neither had parliamentary experience; both were Meighen's friends. They represented no threat.

Since Rogers' downfall Meighen had become the principal spokesman for western Conservatism within the cabinet. With the new franchise western Conservatism promised to be a sizable component of any new government. If, however, the four western Liberals entered the government, Meighen's base would be severely reduced. Almost certainly, Liberals would outnumber Conservatives among the western ministers in a new cabinet. As a spokesman for western Conservatism, Meighen knew that such a development would 'be perilous indeed.'[60] Rogers might then carry the western Conservatives with him and leave Meighen defenceless in the face of a rank-and-file revolt. On his own initiative, Meighen therefore begged Pitblado and Andrews to enter the government, but to no avail. They refused and urged him to accept the western Liberals who were publicly offering themselves. More importantly, Meighen failed to convince his chieftain. On 25 September Borden wrote in his diary: 'I am beginning to feel that we should take them in as our first duty is to win, at any cost, the coming election in order that we may continue to do our part in winning the War and that Canada not be disgraced.' The strength of Borden's conviction overcame the logic of Meighen's argument.[61]

Sir Wilfrid Laurier made a final, brilliant attempt to sabotage the coalition. After Borden had appointed Ballantyne as minister of public works and Guthrie as solicitor-general as the first stage of cabinet reconstruction, rumours immediately arose that Laurier was planning to resign. One well-informed source claims that the prominent Nova Scotia MP, E.M. Macdonald, had asked an Alberta MP whether Laurier's resignation would 'satisfy' western conscriptionist Liberals.[62] Within two days even Borden, who should have known the political uses of a resignation threat, had come to accept that Laurier's departure was imminent. Western Liberals were openly gleeful. As Calder told Rowell, Laurier's resignation would 'materially change' the situation.[63] In desperation, the conscriptionist Liberals took the bait.

Laurier himself orchestrated subsequent events to his great advantage. He met with Pardee, E.M. Macdonald, Carvell, George Graham, and Gouin in Montreal on Sunday 30 September and told the group that he intended to resign. Gouin,

60 Meighen to Pitblado, 26 Sept. 1917, BP, v. 15.
61 John Haig to Meighen, 1 Oct. 1917, BP, v. 77; Pitblado to Meighen, 1 Oct. 1917, PAC, Meighen Papers, v. 2; Borden Diary, 25 Sept. 1917.
62 Alex Smith, Ontario organizer, to Laurier, 1 Oct. 1917, Laurier Papers, v. 713; see also Vivian Bartram to Dafoe, 15 Oct. 1917, Dafoe Papers.
63 Borden to Perley, 3 Oct. 1917, BP, v. 77; Calder to Rowell, 4 Oct. 1917, Sifton Papers, v. 205.

fearful of such an action, promised that he would not support demands for repeal of the Military Service Act, a pledge which delighted Laurier. The others, however, remained silent. Immediately, Calder, Macdonald, Pardee, and Carvell decided upon a new leader — Carvell — and sent word to their allies of their good fortune. But on Tuesday evening, when the conscriptionists met Laurier again, the Liberal leader was in a different mood. Buoyed by a 'shower of representations' pleading with him to remain, Laurier counter-attacked. The conscriptionists' proposal, he argued, meant that he could not be Liberal leader because of his origin.[64] Because of this he would not resign without consulting 'friends' in Montreal and Toronto. On Thursday night the Liberal insurgents knew that Laurier's resignation was 'off.' Calder, Pardee, and their allies had played a dangerous game, and they had lost once again. They had to act quickly to escape political extinction; as Calder warned Rowell: 'Caesar is no longer disposed to wait.'[65] The conscriptionist Liberals hurried across their Rubicon.

On 12 October a Union coalition was announced. N.W. Rowell, a last-minute addition, became president of the Privy Council and vice-chairman of the newly formed war committee of the cabinet. General S.C. Mewburn was the new minister of militia and defence. The westerners, Sifton, Crerar and Calder, took the customs, agriculture, and immigration and colonization portfolios respectively. Hugh Guthrie remained solicitor-general. When Frank Carvell decided to join the Unionists as minister of public works, Ballantyne moved over to the marine, fisheries, and naval service portfolio. Two other latecomers, Gideon Robertson, a Labour representative, and A.K. Maclean, a veteran MP who entered when Premier Murray of Nova Scotia refused, had to accept office as ministers without portfolio. The Tories lost Sir George Perley, who was finally appointed high commissioner to Britain, Douglas Hazen, who moved to the Supreme Court of New Brunswick as chief justice, and W.J. Roche, who eventually became head of the Civil Service Commission. The dying Frank Cochrane inexplicably stayed in the cabinet as minister without portfolio. Overall, there were twelve Tory ministers, nine Liberals, and one 'Labour.' Most of the senior portfolios, including finance, railways and canals, and trade and commerce, continued to be held by Tories. The Liberals seemed both outnumbered and outranked.

64 See Laurier to D.D. Mackenzie, 18 Oct. 1917, Laurier Papers, v. 714. The account of the meeting is drawn from Pardee to Rowell, 6 Oct. 1917, Rowell Papers, v. 3; King Diary, 6 Oct. 1917. Skelton barely mentions the Laurier resignation incident. *Laurier*, II, chap. 19.
65 Calder to Rowell, 4 Oct. 1917, Sifton Papers, v. 205. Calder's meeting with Laurier when the resignation rumour was squelched is described in Allan Turner, ed., 'Reminiscences of the Hon. J.A. Calder,' *Saskatchewan History*, XXV (Spring 1972), 72-3.

Yet this political marriage possessed more equality than its surface appearance indicates, and the examination of the terms and machinery of the Union government in the following chapter will substantiate this. When one considers the bargaining position of the conscriptionist Liberals in October 1917, the acquisition of nine portfolios was a remarkable achievement, one obtained as a result of Borden's generosity and his frustration with anti-coalition elements within his own party,[66] and as a result of the Liberal control of all provincial governments except Ontario's.

In the late spring, when Borden first announced his plans for a coalition, conscriptionist Liberals were able to claim with much justification that he had adopted their programme. One and all interpreted the Borden proposal as a betrayal of Conservative weakness and a recognition of Liberal strength. Who could doubt that the vigour of the conscriptionist Liberals would overwhelm the exhausted Borden ministry? So impressed were the Liberals favouring coalition with the weight of their arguments that they assumed that Laurier would have to give in. Their strategy failed and their campaign lost its impetus. During the second stage of negotiations, the conscriptionist Liberals were out-manœuvred by Laurier and his allies. The plan for a national Liberal conscriptionist convention, which Rowell correctly regarded as essential to their hopes, was continually frustrated.[67] Their unity was undermined by the bitterness arising from the Toronto and Winnipeg conventions. In this second stage the conscriptionist Liberals, thwarted in Ottawa by Laurier's prestige, sought to employ lower levels of political influence to gain a compromise. Rallies, picnics, declarations, and resolutions were their main artillery, but the attack was too sporadic and could not breach the solid wall of Laurier's position. By mid-August, then, the conscriptionist Liberals had lost their fight to gain control of the Liberal party and to take it as a single body into a coalition government.

In the third and final stage they fought to salvage their political future. For the conscriptionist Liberals, coalition with Borden was a second choice; their exhilaration when rumours of Laurier's retirement spread are proof of this. In this light, their final entry into the coalition is best seen as an attempt to prevent a long-term Liberal catastrophe in which both federal and provincial Liberals would be 'annihilated' in much of English Canada.[68] Thomas Crerar was more

66 Borden's frustration with his Conservative colleagues was indeed great. See his *Memoirs*, II, 751, 756-60; and Borden Diary, 1-12 Oct., *passim*.
67 Rowell continued to hope for such a convention until the very end. See Rowell to Maclean, 27 Aug. 1917, Rowell Papers, v. 3.
68 Pardee to Rowell, 6 Oct. 1917, Rowell Papers, v. 3. This is a most revealing letter on the aims of the conscriptionist Liberals.

explicit and prophetic. Writing in late August he thought that a 'straight party election' might return Laurier and reject conscription. But in the following election, after the soldiers' return, the Liberals would be swept from office and remain in opposition for 'the next 12 or 15 years.' He continued:

The Tory Party would have the credit of having stood by the boys in the trenches, would pose as the party of loyalty and would carry the soldier vote ... I believe that this can be almost altogether avoided by the formation of a Union Government at this time, particularly if the element that goes in is strong enough to dominate the Conservative group who would be in it. Such a Government could not last beyond perhaps a year after the war is over, since they would be practically certain to split on domestic issues. I think then the opportunity would come to create a really Progressive Liberal administration free from the present reactionary influences that operate within the Liberal Party. I think such a program would hold the West almost solid in the future for Liberalism, in fact, make it a citadel of Liberalism in Canada.[69]

Refuges had to be found, and Borden offered the safest haven. In a coalition the conscriptionist Liberals might keep their unity and later emerge to recapture the Liberal party when the aged Laurier finally departed from the political stage. Then a new Liberal party might emerge in place of the Quebec-dominated Laurier party. Even the apostate Sifton cherished such dreams of a future reconstructed Liberal party which would have the Canadian west as its stronghold. The ex-interior minister chastised Dafoe when he promised his support fully to Borden: 'It occurs to me to say that I think it would be well for you to be cautious in writing any one. The possibilities of the future hardly include the idea that the Free Press can support a party dominated by the Conservatives for any length of time and it might be awkward for you to feel that you had discussed matters too fully with the enemy.'[70]

A nagging question remains: why did Borden assist the conscriptionist Liberals in their goals? First, wartime tends to magnify the weaknesses of politicians. Winston Churchill described this process: 'The feeble or presumptuous politician is portrayed cowering in his office, intent in the crash of the world on Party intrigue or personal glorification, fearful of responsibility, incapable of aught save shallow phrase-making.'[71] Such a portrayal of Borden was most common in the Canadian press in late 1916. But in 1917 Borden, like Lloyd

69 Crerar to H.B. Cowan, 27 Aug. 1917, Crerar Papers, box 36.
70 Sifton to Dafoe, n.d. (Oct. 1917), Dafoe Papers.
71 *The World Crisis, 1916-1918* (New York, 1923), I, 244.

George, learned that he could save himself and, incidentally, his party by appearing to care for neither. He transferred the image of the selfish and bumbling politician from himself to his Liberal opponents. Paradoxically, he succeeded as a politician by appearing not to be a politician.

Secondly, Borden saw that the Liberals who entered his government were not sufficiently strong to threaten his control — they brought with them no Trojan horse. On the other hand, he believed he could use them to secure long-term ends which had previously been elusive. As we have seen, the Conservative party had been particularly immalleable to Borden's attempts to mould it. Now, the Liberals, dependent upon Borden for their position, afforded him the added strength necessary to break down the areas of the party previously insensitive to his touch. A Union government could be a government more truly Borden's than his Conservative government elected in 1911 had ever been.

Thirdly, Borden was unquestionably concerned with his place in history. He realized that his place would not be a large one if he left politics in 1917.[72] His pre-war administration had been marked by legislative failure and party division. Neither was his war record very distinguished. After all, the memory of the pomposity of Sir Sam Hughes, the rampant profiteering, and the tragedy of the Ross rifle would not evade the future historian's caustic pen. Borden would undoubtedly have been portrayed as a Canadian Asquith, without the advantage of Asquith's distinguished peacetime record. In 1917, however, Borden at last saw a way of retrieving his own reputation by linking it to the success, the courage, the daring, and the brilliance of the Canadian Corps. Borden saw that his 'duty' was 'to form a Government based upon the support of all elements of the population who are desirous of standing behind a Government prepared to throw the full effort of Canada into this War and maintain that effort.'[73] From an individual groping for a sense of his role, Borden had become the leader of a threatened community, deriving from it an explosive energy and a new range previously inconceivable.

72 Borden's vanity is well known, and his *Memoirs* are a splendid testimony to it. In 1917 Sifton, a skilled flatterer, encouraged him by pointing out that 'a coalition Government if established will be the greatest political event ever accomplished in Canada.' *Memoirs*, II, 756. Richard Blain, Tory whip, is reported to have said of him: 'Borden will not resign. He likes the position; he likes the honours and he likes the money.' Cited in Ford, *As the World Wags On*, 136.

73 Borden to W.H. Thorne, 13 Oct. 1917, BP, v. 140.

9

The coalition agreement

A wartime coalition is like a marriage: the protagonists widely proclaim it as a sacrament, a covenant between man and God. Privately, however, the partners carefully agree upon a covenant between themselves, which sets out their respective duties and rights. The Unionists were no exception. After the euphoria surrounding the announcement of the coalition, the first concern of the coalitionists was to work out an agreement on programme, political responsibilities, organization, and finances.[1] Most of this pact has escaped the notice of historians, primarily because so little of it was publicized and because its details have remained hidden in widely dispersed sources. Yet the significance of the bartering between the Liberal and Conservative Unionists is great. More than anything else, it reveals the major difficulties they had to overcome, the fundamentally different visions of the future of Canadian political development held by various Unionist leaders, and, most important, the internal reasons for the eventual collapse of Unionism. Since the programme was the element which received the earliest and widest approval by the Unionists, it is our first concern.

PROGRAMME

The need for immediate consideration of a programme arose from the strong opposition to Unionism by two groups, Laurier Liberals and Rogers Tories. To

1 That such an agreement did not precede the announcement is rather surprising. The only conditions imposed by the western Liberals were full information on decisions and a 'fifty-fifty' split on the war committee of the cabinet. They probably realized that such minimal demands would assure belief in their good faith and strengthen their position with the suspicious Tory caucus. They also knew that Borden, because of his situation and character, would be a fair arbiter. See Allan Turner, ed., 'Reminiscences of the Hon. J.A. Calder,' *Saskatchewan History*, XXV (Spring 1972); Henry Borden, ed., *Robert Laird Borden: His Memoirs* (Toronto, 1938), II; and PAC, Borden Papers (BP), Borden Diary, Oct. 1917.

prevent local party leaders from withdrawing from politics altogether or, even worse, openly attacking Unionism, Sir Robert Borden and his colleagues believed that they had to issue the type of platform which would encourage broad participation at the constituency level. Through the platform, the Unionists expected to appeal to, and to recruit for active political work, the many prominent and talented individuals who had previously shunned political involvement. This sudden infusion of newcomers would create *une grande peur* which would force the disgruntled to acquiesce. That, at least, was the Unionist hope.[2]

Borden presented the Unionist programme on 18 October 1917, less than a week after the announcement of coalition. 'The lines of policy to be followed,' he declared, 'chiefly relate to the prosecution of the War and to the consideration and solution of problems arising during its progress or which will supervene upon the conclusion of peace.' The pretext for breaking traditional ties was unambiguously presented; so was the consequence of retaining them: 'The Union Government has been formed with a desire to give representation to all elements of the population supporting the purpose and effort of Canada in the War.' A successful war effort was therefore clearly identified with the interests of the nation as a whole and, most significantly, with the fate of Unionism. A Unionist victory would be the consecration of the nation, marking the end of a fragmented, artificial colonial society and the emergence of a fully fledged member of the international community.[3]

Domestically, the nation would be purged of its narrowness, its corruption, and its uncertainty. Not surprisingly, the second item of the programme was a pledge to abolish patronage, 'to make appointments upon the sole standard of merit.' The implementation of this promise not only underlined the political 'selflessness' of the Unionists but also broke down the powers of entrenched local organizations. Even before the new government was announced, Borden had told his interior minister, W.J. Roche, a future civil service commissioner, that the time for the long promised reform had finally come and that Roche

---

2 Early indications were that Rogers intended to oppose Union government. A letter from David Boyle, a *Winnipeg Telegram* reporter, suggests this, as does the *Telegram* itself in mid-October (13, 15, 16 and 17). In the end, however, he gave in and worked for the Unionists. Boyle to Rogers, 7 Oct. 1917, PAC, Meighen Papers, v. 2.

3 The programme may be found in J.C. Hopkins, *Canadian Annual Review, 1917* (Toronto, 1918), 587. There is, of course, much truth in Frank Underhill's well-known statement, 'With every world war Canada is made into a nation over again.' This was particularly the case in 1917 when the Unionists hoped to channel the nationalism aroused by the success of the Canadian Corps into the political campaign. Underhill, 'Canada and the Last War,' in Chester Martin, ed., *Canada in Peace and War* (Toronto, 1941), 149.

should draw up plans for the change. With a stroke, Borden sought to begin a political revolution from above.

The rest of the programme strongly echoed Borden's Halifax Platform of 1907, which the Tories had largely ignored since acquiring power, and the various platforms of progressive provincial Liberalism. An open bid for the support of the various reform groups, such as the female suffrage movement, was made, and a willingness to widen the compass of state action was most apparent. The Union government would use its extraordinary powers to cut out ancient sores from the Canadian body politic, as well as to safeguard Canada's material and moral commitment to the war. Women would have the franchise; new lands would be cultivated; profiteering would end; and the earth would yield greater abundance. The brew was a strong one, and the vision of the future was, perhaps, confused. Yet even a veteran journalist like James Brierley, who had seen many political visions come and pass away, thought that only our imaginations created limits upon the possibilities for Union government. Brierley suggested that '... policies quite Utopian in normal times may be not merely practicable but obligatory. It is not too much to say that no other Administration ever had it within its power, as this one has, to make dreams come true ...'[4] So great were the expectations for the Union government, and these its programme reflected and inspired.

POLITICAL TERMS

The programme was a portion of the political terms, the articles of confederation, agreed upon by the Unionist Liberals and the Conservatives. On 17 October N.W. Rowell — who, rather curiously in light of his sophomoric political performance, became the Liberal spokesman in the cabinet — sent a memorandum to Borden outlining the type of platform acceptable to the Liberals.[5] Much of the substance and some of the sentences of this memorandum found their way into the platform presented by Borden on the following day. Of more concern to the Liberals, however, were their political responsibilities and jurisdictions. They fought desperately to maintain the appearance that they had

---

4 Most remarkable is the fact that Brierley wrote this after the election, a period when doubts normally have seeped in. It is typical of the flamboyant rhetoric of the Unionists. 'The Union Government's Opportunities,' *University Magazine*, XVII (Feb. 1918), 14.

5 BP, v. 226. Rowell's platform omitted the transportation development, the immigration, the encouragement of co-operation, and the resource development planks. But he of course demanded 'the elimination of patronage.'

entered the cabinet as equals, although, as we have seen, they were badly out-numbered. The result was frequent and bitter quarrels which exasperated the prime minister. The roots of this conflict lie in the final stage of the coalition negotiations.

In the frantic last days of September, Sir Clifford Sifton had told J.D. Reid that all the westerners asked was 'fifty-fifty' representation in a 'war cabinet.' This was not obtained. A war cabinet modelled on Lloyd George's in England was never formed in Canada. Instead, the Liberals were granted a semblance of their wish by means of a ten-member war committee of the council which included five Liberals, and a reconstruction and development committee, also with ten members of whom four were Liberals. But as Sifton pointed out to Sir John Willison, these bodies bore little resemblance to a small war cabinet, and they were much too unwieldly to possess real decision-making capacity.[6] The Liberals knew that they had not got what they had asked for and continued to argue for equal representation within the cabinet itself, and Borden acquiesced in their pleas. This promise won Borden little favour among his Conservative colleagues, but it did enable him to acquire some new Liberals of considerable importance.[7] One of these was Frank Carvell, the first addition after the consummation of Union; Rowell's persistence had won out over the objections of the New Brunswick Conservative Douglas Hazen.[8] Carvell, Rowell promised and Borden hoped, would bring with him the support of the powerful Liberal organization of New Brunswick. Unfortunately, he also brought a reputation for extreme partisanship which made his appointment particularly odious to New Brunswick Conservatives, so much so that Arthur Ford claimed that 'the entrance of Mr. Carvell ... created almost as much amazement and excitement in New Brunswick as if German warships had bombarded Saint John.'[9]

Perhaps the shock induced by seeing his fellow Maritimer joining the Union government led Premier George Murray of Nova Scotia openly to support Union. Although Murray himself refused to leave the premier's office, he urged Borden to accept in his place A.K. Maclean, a Nova Scotia MP. Maclean thereupon became vice-chairman of the reconstruction and development committee and a minister without portfolio, a position less senior than he had wanted. With Maclean's entry the Liberal segment of the government was

6 16 Oct. 1917, PAC, Willison Papers, v. 74.
7 See Calder to Borden, 29 Oct. 1917, BP, v. 77; and the *Globe*, Toronto, 13 Oct. 1917.
8 Rowell to J.J. Warren, 13 Oct. 1917, PAC, Rowell Papers, v. 3. Hazen did not want to leave. See W.H. Thorne to Borden, 13 Oct. 1917, BP, v. 140; and Foster Diary, 20 Oct. 1917, PAC, Foster Papers.
9 *As the World Wags On* (Toronto, 1950), 96.

notably more impressive than it had been, although it was still numerically weaker than the Tories.[10]

A final attempt to strengthen Liberal ministerial representation occurred in late October. Premier H.C. Brewster of British Columbia, whose ambiguous position during the summer and autumn seemed to preclude his entry into the government, changed his mind and decided that he would like to become the Unionist minister of fisheries and mines. James Calder, who had become the spokesman for western Liberalism, strongly urged the prime minister to admit him, and Borden seemed favourably disposed, believing that west coast Liberalism must have a place in a Union government. In the absence of strong Liberal Unionist leadership, British Columbia had become by the end of October 'a seething mass of suspicion, dissatisfaction and unrest.' As a result there was 'a strong [anti-Unionist] undercurrent operating that [might] break loose at any time.' Brewster's presence in the cabinet would be a dam against this force.

Yet even Calder admitted Brewster's liabilities. His refusal to support Union openly had itself caused many of the difficulties in the western province. To take in Brewster would be to reward indecision and even lack of principle.[11] Unlike the Ontario Liberals such as Rowell, who had spoken from platforms with the Tory Premier Sir William Hearst during the summer of 1917, Brewster had shunned such patriotic co-operation. Furthermore, his presence in Ottawa would deed the west to the same Liberals who had been fighting for their political lives only a few weeks before. W.J. Bowser, the leader of the fragmented British Columbia Tories, sensed the threat and warned Jack Reid that he must fight Brewster's admission:

Calder has stated privately he has information Brewster to be included as Minister of Fisheries. If carried through will be unfair distribution of Western portfolios giving Liberals four and Conservatives only two. Thus Liberals secure portfolio with only three candidates. He will bring no Liberal strength to Government but will create great soreness among Conservatives who are all enthusiastic because Liberals pressing only for purpose [of] getting rid of him in Provincial affairs. He has refused to this date to declare for Union government. Block if possible.[12]

10 The Tories had thirteen ministers, the Liberals nine, with Robertson, an independent Liberal. Hopkins, *Canadian Annual Review, 1917*, 584; Murray to Borden, 18 Oct, Borden to G.H. Perley, 12 Oct. 1917, BP, v. 77. Crothers was supposed to leave the cabinet to free a portfolio for Maclean, but for some reason he remained.
11 Borden to Meighen, and Calder to Borden, both 29 Oct. 1917, BP, v. 77; Calder to Rowell, 1 Nov. 1917, Rowell Papers, v. 4.
12 Telegram, Bowser to Reid, 30 Oct. 1917, BP, v. 77. On the confused British Columbia political situation at this time, see Calder to Borden, 1 Nov. 1917, BP, v. 150.

Reid had no veto, but Arthur Meighen, the new and suspicious guardian of Tory interests in the west, did.[13] Brewster enjoyed another Victoria winter.

The Brewster incident points to one of the most difficult and certainly one of the most fundamental questions which plagued the architects of Union: how did one recognize a Unionist? Brewster was finally unacceptable because he had not firmly committed himself to conscription and coalition. In a year when suspicions abounded, the test had to be a difficult one, and Brewster's late conversion did not pass muster. Even the commitment of Rowell, a supporter of conscription in January, was questioned when he seemed to moderate his tone.[14] But if Rowell was imperfect, what could be said about the large number of flawed individuals who sought safety under the Unionist umbrella in October? Borden and the Unionist leaders handed down a creed which Unionist followers were required to accept. Whatever their previous views, full adherence to Unionism and conscription and complete rejection of Liberalism were the first articles of this creed.

One who upon testing the creed found it too rigid for his latitudinarian ways was the Liberal candidate for North York, William Lyon Mackenzie King. Not for the last time, King found his refuge in ambiguity. An early supporter of conscription, he retreated when he saw that Laurier would never tolerate such a measure. From Kingsmere, his cottage in the Gatineau Hills north of Ottawa, King slinked in and out of the political rough and tumble, never failing to keep one eye around the corner whenever he retreated. After coalition was achieved, he asked Rowell whether, if he were to stand for Union and for conscription 'as passed,' he would be permitted by the Unionists to run 'as a Liberal' against J.A.M. Armstrong who had received the Conservative nomination without a special Unionist convention. Rowell said no: King had to accept Borden as a leader and Unionism as his party. The price was too high; King remained a Liberal.[15]

Like the early Christians who learned that commitment to a creed did not end heresy, the Unionists had to develop formal institutions to prevent chaos and to decide how the constituencies would be apportioned. Although no public announcement was ever made, a complex agreement on control of the local constituencies was worked out. The first principle was admirably simple: 'Where

13 Borden to Calder, 30 Oct. 1917, BP, v. 77. Burrell was also opposed to Brewster: see Calder to Borden, 12 Nov. 1917, BP, v. 140. Other BC Liberals were also rejected: Burrell to Borden, 2 Nov., Calder to Borden, 3 Nov. 1917, BP, v. 77.
14 Sifton warned Dafoe: 'Don't waste any bouquets on Rowell.' 15 Oct. 1917, PAC, Dafoe Papers, microfilm copy.
15 King to Laurier, 17 Oct. 1917, PAC, Laurier Papers, v. 714.

a Member in the late Parliament gave consistent support to all war measures and particularly to compulsory military service and for Union government ... whether Liberal or Conservative he as sitting Member should be recognized as the Government candidate ...'[16] Obviously this rule was irrelevant in many constituencies where the member had opposed conscription or had supported it but had chosen not to stand in the 1917 election. In such cases, a joint convention of Unionist Liberals and Conservatives would meet to choose the Unionist nominee. If a candidate had already been nominated by either party, he had to resign and face a bipartisan convention. Fair, logical, and shrewd, these principles could theoretically settle all questions of political jurisdiction and interest. As one might expect, they did not.

First, the members of both coalition groups pointed out that the results of the 1911 election were a most unreliable indicator of the probable fate of the parties if an election had occurred in early 1917. The Tories, for example, could never have hoped to win almost thirty seats in Quebec; they would have been fortunate to capture five. Neither could the Liberals have made virtually a clean sweep of the Prairies as they did in 1911. The Tories' chief bargainer, Jack Reid, argued that the Conservatives would have won the election without the accession of the Liberal Unionists.[17] Rowell, on behalf of the Liberal Unionists, countered that it was they who had made the greater sacrifice and who should therefore be given special protection.

The result of this disagreement was an infinitely complex allocation of the constituencies of each province between Liberal and Conservative Unionists. According to Reid, the Maritime and western Liberals accepted that 'the representation [of the two parties] should be in the same [overall] proportion as it was at the time of dissolution.'[18] In practical terms, this meant that in Saskatchewan where the Liberals controlled all seats at the dissolution, six seats would be granted to the Tories.[19] The Unionist Liberal organization in that province would be responsible for finding those seats. In British Columbia, where the Tories had held all the seats, this unpleasant task fell to the Tories.

16 Borden to Senator George Lynch-Staunton, 25 Oct. 1917, BP, v. 79; Foster Diary, 31 Oct. 1917; and 'Basis as to Candidates,' Rowell Papers, v. 4.
17 (J.D. Reid), 'Memo for Sir Robert,' 24 Oct., John Godfrey to Borden, 30 Oct. 1917, BP, v. 79.
18 This meant, of course, that the Tories would predominate in the Unionist caucus. This agreement shows that the Unionists expected to win almost every seat outside of Quebec, a province which was excluded from calculations on the proportion.
19 Meighen to Donald McLean, n.d. (Nov. 1917), Meighen Papers, v. 11. See also David Smith, *Prairie Liberalism: The Liberal Party in Saskatchewan, 1905-71* (Toronto, 1975), 62-5.

Martin Burrell and the provincial Tory leader W.J. Bowser therefore agreed to obtain four of British Columbia's thirteen seats for Unionist Liberals. The local Tories, however, proved much more intransigent than Unionist Liberals in Saskatchewan, where the superbly efficient provincial Liberal machine had little trouble in securing the six Conservative seats.[20] Although the obstructions were great, Borden forced Burrell and Bowser to persist in order that his public promise that 50 per cent of the seats west of Ontario would have Liberal Unionist candidates might be fulfilled.[21]

If anything, the Maritimes presented greater hindrances to the appropriate division of constituencies than the west. Frank Carvell allocated the New Brunswick seats and, while even his staunchest enemies admitted his fairness, he was unsuccessful.[22] The almost certain loss of four French-Canadian constituencies in New Brunswick and the reduction of the number of constituencies through redistribution made Carvell's task virtually impossible. Local members and candidates defied his pleas, and found that the intense traditional bitterness between New Brunswick's Tories and Liberals permitted them to act independently of Unionist control. Ultimately, the attempt to impose order completely broke down.

Carvell lacked the assistance of a strong Liberal provincial organization, unlike A.K. Maclean in Nova Scotia who had the full support of Premier Murray's provincial machine. Maclean also had the aid of W.S. Fielding, the historic leader of Nova Scotia Liberalism who had finally endorsed Union government on 22 October.[23] (To obtain such a distinguished convert, the Unionist creed was relaxed somewhat.) Maclean, then, had little trouble controlling the constituencies, but whether the object of that control was entirely the good of Unionism is quite another question. There is much evidence that the activities of Murray and Maclean were calculated to serve certain other long-term ends of Nova Scotia Liberalism as well. The extraordinary manipulation carried out is well-documented in a letter from the Laurier Liberal candidate G.W. Kyte to Laurier:

20 Bowser to Borden, 5 Nov., Burrell to Borden, 2 Nov. 1917, BP, v. 77. The BC Tories argued that they would have won every seat again in their province, and that the Tories would surely have won six seats in Saskatchewan with the new franchise.
21 Borden announced this publicly in order to win Liberal Unionist good will. See Hopkins, *Canadian Annual Review, 1917*, 637.
22 See W.H. Thorne to Borden, 5 Nov. 1917, BP, v. 136. For the difficulties in New Brunswick, see Hopkins, *ibid.*, 606. The local Liberal government was heavily dependent on Acadian support, and refused to co-operate with the Unionist campaign.
23 *Ottawa Journal*, 23 Oct. 1917; Bruce Fergusson, *Mr. Minister of Finance: Hon. W.S. Fielding* (Windsor, NS, 1971), II, chap. 9.

It looks now as though you will have one-half of the members from Nova Scotia after the election. McKenzie, Chisholm and Sinclair are sure to be elected against Union Government. Premier Murray and A.K. Maclean are putting through a deal which if successful will assure my election in Richmond and South Cape Breton as a supporter of yours — the other to be the Tory Union Government man J.C. Douglas ... Ned Macdonald will probably be elected in Pictou as a result of a deal with Cumberland County. Murray is trying to get Liberals elected irrespective of whether they are Unionist. In this way he is helping your supporters in the last Parliament to get back.[24]

Unlike most Liberals in the west and Ontario, Nova Scotian Liberals generally considered Union government to be an aberration created by the war and destined to disappear when the conflict ended, leaving few traces upon the traditional political system. In 1917 exceptional rules governed the contest, but the game remained the same.

Paradoxically, most of the Conservatives' anger was directed against the Ontario Liberal Unionists, not their Maritime counterparts. The Tories had won seventy-two of Ontario's eighty-six seats in 1911. Therefore, when Rowell demanded that the Liberal Unionists be granted 'at least' twenty seats in Ontario, he was asking that some Conservative members, supporters of conscription and Union, should resign. More outrageous in the eyes of the Tories was Rowell's insistence that the Unionist Liberals be given full control of these constituencies; not even a government minister should enter the constituencies without Rowell's permission. An infuriated Reid damned the proposal as 'too absurd to discuss.' Furthermore, Rowell wanted permission to endorse whomsoever he thought fit, even George Graham, an open opponent of Union government.[25] However absurd Rowell's scheme seemed to Reid, it nevertheless won favour with the ultimate arbiter of political fate in 1917, the prime minister.

Borden accepted Rowell's argument because he saw, as Reid did not, that Rowell had to convince wavering Ontario Liberals that 'they have lost nothing by Union.'[26] Thus some Conservatives were asked to step aside in favour of

---

24 Kyte to Laurier, 4 Nov. 1917, Laurier Papers, v. 716; see also Kyte to Charles Murphy, 10 Nov., *ibid.*, and Kyte to Laurier, 18 Oct., *ibid.*, v. 714.

25 (J.D. Reid), 'Memorandum for the Prime Minister,' 19 Oct. 1917, BP, v. 79. Rowell probably wanted such absolute control for long-term bargaining advantage. See also Foster Diary, 31 Oct. 1917; and 'Memo for Sir Robert,' 24 Oct. 1917, BP, v. 79. At the very time Rowell was pressing Graham's claim, Graham was publicly denouncing Union government. See *Toronto Star*, 24 Oct. 1917.

26 John Godfrey to Borden, 30 Oct. 1917, BP, v. 79. Godfrey attempted to act as Rowell's advocate in this instance.

Liberals. Reid angrily charged that Borden was 'under [Liberal] control,' adding that he had 'a strong impression an understanding exists between Pardee, Graham, Rowell and [Duncan] Ross and others to continue their objections until nomination day and split then and likely go out. They gain time, break up our Ontario organization and too late for us to reorganize.'[27] Reid's impression was to prove as false as Rowell's apparent victory. The real loser, however, was the Unionist party in Ontario.

Borden was unable to force a sufficient number of Conservatives to resign or to support Liberal Unionists of such dubious credentials as George Graham. The break with the rule that any standing member who had supported conscription and coalition should be chosen as Unionist candidate created chaos which the Unionists could not afford. Rowell's demands also set off a strong Tory reaction, and Tories refused to rally behind Liberals at all and called for 'Unionist conventions.' The ironic outcome of Borden's generosity and Rowell's plea for fairness was a lasting suspicion of Rowell among both Conservative and Liberal Unionists, the former because Rowell asked too much for his party and the latter because he could not fulfil his promises. Rowell was never to reclaim the stature he possessed in the first days of Union government. The earliest advocate of coalition had become its first victim.

Two examples of the frustrating attempt to manipulate Ontario Unionist sentiment in order to obtain what Liberal Unionists considered fair terms will suffice. The first shows the inconsistency of the principle of support for a sitting member, and the second indicates the remarkable truculence of long-entrenched local organizations.

While in the midst of his campaign W.B. Northrup, Tory member for East Hastings since 1900, suddenly learned that Borden had endorsed T.H. Thompson as Unionist candidate. In doing this, Borden broke the pledge he had made to Tory backbenchers that sitting members who had voted for conscription would be endorsed. More surprising is the manner in which Thompson was named. No Unionist convention was held; Borden simply acted by fiat. The astonished Northrup protested, refused to resign, and warned Borden: 'I wish for the sake of the Government you would have some reliable friend ascertain the comments being made in Toronto and Ottawa on your action.'

Unfortunately for Northrup, the comments must have been mere small talk and not threats. Borden would not budge: he coolly informed Northrup that Thompson had been selected by 'a committee' although the membership and

27 'Memo,' n.d. (Oct. 1917), *ibid.*

nature of this committee were not identified. All Borden would say was that Northrup was unacceptable to this mysterious group, and that he should not regard the action as 'an attack' upon himself.[28] Northrup knew he was beaten; a few days before the election he resigned. For his troubles he received a bauble, the clerkship of the House of Commons.

Northrup's withdrawal was relatively straightforward when compared to the confused behaviour which took place in two neighbouring Ontario ridings, Brant and Brantford. Early in the campaign Calder, Reid, and Rowell had agreed that Brantford should be Tory and Brant Liberal, and that the candidates should be W.F. Cockshutt and John Harold respectively. Unfortunately in both ridings other prominent candidates also entered the race and pledged themselves to support Union government. In Brantford a Liberal Unionist meeting had nominated the former Liberal MP, Lloyd Harris, while in Brant the Tories nominated Harry Cockshutt, the brother of W.F. Cockshutt. Harris withdrew immediately when told he would receive no endorsement, but Harry Cockshutt persisted with the full support of his brother. The desperate Liberal Unionists in Brant called for a joint convention, but the Tories rebuffed them. They then appealed to the prime minister for help.[29]

Borden, however, had seriously compromised his position. Harry Cockshutt produced a letter from the prime minister, written after the formation of the Union government, which informed him that he would be the Unionist candidate with Borden's full support.[30] Faced with this embarrassing document Borden hesitated, but then endorsed Harold once again. The latter won the election by a small margin, but the bickering and strain did little good for the reputation of the Unionists or, for that matter, of Borden.

To summarize, the political terms agreed upon by the Unionists were doomed, first by their own complexity, and secondly by their widespread local rejection. In the end, the mechanical distribution of constituencies collapsed in most of Canada, and the attempt to allocate seats itself destroyed nascent Unionist organizations in many constituencies. The result was disastrous. The political terms meant that the Unionist Liberals possessed too much strength for complete Conservative dominance of the Union, but too few resources to permit a merger. Rather than join in an effort to create a united party, the Liberal

28 Northrup to Borden, 26 Nov., Borden to Northrup, 29 Nov. and 11 Dec. 1917, BP, v. 79.
29 Rowell to Borden, 14 and 19 Nov. 1917, Rowell Papers, v. 4.
30 Cockshutt to Borden, 4 Dec. 1917, BP, v. 79; *Toronto Star*, 10 Dec. 1917.

Unionists jealously and nervously guarded their independence; they failed to secure the number of seats they desired, but they did create a lasting resentment among their Tory colleagues.

ORGANIZATION

The failure of the Unionist leaders to attain their early goals can be attributed largely to the weakness of national Unionist organization. Since electoral victory is usually taken as a reliable indicator of a strong political organization, contemporary observers as well as later historians have tended to ascribe great effectiveness to the Unionist organization.[31] In fact, the organization lacked direction, was rent by schism, and was most ephemeral. Within the constituencies no Unionist organization ever took root, primarily because the national Unionist leaders did not nourish the early growths of bipartisan sentiment which appeared during the summer and fall of 1917. To all outward appearances Unionism seemed fully vigorous in December 1917, but decay was already spreading rapidly in the less visible portions of its structure.

This organizational weakness arose even though the Unionist ministers had made a strong organization their first priority. As soon as he entered the government Calder drew up a rough plan for a tight, centralized organization:

Matters Political.
1. Organization: (a) Arrange for sub-committee of Cabinet to have general control.
   (b) Central control of organization —
       Maritime Provinces —
       Quebec —
       Ontario —
       West —
New literature should be prepared. Should be Union Central Office in each province. Election officials by joint appointment. Plan of campaign in each province. Should decide policy on inflammatory appeals.
N.B. Eliminate Sifton

31 See *Manitoba Free Press*, 19-24 Dec. 1917; Hopkins, *Canadian Annual Review, 1917*, 602-43; J.W. Dafoe, *Clifford Sifton in Relation to His Times* (Toronto, 1931), 438; R.M. Dawson, *William Lyon Mackenzie King* (Toronto, 1958); and O.D. Skelton, *Life and Letters of Sir Wilfrid Laurier* (London, 1922), II. Skelton wisely blames the weakness of Liberal organization more than the strength of Union organization; in substance, however, he agrees.

Provincial Committees – to control conventions, selection of candidates, selection of election officials etc.[32]

This plan was never followed, but not because there were insufficient skilled organizers in Unionist ranks. Among the Liberal Unionists Calder, Carvell, Maclean, and even Rowell were well known for their abilities in this regard. While it is true that Rogers and Cochrane were no longer of much help, such shrewd political manipulators as Reid and Senator James Lougheed still remained, as did the most talented of all, Sir Clifford Sifton, who, though not in the cabinet, was most eager to assist.

Borden, too, wanted a potent organization which would bind together Conservatives, Liberals, and the many reform groups which had done so much to bring Union government into existence. But he did not want an organization dominated by remnants of the old Tory machine which had defied him so often in the past. Seeing that this might occur in any centralized national organization, he was forced to accept a highly decentralized structure. Neither Borden nor the Unionist Liberals could afford to let a strong Tory-dominated organization run the campaign, whatever the short-run advantages. After the election, they knew it could be very easily turned against them.

Thus the Unionist organization was feudal in character with weak and often purely nominal lines of control. At times this was effective, as in Saskatchewan where the superb, wealthy Liberal provincial organization handled the Unionist campaign. On the other hand, British Columbia never achieved any organization above the constituency level, and only the great strength of the Unionist impulse in that province permitted a Unionist victory. Borden continued to hope that a new structure, freer and more effective, would naturally emerge from the common experience of the election, but this dream was never realized.

The decentralized character of the organization suggests that it is best examined by region. Such an examination is greatly facilitated by a sketch of much of the Unionist organization in, of all places, the papers of W.F. O'Connor, who acted as the equivalent of the chief electoral officer for the Dominion in 1917.[33] (Peculiar political years leave unusual historical legacies!) Whatever its origin, O'Connor's list is invaluable since it identifies, for most of the nation, the political organizer in charge of a province, region, or constituency. Furthermore, it substantiates the thesis that the 1917 Unionist campaign substituted enthusiasm for careful direction, diversity for unity. Unfortunately, there are some

32 'Memo,' n.d. (mid-Oct. 1917), BP, v. 114.
33 'Election – 1917,' PAC, O'Connor Papers, v. 7.

areas where the list offers no help and our information comes only in small pieces. Nova Scotia is the most notable of these areas and a good place to begin.

Nova Scotia was a cauldron of conflicting political passions in 1917. Even though Fielding, Maclean, and Murray favoured Union, they were unable to carry their colleagues with them. Often they compromised, as the Kyte letter to Laurier cited above clearly shows. This evidence of Liberal Unionist compromise and the absence of any Conservative leadership in the province (Borden, the sole Tory minister from the province, remained above, not a part of, the battle) led the Tories to resist pressures to withdraw candidates in favour of Liberal Unionists.[34] Borden, who himself moved to the constituency of Kings in order to free Halifax for Maclean, later recalled the difficulties: 'There were many excursions and alarums in Nova Scotia with respect to the selection of candidates. The party spirit in that Province was intensely strong. With great difficulty I secured the withdrawal of the Conservative candidate and the election of Mr. Fielding by acclamation in Queens-Shelbourne. It was impossible to make any arrangements with the Halifax Liberals although their leading men were anxious to accept my proposal for one Liberal and one Conservative.'[35]

In the end, no organization congealed in Nova Scotia. Murray himself, after announcing for Union, never went out on the hustings for the Unionist cause. Fundamentally, Nova Scotia Unionism lacked the enthusiasm which drew new men into politics elsewhere, especially in Ontario and the west. There was a remarkable measure of shrewd calculation in the decision of Nova Scotia Liberals to support Unionism. Fielding, for example, took care to limit his support to 'measures for the Prosecution of the War while reserving [his] freedom of action.'[36] When asked to speak for the Unionists, he adamantly refused, citing the Irish proverb; 'It is easy to bear another man's toothache.' Never, he told the Unionists, would he speak against his erstwhile Liberal colleagues.[37] According to one report of a meeting where the Liberal Unionists and anti-Unionists decided their tactical position, Maclean joined the government because 'there was considerable sentiment in favour of the idea, that as a fairly representative, Union government has been formed, it might be as well for the Nova

---

34 F.B. McCurdy, the parliamentary secretary of the Department of Soldiers Civil Re-Establishment, did much of the campaign work in Nova Scotia for Borden, but with mixed results. BP, Borden Diary, Nov. 1917, *passim.*
35 Borden *Memoirs*, II, 761. See also Hopkins, *Canadian Annual Review, 1917*, 607, 624-5; *Halifax Chronicle*, 4 Dec. 1917; and Foster Diary, 12 Nov. 1917.
36 Cited in *Halifax Chronicle*, 25 Oct. 1917.
37 Fielding to Charles Tanner, 3 Dec. 1917, Public Archives of Nova Scotia (PANS), Fielding Papers, v. 524.

Scotia Liberals to be represented in it.'[38] This is scarcely the tone of emotional commitment; Union government in Nova Scotia was only a grudging partnership for distinct and temporary ends. Annulment was as certain as the war's close.

Prince Edward Island was also absent from O'Connor's list. One assumes that the reason for the omission is similar to that of Nova Scotia; no real Unionist organization existed. According to A.E. Arsenault, the Conservative premier of the province, 'not one Liberal public man nor Liberal newspaper supported Union.'[39] Like the phantom causeway, Union sentiment never crossed the Strait of Northumberland.

New Brunswick, however, is a different matter, and in this province, notorious for its political mayhem, the Unionists made a surprisingly energetic attempt to create a provincial organization. The credit for this goes to Frank Carvell, who, according to the O'Connor list, took charge of every constituency except Northumberland. Carvell immediately learned that three constituencies, Kent, Restigouche-Madawaska, and Gloucester, which contained French-Canadian majorities, were 'hopeless.' Another, Westmorland, was very doubtful, and in fact no Unionist candidate was endorsed in that riding.[40] In the seven remaining ridings, Carvell sincerely tried to follow the Unionist formula of holding joint conventions in open constituencies, but he found it almost impossible to keep New Brunswick Liberals and Tories, fresh from a bitter provincial encounter, together in the same room.[41] Not surprisingly, he frequently despaired, especially when he discovered that the provincial Liberal government would offer no help at all. Although Premier Walter E. Foster was personally

38 Kyte to Laurier, 16 Oct. 1917, Laurier Papers, v. 714.
39 Arsenault to Borden, 18 Dec. 1917, BP, v. 227.
40 I have not been able to discover why Northumberland was omitted; probably local resentment of Carvell was responsible. The 1921 census shows why these constituencies were lost:

	Total male population	French-Canadian male population
Restigouche-Madawaska	22,258	17,009
Gloucester	19,697	16,703
Kent	12,317	9227
Westmorland	26,959	10,148

Canada, *Census of 1921* (Ottawa, 1924), I, 361-2. In Westmorland a 'win-the-war' Tory, O.B. Price, fought A.B. Copp, a Laurier Liberal, for whom Carvell had originally tried to secure the Unionist nomination. W.H. Thorne to Borden, 5 Nov. 1917, BP, v. 136.
41 The provincial campaign had been fought on the issue of corruption, always one with considerable 'meat' in New Brunswick. The Liberals narrowly won. Hopkins, *Canadian Annual Review, 1917*, 700-1.

sympathetic to Union, his hands were tied by the dependence of the provincial party upon Acadian support. Still, by election day Carvell's efforts had dispelled most of the gloom, and New Brunswick Unionists confidently predicted they would win at least six of the seven possible seats.[42]

No such optimism arose in Quebec where the Unionists made only a token appeal. Throughout the summer Quebec had bitterly opposed conscription and coalition. When the Union government was formed, Borden tried but failed to obtain significant French-Canadian representation in the new cabinet. He did little better with Liberal English-Canadian representation in Quebec. C.C. Ballantyne, a paint company executive, had no popular following among Quebec Liberals; indeed, he had never held any public office apart from that of mayor of Westmount. Furthermore, his selection greatly offended the sensitive C.H. Cahan whose position he took as government candidate in St Lawrence-St George.[43] Ballantyne brought neither widespread support nor his own riding, but he did set off a serious squabble among Montreal Tories.

The Ballantyne affair is another indicator of the extent to which Quebec, both English and French sectors, was *terra incognita* to Borden and his advisers. In 1917 the Unionist organization in Quebec never extended beyond a few English-Canadian constituencies. Much of the old Conservative organization had already joined the Liberals in the summer at the prompting of Senator Auguste Landry.[44] What remained was badly split by quarrels which often had very little to do with conscription. From the days of Sir John A. Macdonald the CPR and related Montreal financial and manufacturing interests had generously supplied the Quebec Tories with men as well as money. In 1917, however, the support of the great railway was not available because of the railway nationalization policy adopted by the Conservative government over the very fervent objections of the CPR and its president, Lord Shaughnessy. Although the CPR publicly espoused neutrality, and some of its officers privately assisted the Unionists, there is much evidence that the Liberals were the true beneficiaries of the company's largesse.[45]

---

42 Carvell to Borden, 16 Nov. 1917, BP, v. 136. See also A.K. Cameron to Walter Cameron, 21 Nov. 1917, PAC, Cameron Papers, v. 2. According to Cameron, Carvell believed that Laurier would win 'at least 105 seats.' Also Hopkins, *Canadian Annual Review, 1917*, 701, 710. The 'predictions' of the Unionist central office were published in the *Manitoba Free Press*, 15 Dec. 1917. The Unionists took all seven seats where the Acadians were not a factor.

43 H. Morgan, *Canadian Men and Women of the Time* (Toronto, 1912), 56; and Borden to Cahan, 17 Oct. 1917, BP, v. 28.

44 Gouin to Laurier, 24 Aug. 1917, Laurier Papers, v. 712. Gouin relayed to Laurier a bargain made between the defecting Tories and the Liberals over several constituencies.

45 J.P.B. Casgrain reported a conversation at the Mount Royal Club in Montreal in which Shaughnessy indicated he favoured a Liberal victory. He also claimed that a company

With the overwhelming majority of the province adamantly opposed to conscription and much of the traditional Conservative financial and organizational apparatus hostile to nationalization, only a minimal organization was developed. The O'Connor list shows the haphazard Unionist effort in the province. Albert Sévigny, distrusted by his colleagues and himself taking refuge in the constituency of Westmount, looked after most of eastern Quebec and some of the Eastern Townships. Charles Doherty, never known for his political skills, handled much of the remainder, including most of the Montreal constituencies. So low were the Unionists' hopes that High Commissioner George Perley continued to be responsible for his old constituency of Argenteuil although he never set foot upon Canadian soil, much less that of Argenteuil, in 1917! Nominal co-ordination of the campaign was exerted by a Quebec electoral committee chaired by Senator George Foster. Yet Foster himself admitted that he had little success, adding that the only effective sector of the Unionist organization was a quasi-official women's patriotic group.[46] These women undoubtedly made a useful and notable contribution, but they were scarcely the nucleus of a permanent organization.

In Ontario, as so often in Canadian history, the problem was the reverse of that in Quebec: too many wanted to play some role in the campaign. N.W. Rowell had brought with him the greater portion of the highly primed and well-manned Liberal organization.[47] Moreover, numerous 'amateurs,' long active in patriotic groups, sought involvement in the Unionist campaign. Yet the Conservative organization was so strong that it was prepared to give up nothing. As we have seen Borden tried to solve this problem by granting several ridings to the Liberals. Yet the overall control of the province had to remain with the Tories, and the O'Connor list verifies that it did: J.D. Reid is revealed to be in charge of all Ontario constituencies, sharing a few with others (one very curious example of this was Prescott where Sévigny aided

official said: 'If you want to please the company vote for Laurier.' Casgrain to Laurier, 2 Nov. 1917, Laurier Papers, v. 717. See also Laurier to F.L. Beique, 18 Jan. 1918, *ibid.*, v. 720; E.M. Macdonald to Laurier, n.d. (fall 1917), *ibid.*, v. 705; and E.M. Macdonald, *Recollections: Political and Personal* (Toronto, n.d.), 339.

46 George Yates, secretary to the prime minister, 'Memo,' 19 Dec. 1917, BP, v. 227, reported: '... Senator Foster says that Mrs. Holt is the one woman who elected your three Ministers and you should give her a good letter. She had the hundred and fifty women working for three weeks.' Men received an appointment or a contract; women received a letter.

47 This is confirmed in Murphy to George Gibbons, 3 Nov. 1917, PAC, Gibbons Papers, v. 1; Laurier to W.A. Charlton, Laurier to C.W. Kerr, both 29 Oct. 1917, Laurier Papers, v. 715.

Reid). In the Liberal Unionist constituencies, Rowell represented local interests in negotiations with Reid.[48]

Borden saw the dangers of rivalry between the two official wings of the party, and tried to introduce into electioneering another element made up of members of the numerous war-related voluntary groups of Ontario. These organizations, he hoped, might form the basis of a permanent Unionist organization. One might also suggest that their vision of a political party coincided more closely with Borden's own than that of the Ontario Liberals and Tories. How, then, did Borden employ this reservoir of talent and enthusiasm?

First, he encouraged newcomers to take advantage of their previous non-involvement and stage 'non-partisan' public meetings and issue 'non-partisan' declarations which would secure wide publicity.[49] This, it was expected, would facilitate the breaking of party ties by those hesitant to shed their old political raiment. Also, such extensive publicity would create the desirable impression of a ground-swell from below in favour of Union government, and would undermine the Liberal charge that Union was merely the shotgun marriage of two desperate political factions. Borden also knew that a non-partisan air would encourage normally neutral groups, notably the churches, to lend their support to the cause, and this did in fact occur. Michael Bliss has described how the Methodist Church in the First World War sent forth its Christian soldiers under the Unionist banners.[50] Among Protestant congregations, the Methodists stood out only because of their numbers and their stridency. Most of the other Protestant churches marched in step. Bishop J.F. Sweeney of Toronto in a pastoral letter openly urged Anglicans to support Union 'because it is non-partisan – being composed of the best men on both sides of politics,' and 'because its *raison d'etre* is to "win the War." '[51]

The newcomers had another, more 'political,' function. They were to act as a buffer between traditional Liberals and Tories at the numerous Unionist conventions to choose candidates. Borden, working closely with John Godfrey, president

48 Other shared constituencies were Elgin West (Crothers); Lanark (Hanna); Muskoka (Wright); Peterborough West (Burnham); and Simcoe South (Boys).
49 A description of such activities can be found in Hopkins, *Canadian Annual Review, 1917*, 602-3.
50 'The Methodist Church and World War I,' *Canadian Historical Review*, XLIX (Sept. 1968), 213-33. An excellent example of Methodist polemic can be found in their official publication, the *Christian Guardian*, 12 Dec. 1917.
51 Cited in Hopkins, *Canadian Annual Review, 1917*, 630. The Catholic Church was understandably neutral in the election contest, although Bishop M.F. Fallon, a leading opponent of bilingual schools in Ontario, strongly supported Union.

of the powerful Ontario Win-the-War League, managed to flood many conventions with well-disciplined leaguers, who upheld Borden's interest in the centre of the Tory-Liberal Unionist antagonism. At Borden's insistence and thanks to his own talent, Godfrey won a place with Reid and Rowell as a member of the triumvirate which eventually directed the Unionist campaign in Ontario.[52] For all the jealousy and divisions, the Unionist organization in Ontario perhaps offered the strongest grounds for the belief that a lasting Unionist organization, quite unlike party structures in the past, would emerge in the 1917 battle.

In the west, piecemeal efforts were made to combine old party organizations, but with limited success. In Manitoba, where a strongly Unionist Liberal provincial government was in the midst of a controversial investigation of the previous Tory government, there was little co-operation between the two parties. Arthur Meighen's veto of the entry of provincial Liberal A.B. Hudson into the federal cabinet meant that, unlike Ontario, Saskatchewan, and Alberta, Manitoba Liberalism lacked a cabinet representative. (T.A. Crerar, although a Liberal, had no political experience and was chosen because he was president of the powerful Grain Growers' organization.) As with many of Meighen's actions, this refusal to admit a Liberal counterpart from Manitoba ultimately worked to his own disadvantage. When Meighen as spokesman for Tory interests throughout the west was unable to devote proper attention to his own province, Robert Rogers returned to play a large part in a Unionist organization of which he fundamentally disapproved.[53] Perhaps it was the certainty of Union success in Manitoba which fostered such carelessness. Nowhere did Liberals so enthusiastically support the government. But co-operation was minimal and no kernel of a future Unionist organization developed.

In Saskatchewan, James Calder, the provincial government's former political organizer, took the core of his old machine with him when he went over to Unionism. Because of the weakness of the provincial Tories the entire campaign was left to Calder who soon dispelled the Tories' suspicion by showing great fairness. First, he agreed to form a joint National Government Association of Saskatchewan and to leave decisions on candidates to its local members with one notable exception. Although Unionist conventions were to have complete freedom to choose candidates, Calder insisted that at least six of those chosen must

---

52 Godfrey to Sifton, 9 Nov. 1917, PAC, Sifton Papers, v. 205; Godfrey to Rowell, 30 Oct. and 5 Nov. 1917, Rowell Papers, v. 3; and Godfrey to Borden, 30 Oct. 1917, BP, v. 79. Godfrey toured the province, acting as a 'trouble-shooter' for Borden.

53 The O'Connor list shows that Rogers assisted or acted as the principal in eight of fifteen constituencies.

be Conservatives, as Meighen had demanded.[54] To the surprise of all, these conventions selected not six but eight Tories along with eight Liberals. Calder's good-will was unquestioned — at least by the Tories.

Calder's former cabinet colleagues took little part in the campaign because the cabinet was badly split on conscription and Union. At the last moment, however, Premier W.M. Martin, a long-time supporter of conscription, publicly announced his personal intention to vote Unionist.[55] It was, perhaps, the hesitant and sometimes defiant attitude towards Union government shown by many provincial Liberals which permitted the Conservatives to win the endorsement in eight constituencies. For Calder, the situation was perilous, and raised the question of what he was to do after the election. He knew that the machine would be restored to provincial Liberal hands after the election, and there would then be little chance for a permanent structure to sustain Unionism in Saskatchewan.

In Alberta, a similar situation developed. Arthur Sifton's former government failed to unite behind his decision to go to Ottawa. Like Calder, Sifton brought the core of the provincial organization with him, but it lacked the effectiveness of Saskatchewan's. Liberal Unionists, including the early supporter of conscription and coalition, Michael Clark, were rejected by conventions which chose Liberal Unionists with very dubious credentials instead. In Calgary, Alexander Allan, the president of the Provincial Liberal Association, held an anti-Unionist convention which over five hundred Liberals, many of them very prominent, attended.[56] As a result of such embarrassments, Sifton's position as provincial Unionist leader was seriously weakened, and the result was a majority for the Conservative Unionists among the endorsed candidates. Although an election victory was almost certain, particularly after Henry Wise Wood of the United Farmers of Alberta placed his prestige behind Unionism, the Alberta Unionists remained only a loose coalition of disparate groups which were to disappear soon after the election.

British Columbia was a Tory province federally, although in 1916 it had become Liberal provincially. Martin Burrell, the only minister from the province, was faced with a situation far beyond his political capacities. Although Calder gave him some valuable assistance, Burrell found it quite impossible to manage the constituencies. The Tories therefore carried all but one of the thirteen

54 *Manitoba Free Press*, 26 Oct. 1917. See Roger Graham, *Arthur Meighen: The Door of Opportunity* (Toronto, 1960), I, 175, for a full discussion of Meighen's role in the campaign.
55 *Manitoba Free Press*, 10 Dec. 1917.
56 *Edmonton Bulletin*, 2 Nov. 1917. The opposition to Unionism rallied behind C.W. Cross, the provincial attorney-general; the provincial government in Alberta was itself more a coalition than a united party.

constituency conventions. By election day, Liberal and Conservative Unionists were openly antagonistic and fighting each other rather than Laurier Liberals.[57] The task of campaigning, however, was efficiently carried out by voluntary groups, especially the Win-the-War Leagues and the Great War Veterans' Association. Burrell and Borden hoped that these groups would congeal to form a lasting political association, but the campaign with its tremendous tensions meant that newcomers to political participation had a frustrating initiation which repelled them rather than attracted them to politics.

Two aspects of the organization remain to be considered: the threads which linked these provincial efforts and the financial foundations which supported the Unionists. Calder's October plan for a highly structured national organization was not realized for two reasons. First, the calendar would have won the race to create such a national organization. Secondly, such a national organization set up in a brief span of time would necessarily have relied upon the old party organizations. This, above all, Borden wanted to avoid. Since Borden believed that victory was certain, he was willing to make do with a very loose organization which he expected would spur widespread popular participation. Very likely Borden wanted Unionism to become a movement; not a party but a broad popular upheaval which would fundamentally alter the Canadian political system.

The eclecticism of the national party direction substantiates this impression. Rather than selecting party regulars to admister the national campaign effort, men who would be the building bricks of a future party bureaucracy, Borden turned to mavericks whom he surely knew would leave Ottawa in January 1918. Sir Clifford Sifton, for example, was at Borden's side throughout the campaign, except when he journeyed out of Ottawa to administer harsh justice to re-calcitrant Tories or Liberal Unionists. Another maverick was Sir John Willison, the Unionist publicity director. His office provided most of the meagre co-ordination for the national campaign through its publication of propaganda and its operation of a speakers' bureau.[58] Other men of similar backgrounds, such as Godfrey or the publicist Arthur Hawkes, also spent December 1917 in Ottawa working on the Unionist campaign. In every detail, then, from remote

---

57 J.S.H. Matson to Borden, 2 Nov., Calder to Borden, 3 Nov. 1917, BP, v. 77; H.C. Brewster to J.W. McIntosh, 29 Jan. 1918, PABC, Brewster Papers, Premiers Correspondence.

58 Hopkins, *Canadian Annual Review, 1917*, 610. Unfortunately one finds no description of Willison's work in this position in A.H.U. Colquhoun, *Press, Politics and People* (Toronto, 1935); and there are no interesting documents on the Unionist publicity committee found in the Willison Papers.

constituency to the central office, the Unionists were quite unlike a traditional Canadian party.

The financial basis of Unionism was similarly irregular, although details are, as usual, hard to find. The general impression, however, is that the local organizations were largely self-sufficient, much more so than in earlier elections. Volunteer labour was abundant and local funds ample in most of Canada, apart from Quebec and the Maritimes, where local resources were inadequate. For this reason Borden was forced to appoint a fund-raising committee for eastern Canada which was chaired by Lord Atholstan (Hugh Graham) and another Montreal millionaire, Lorne Webster. Borden requested that Atholstan raise the astonishing sum of $1.5 million, an amount five times that available to the Tories in the 1904 national campaign. The committee's task was not easy: the usual subvention from the CPR was unlikely, and Atholstan's frantic appeals to Borden to conciliate the railway did not succeed. Atholstan was accordingly forced to seek out new sources, and the remarkable absence of complaints indicates that he was successful. Individual contributions were staggering: Thomas Cantley, a Nova Scotian steel magnate, contributed $50,000 himself. Atholstan even turned to Lord Northcliffe for financial assistance for the Canadian campaign.[59] Whether Northcliffe complied is unknown, but another British press lord did: Lord Beaverbrook aided Unionists in his native New Brunswick and among the soldiers in Europe.[60] The 1917 election was, in every respect, an extraordinary election, but this appeal to Britain must rank as its most unusual aspect. Only one feature rivals it in this respect: the campaign for the soldier vote.

After the fall of Hughes, the government soon learned how unpopular Sir Sam had made it among the overseas troops. There was also, inevitably, disillusion arising from the miserable condition of life in the trenches and the apparently endless war. Captain Earle Logan, for example, told Perley that, while censoring letters in September 1917, he had found that 70 per cent of the soldiers were advising their relatives to vote against conscription. The men were 'fed up' and did not want their relatives to serve. A disaster would befall the

59 Borden to Atholstan, 3 Nov., Atholstan to Borden, 31 Oct., and n.d. (Dec. 1917?), BP, v. 327. Pages 193300-10 of the Borden Papers are a rough collection of notes by Atholstan on the railway question. Cantley to Borden, 19 Dec. 1919, BP, v. 16. Caird to Northcliffe, 26 Nov. 1917, Beaverbrook Library, London, Lloyd George Papers, F 23/1/29.
60 Borden to Perley, 1 Sept. 1917, BP, v. 145. See also A.J.P. Taylor, *Beaverbrook* (New York, 1972), which indicates Borden had wanted Beaverbrook to return to Canadian politics.

Union government, Logan argued, unless it undertook extensive 'educational' work immediately.[61] Yet the government could not even estimate the number of troops in Europe to the nearest ten thousand.[62] How, then, could it ever accomplish the necessary 'education' within the short period? The answer was obvious, unfortunate, and illegal: they could work through the military hierarchy.

A decision was made at the highest level that the soldiers' vote, which was more valuable than a civilian ballot because of its portable character, had to be marked for the government candidate. Every regiment and platoon was organized, and F.B. McCurdy, a parliamentary secretary, acted as the liaison between the European organization and Ottawa, while Canada's high commissioner, Perley, agreed to exercise overall direction from his office in London. Harold Daly was attached to Perley's office, and acted as a general manager of the operation. Lieutenant-Colonel Joseph Hayes was Daly's representative at the front in France. Assisting them was Hector McInnes, a civilian and a valuable cloak for Sir George Perley. Since the campaign in Canada lacked national direction, provincial Unionist organizations were asked to name some officers already present in Europe to organize the soldiers, and an organization, parallel to each provincial one, was formed. The officers selected were told to ask for a furlough and, *mirabile dictu*, this request was immediately granted. To assist the officers, the Beaverbrook presses in Britain turned out reams of Unionist propaganda which flooded barracks and trenches throughout England and France. By early December there was little doubt of the outcome. The organization among the soldiers was a masterful blend of efficiency and enthusiasm, if not of probity and permanence.[63]

It is appropriate that this chapter which is concerned with the failure to develop a new Unionist organization should end with a discussion of the military voter. For all its abnormalities, the soldiers' organization might well have been the most 'normal' feature of Unionist organization. At least it was staffed by old

61 Logan to Perley, 7 Oct. 1917, BP, v. 79. On 24 Oct. Borden told Rowell that brothers and fathers of those at the front should be exempted lest the soldiers oppose conscription. Borden to Rowell, 24 Oct. 1917, BP, v. 226.
62 See PAC, Loring Christie Papers, v. 2, file 4, and v. 25, file 95, where Christie, a Borden aide, tries to determine the numbers of Canadian soldiers.
63 Perley was initially reluctant to aid because of his office, but he finally agreed to act. Reid to Perley, n.d. Perley hoped that 'we can manage in such a way as to avoid serious criticism.' Perley to Borden, 18 Nov. and 10 Dec., also McCurdy to Hayes, 30 Oct., McInnes to Blount, 23 Nov. 1917, all in BP, v. 79. According to McInnes, the officers were all 'sympathetic' but they felt rather guilty about open partisanship. Also PAC, Harold Daly Papers, Memoirs.

Tory party workers. In Canada itself, Unionist organization was a peculiar hodge-podge of the formerly apolitical, Tory workers, and scattered but numerous ex-Liberals. This was, as we have seen, largely intentional. The pre-war Canadian political party normally had a relatively low level of participation, and because of this the Liberal and Conservative parties were weakened in their position vis-à-vis powerful institutions or social groupings. Thus, a railway could determine the economic policy of a party, not because of its own intrinsic economic power but because of the weakness of political parties (that is, the national party not the constituency party). Borden had therefore concluded early in his career that the means of freeing his party from dependence on such influences was to increase the level of political participation. To do this, he had to undercut those closely associated with the old Tory organization. He did this by abolishing patronage, by introducing new men, and gradually eliminating the old.

Yet Borden also depended on Lord Atholstan, overlooked unfair appeals to race and religion, and permitted the notorious activities of his party organization among the soldiers. One might certainly suggest blatant hypocrisy and ask how Borden, on the one hand, could regard his cause in 1917 as sacred, and, on the other hand, employ such profane means. This type of question, so cherished by many journalists today, would simply lead us to a crude form of psychohistory and ultimately into a *cul de sac*.[64] Still, some conclusions are possible.

Borden, in common with many other Canadians during the First World War, came to believe that the war would inspire a national regeneration. 'Shall we not hope, and indeed believe,' he asked in 1917, 'that this war may prove to be the birth-pang attending the nativity of a truer and nobler civilization?'[65] But if the war were lost, if Canada failed and turned in upon itself, rejecting its past and its future, this new civilization would be still-born. Borden and his followers therefore defined citizenship as a willingness to serve: those who refused must be denied its privilege. No 'adherence to tradition or system or ... personal considerations' should obstruct the nation's path.[66] White was right and black was wrong. As Wilfred Campbell wrote in a 1917 poem:

64 Thus Robert Coles has written of one of the worst examples of this genre: '[This study is] an instructive lesson in how psychological words and phrases presented as a means of scientific exposition can become in certain hands instruments of moral condemnation and even malicious abuse.' 'Shrinking History – Part Two,' *New York Review of Books*, XX (8 March 1973), 25.

65 Borden, *The War and the Future*, ed. Percy Hurd (London, 1917), 160.

66 Borden, *A Speech before the United Kingdom Branch of the Empire Parliamentary Association at London England, June 21, 1918* (Ottawa, 1918).

We are either on God's side or evil's,
We are either perjured or true; —
And that, which we set out to do in the first place,
That must we do.[67]

And that Borden did; he knew no other.

---

67 'Our Dead,' in J.O. Miller, ed., *The New Era in Canada* (Toronto, 1917), 348.

10

The plebiscite on conscription

The political scientist V.O. Key has described democratic elections as 'collective decisions' to which politicians must 'as a matter of course attribute decisional content.'[1] Recent research suggests that politicians are generally correct in believing that the people's decision is a statement of policy preference, particularly when the parties vividly present the alternatives which they represent. 'Confused voters reflect confused parties; clarity among the voters follows clear-headed parties.'[2] In 1917 the parties' positions were clear, and Sir Robert Borden, his colleagues, the press, and, probably, the Canadian people saw in the results of the general election an unmistakable decision. Very simply, a vote for Union meant 'an order for full steam ahead' for Unionist war policy, and, in particular, for the policy of conscription.[3] The campaign had relentlessly focused upon this single issue, shunting other issues to remote corners.

On the hustings and in their press, in public and in private, the Unionists emphasized the importance of the distinction between government and opposition. Thus, Unionist Liberal Frank Carvell argued that 'The real question before the electors of Canada to-day is whether or not this Dominion will do its full duty, not only to itself, the Empire at large, and the civilization of the world, but to the soldiers who have already gone forward, many of whom have made the supreme sacrifice ... We have allowed all matters of local and political interest to Canada to remain in abeyance until peace has been declared, and to

1 V.O. Key, *Public Opinion and American Democracy* (New York, 1967), 472-80.
2 See Gerald M. Pomper, 'From Confusion to Clarity,' *American Political Science Review*, LXVI (June 1972), 428.
3 James Brierley, 'The Union Government's Opportunities,' *University Magazine*, XVII (Feb. 1918), 15. On the need for a clear position, see R.L. Borden, *Letters to Limbo*, ed. Henry Borden (Toronto 1971), 11.

devote our whole attention to the energetic prosecution of the War.'[4] And in sombre tones Andrew Macphail of McGill University warned voters of the responsibility they had in the polling booth: 'When you go into your secret place on the 17th of December, and cast a furtive ballot, what you secretly do will be proclaimed before God and the Army.'[5] Even less elegant and much blunter was the cartoon caption in the *Manitoba Free Press* two days before the election: 'Make every ballot a bullet for Bill.'

The Unionist campaign moved towards its climax with an ever increasing intensity. In the large halls of Canada's few cities and in the clapboard town halls of the numerous small towns, Unionists spoke of the meaning of the war with great solemnity, often employing the rich and powerful imagery of Protestant Christianity. Gone were the joint political meetings of the past, so familiar to us from Leacock's *Sunshine Sketches*, where both candidates performed on the same platform while their supporters jousted in the crowd. Now Unionists met only with Unionists, and, instead of the boisterous atmosphere of the old meetings, there was 'a strange and silent earnestness.'[6] The didactic, grave speeches of the politicians who normally bantered with their audience undoubtedly gave Unionist gatherings a sense of fear, conviction, and solidarity. Perhaps Northrop Frye's description of a 'garrison mentality' best identifies the dominant atmosphere of the Unionist campaign. 'A garrison,' Frye writes, 'is a closely knit and beleaguered society, and its moral and social values are unquestionable. In a perilous enterprise one does not discuss causes or motives: one is either a fighter or a deserter.'[7] There is an acute, overwhelming sense of shared interest. The war acquires a mystical nature endowed with its own eschatology. Values are group values, and real terror comes when the individual is apart from the group.

This concept partially, but not wholly, explains the intense focus of the Unionist campaign upon the war, which seems rather curious on political grounds since it implied that once the war was over the *raison d'être* of the Union would vanish. Yet, although the original Unionist statement of policy in October set forth a wide-ranging programme, embracing such causes as civil service reform and resource development, by December these further planks had become almost superfluous. Three factors combined to bring this about.

4 Cited in J.C. Hopkins, *Canadian Annual Review, 1917* (Toronto, 1918), 606.
5 'In This Our Necessity,' *University Magazine*, XVI (Dec. 1917), 480.
6 *Manitoba Free Press*, 19 Dec. 1917. 'The Union meetings were quiet. There was none of the boisterous applause which used to mark campaign meetings in this country ...'
7 'Conclusion to a *Literary History of Canada*,' *The Bush Garden: Essays on the Canadian Imagination* (Toronto, 1971), 226.

The first of these was the discovery by Liberal Unionists that the stream of partisanship ran very deeply in Canada, and that many of their expected followers had not moved with them to the Unionist side. It was therefore natural that Liberal Unionists became particularly anxious to emphasize the powerful war issue, which they saw as a magnet of extraordinary strength for English Canada. Thus the leading Liberal Unionist journal, the *Manitoba Free Press*, editorially proclaimed on 15 December that there was 'Only one issue: fight or quit.' Paradoxically, by narrowing the issues, the appeal became broader, and the Liberal Unionists effaced from their minds any consideration of what would happen when the war ended.

If the Liberal Unionists had to concentrate on the war at the expense of secondary issues in order to win converts, the Tories did so in order to maintain their strength. Union government had bitterly alienated many Tories who profoundly distrusted Liberal Unionist motives. These disillusioned Conservatives, largely grouped about Robert Rogers, assisted individual Tory candidates while persistently sniping at the Liberal Unionists and often at Borden himself as the architect of the disastrous political marriage. No better expression of this point of view exists than in the Rogers-controlled *Winnipeg Telegram* whose erratic behaviour betrayed a political ship lost in a storm. Only in December when it became clear that the election was nothing less than a plebiscite on conscription did the Rogers faction fully join in the battle. A letter from Sir Edward Kemp to Borden containing 'a description by a lady friend' of R.B. Bennett's greater than normal confusion reveals how even the most reluctant were forced to enter the fray.

1. I am a hearty supporter of Union Government.
2. I am entirely opposed to Union Government because they have included A.L. Sifton, my arch-enemy who is a thorough rogue.
3. Nevertheless, I am entirely in accord with Union Government, and will raise my voice in support of R.L. Borden because he has achieved the miracle of Union Government.[8]

Such contradictions abounded in the Tory ranks. Many Conservatives were firmly opposed to prohibition, women's suffrage, and civil service reform, all

8 Kemp to Borden, 31 Jan. 1918, PAC, Borden Papers (BP), v. 96. Bennett did not run in 1917 because he expected Borden to appoint him to the Senate. In Bennett's eyes this appointment fell through when he strongly criticized Borden's attempts to form a coalition. In 1918 he became an even stronger critic of the government, comparing it to the corrupt governments of post-Augustan Rome. See Bennett to Borden, 17 April 1918, BP, v. 327.

elements of the Unionist platform. Indeed, Roger Graham tells us that Arthur Meighen favoured neither female suffrage nor the end of patronage.[9] On the other hand, the senior Tory minister, Sir George Foster, whose own career was replete with scandal, rejoiced in the abolition of patronage and the bar.[10] Surprisingly, the divisions within the cabinet did not follow party lines, but regularly found former Liberals and Tories arrayed on the same side.[11] On one subject alone – the war – all agreed. The Conservatives therefore found that the Rogers faction and others offended by Unionism would put forth far greater effort when the war was treated as the overwhelming issue and other areas on which Liberal Unionists and Borden had reached agreement in October 1917 were obscured.

Borden was compelled to concentrate on the war; Laurier chose to do so. Here is the third and perhaps the most powerful reason why the election of 1917 became a plebiscite on conscription. For Laurier an election on the conscription issue was truly a godsend. The leader of a party very much in search of a direction and, like Liberals elsewhere, severely discomfited by the need to come to terms with modern industrial society, the septuagenarian Laurier found a fight against conscription one which could be carried out on familiar terrain. He could attack Toryism and 'its undying spirit of domination' as he always had. He could remain true to 'Liberalism,' to the liberalism of Gladstone and Morley, Mackenzie and Blake, to the traditional values of individual freedom, liberty, and resistance to oppression.[12] The complexities of a new age, of labour, of civil service reform, of prohibition, of female suffrage, and of 'positive freedom' could be ignored.

Laurier could also solidify his hold upon the French Canadians and the new immigrants to Canada by becoming a martyr to conscription. Canadian Liberalism would be the voice of the oppressed and the bitter opponent of the 'would be aristocracy of the country.'[13] Laurier knew that Unionist strength

---

9 *Arthur Meighen: The Door of Opportunity* (Toronto, 1960), I, 196.
10 PAC, Foster Papers, Foster Diary, 12 Oct. 1917, 31 Jan. and 14 Feb. 1918.
11 Henry Borden, ed., *Robert Laird Borden: His Memoirs* (Toronto, 1938), II, 753.
12 Cited in O.D. Skelton, *Life and Letters of Sir Wilfrid Laurier* (London, 1922), II, 511. See especially J.T. McLeod, 'The Political Thought of Sir Wilfrid Laurier,' unpublished PhD thesis, University of Toronto, 1965, 304-9, for Laurier's doubts about reform Liberalism. Laurier was in all ways a man of an earlier age. W.L.M. King reported a conversation: 'Sir Wilfrid and Fisher were talking of the present age. Sir Wilfrid was deploring its mechanical aspect, photos for paintings, no originality, he disliked the motor, the telegraph, telephone, the real charm of the world had gone. He would rather have the eighteenth century.' PAC, King Papers, King Diary, 4 Nov. 1917.
13 Cited in King Diary, 12 Oct. 1917. See also Laurier to W.T.R. Preston, 3 Jan. 1918, PAC, Laurier Papers, v. 718.

rested upon English-Canadian intoxication with power, but that such hubris was always ephemeral. By contrast, Liberal ballots in 1917 would be cast by those who felt wronged, and no emotion was more enduring. Henri Bourassa vividly expressed this bitterness that would be lasting: 'Le programme unioniste, c'est l'antithèse de tout ce que nous aimons, de tout ce que nous croyons, de tout ce que nous voulons. C'est la synthèse de tout ce que nous détestons, — hommes, idées, et tendances — dans les deux partis.'[14]

As a Liberal candidate in 1917, Charles G. Power, later admitted, 'the 1917 election was essentially a one-party election, one party only in Quebec and one party only in other provinces.' The Liberal campaign was, accordingly, primarily anti-conscription, support for Laurier, and 'denunciation of his betrayers.' Such a campaign promised and created a future Liberal Quebec based upon a profound sense of injustice among the French-Canadian population of that province. The Liberal campaign of 1917 firmly identified the symbol of that injustice, conscription, with Unionism and with the Conservative party of Canada, and until 1949 the Liberals successfully exploited this grievance to assure their dominance in Quebec.[15]

Thus Unionists by necessity and Laurier by conscious design combined to make the general election of 1917 a referendum on conscription. The Unionists sacrificed the future; the Liberals the present. Unlike many of his followers, Laurier 'knew from the first that with the Wartime Elections Act it would have been folly to expect a victory.'[16] He directed his campaign accordingly, so that in defeat he acquired lasting advantage.

The Unionists, however, so desperately wanted victory in 1917 that they were willing to mortgage the future. Not surprisingly, they began to fear defeat as the campaign progressed. Initially, there had been no doubts. On the morrow of the Union Sir Clifford Sifton exclaimed that the victory was 'complete' and that 'the new government is strong enough to attend to its own business and I shall therefore be free to attend to mine.'[17] Both the elation and the resolve were short-lived. On 8 November a troubled Sifton asked John Godfrey to outline the 'attitude of rank and file electors towards Union.' He proceeded to give the reasons for his request: 'I have heard some very disquieting information lately. I was extremely optimistic when the Government was formed, and I hoped that

14 Cited in Robert Rumilly, *Henri Bourassa* (Montreal, 1953), 590.
15 *A Party Politician: The Memoirs of Chubby Power*, ed. Norman Ward (Toronto, 1966), 61, 55, and 75. See also J.L. Granatstein, *The Politics of Survival* (Toronto, 1967), especially chaps. 1 and 2.
16 Laurier to Preston, 3 Jan. 1918, Laurier Papers, v. 718.
17 Sifton to Dafoe, 15 Oct. 1917, PAC, Dafoe Papers, microfilm copy; Sifton to Willison, 16 Oct. 1917, PAC, Willison Papers, v. 74.

they would strike the right note and dispose of a few pressing questions of great public importance in an effective way.' The 'golden moment,' Sifton claimed, was 'rapidly passing by.' Godfrey in his reply admitted that there certainly was trouble: 'The only thing that has saved the situation in Ontario is the fact that Union Government has practically broken in two Sir Wilfrid's official organization.' Even so, Laurier would probably 'make quite a showing in Ontario.' What had gone wrong? First, the unseemly bickering over constituencies had hampered the growth of a 'real Union sentiment.' The problem, Godfrey perceptively noted, is that 'Rowell has persisted in regarding this thing as a coalition instead of a Union.' Secondly, whenever Godfrey asked, he was informed by constituency workers that strong anti-conscriptionist sentiment existed, especially in the rural areas. Two courses were open. Conscription could be de-emphasized; this, of course, was unthinkable. The other alternative, a direct appeal to the rural areas doubtful about conscription, which, if necessary, would exempt those areas from the burden of conscription, was accordingly chosen.[18]

More than anything else, the Sifton-Godfrey exchange was prompted by the astonishing figures on registration and exemption under the recently passed Military Service Act. By 10 November, the final date for registration, only 21,568 had reported for service, and fully 316,376 had applied for exemption.[19] These claims for exemption came not only from Quebec, where they had been anticipated, but also from the heart of Ontario and other portions of 'loyal Canada.' Borden, like Sifton and Godfrey, saw that many farmers were opposing conscription because it would deprive them of labour at a time when agricultural prosperity was great. On 20 November Borden openly criticized the tribunals created to consider claims for exemption. In Quebec, they had been too lenient; in other provinces, too harsh: 'exemption has been refused to men long engaged in agricultural production without whose labour such production could not be continued.'[20] Accordingly, special representatives of the minister of militia would review the decisions of the exemption tribunals and reverse unfair edicts. Not for the first time, Borden treated Quebec as a province unlike the others.

Pressed by his opponents to justify this action, Borden adopted what Richard Hofstadter in another context has termed the 'paranoid style': the opposition is

18 Sifton to Godfrey, 8 Nov., Godfrey to Sifton, 9 Nov. 1917, PAC, Sifton Papers, v. 205; see also, J.W. Dafoe, *Clifford Sifton in Relation to His Times* (Toronto, 1931), 437-43.
19 Hopkins, *Canadian Annual Review, 1917*, 351.
20 Cited in the *Globe*, Toronto, 21 Nov. 1917. See also C.F. Paul to Rowell, 23 Nov. 1917, PAC, Rowell Papers, v. 4; W.R. Young, 'Conscription, Rural Depopulation, and the Farmers of Ontario, 1917-19,' *Canadian Historical Review*, LIII (Sept. 1972), 289-320; and R.W. Trowbridge, 'War-time Discontent and the Rise of the United Farmers of Ontario,' unpublished MA thesis, University of Waterloo, 1966. Although the farmers

conceived of as an evil conspiracy acting to undermine the nation; hence unusual measures are acceptable.[21] The interests of the nation were ever more closely linked with the interests of Unionism. Even the principle of conscription could be altered to meet the needs of the party. Thus, tribunals were instructed to be exacting when applying guidelines for exemption in Quebec where Unionism had little chance, and to be flexible in the Unionist stronghold of Ontario.[22] Moreover, General S.C. Mewburn, minister of militia, tried to quell the storm of protest in farmers' newspapers in Ontario by promising the exemption of farmers' sons 'honestly engaged in the production of food.'[23] Appeals were also made to the anti-French and anti-Catholic prejudices of the normally Protestant Ontario farmer by linking Laurier with Bourassa and the Catholic Church.[24] Yet all these moves seemed ineffective: Foster wrote in his diary on 27 November, 'wherever a farmer is found an opponent develops.'

Special measures were called for; Sir Clifford Sifton had already thought of one — further assurance of the exemption of agricultural workers by means of an order-in-council. On 3 December such an order was published, stating that whenever an agricultural worker had had his exemption denied by a tribunal, the minister of militia would review his case and exempt the worker if he believed the person was 'promoting agricultural production.'[25] The procedure was

were already suffering from a labour shortage, agricultural prosperity throughout Canada was extremely high. The following is the value of field crops to 1917 from official statistics:

1910	$384,513,795
1914	638,580,300
1915	825,370,600
1916	886,494,900

Hopkins, *Canadian Annual Review, 1917*, 370-1. On wartime prosperity and its effects, see John H. Thompson, ' "Permanently Wasteful but Immediately Profitable": Prairie Agriculture and the Great War,' paper presented at 1976 meeting of the Canadian Historical Association.

21 *The Paranoid Style in American Politics and Other Essays* (New York, 1965). Hofstadter was speaking largely of the American radical right.

22 *Globe*, Toronto, 21 Nov. 1917; Union Government Publicity Committee, *The Farmers' Son and Conscription* (Toronto, 1917).

23 Cited in Hopkins, *Canadian Annual Review, 1917*, 352; and Young, 'Conscription, Rural Depopulation,' 305-7.

24 Borden told his colleagues that Bourassa and Laurier must be linked together and be shown as the traitors they were. Borden to Foster, C.J. Doherty, and J.D. Reid, n.d. (Nov. 1917), BP, v. 16.

25 See Main Johnson Diary, Dec. 1917, MTCL, Johnson Papers, for an excellent account of a secret Sifton trip to Toronto on this matter. See also Godfrey to Sifton, 19 Dec. 1917, Sifton Papers, v. 205. The phrase from the order was cited in the *Globe*, 4 Dec. 1917.

undoubtedly satisfactory to farmers in Ontario, if not to their counterparts in Quebec.

Although Godfrey later, on 19 December, praised Sifton for his 'energetic handling of the situation' which, he claimed, 'saved the day,' the danger was almost surely exaggerated. A close scrutiny of the papers and diaries of Liberals in late November finds little optimism about their prospects in Ontario.[26] While it is true, as O.D. Skelton remarked at the time, that a town-country split on conscription in Ontario was a definite factor, the frantic actions of late November and early December can best be explained by the almost obsessive need for victory felt by Unionist leaders and their increasing irritation at the difficulties of imposing their will on truculent local organizations. Whatever the reason, the action was embarrassing, a betrayal of doubt, and a source of another grievance for French Canadians.

Even more controversial, however, was the late November decision to employ every means available to swing the potentially decisive soldier vote. W.T.R. Preston, the Liberal overseas scrutineer, has left a vivid and, indeed, lurid account of the overseas events in his autobiography. In Preston's words, 'Never can there have been such frauds, never an election such a travesty.' Most of Preston's charges can never be proven, and Roger Graham has shown that in certain matters Preston was quite wrong, perhaps deliberately so.[27] Still, there can be little doubt that gross irregularities occurred, particularly in the directing of votes towards certain constituencies where it seemed that they might be needed. The pattern of the soldier vote is itself almost irrefutable evidence of this. As Godfrey Langlais sarcastically wrote, it appeared that 'Des quatre coins de la planete, une pensée amantée a dirigé le cœur de ces hommes vers le Temiscamingue, terre de prédilection et d'espérance.'[28]

That the tendency for votes to be cast in close constituencies was not accidental is clear from a letter from Joseph Hayes, Unionist scrutineer in France, to

26 The King Diary is especially notable in this regard. Throughout the month of November the Liberal candidate for North York was convinced of defeat for himself and his party in Ontario. The H.H. Dewart (PAC), Charles Murphy (PAC), and Laurier Papers tend to confirm this impression.

27 Preston, *My Generation of Politics and Politicians* (Toronto, 1927), 386; see generally, chaps. 46-7. Graham, *Arthur Meighen*, I, 255. Preston, a former Liberal organizer, was popularly known as 'Hug-the-Machine Preston.' While a civil servant in Ontario he sent a telegram to a winning candidate in a provincial by-election requesting him to 'Hug the machine for me.' A Conservative telegraph operator passed over the message to party officials who promptly published it. Preston retained the sobriquet for life. See P.D. Ross, *Retrospects of a Newspaper Person* (Toronto, 1931), 126-7.

28 Langlais to Laurier, 15 Jan. 1918, Laurier Papers, v. 721 (some accents are missing in the original). Langlais represented Laurier as an agent in Europe for the election. He was speaking of Frank Cochrane's constituency.

F.B. McCurdy. This letter, found in the Borden Papers, is a remarkably frank account of the means used by the Unionists to sway the vote.

Many [officers in charge] lined their men up and told them plainly what they wanted them to do as a matter of duty. Colonel Blois of 25 was one. Also many of the Chaplains took the stump and gave 10 minute addresses before the curtain at the shows each night. Great enthusiasm was worked up by polling day and seemed to increase ... The special places I was asked to secure extra votes for, i.e., loose or non-resident votes were Ottawa 200, North Perth 200, Lennox 300, South Perth 200, South Grey 200, South Hamilton 200, Peel 200, Peterboro West 200, Waterloo North 300, East Hamilton 200, Pictou, Lunenburg, Hants, Digby, Annapolis, Cape Breton South and Richmond. I apportioned all the units in the whole four divisions among these constituencies. I got Stanley Johnson off duty early and set him to work north of Houdan and he was turning all the loose votes in his area into Colchester. It was only yesterday your cable was forwarded from London stating that your opponent had dropped out. Had we known earlier we could have utilized your vote to good advantage elsewhere.

Preston's characteristic hyperbole cannot obscure the large measure of truth which his charges bear.[29]

The farmers' exemption and soldiers' vote incidents are significant in that they undermined the 'respectability' of Unionist political leadership. After all, Unionism had grown out of the intense idealism of the war, and was justified by its integrity, its call to sacrifice, and its difference from the corrupt political parties of an earlier day. Respectability was therefore imperative, especially for the Liberal Unionists. The shoddy tactics of the 3 December order-in-council and the military vote chipped away public confidence in the probity of the Unionist movement. Never again could victory be complete.

On 17 December 1917 the bitterest campaign in Canadian history ended with a decisive Unionist majority. Borden gathered with some intimate friends in the Senate Chamber to learn the results which were beyond his expectations.[30] Only two

---

29 Hayes to McCurdy, 18 Dec. 1917, BP, v. 79. A soldier could vote in any constituency if he was not in Canada when he enlisted, could not name any place where he resided at least 4 of the 12 months preceding service, could not state an electoral district, or if he could not state any place where he had resided in Canada. Obviously only a very small number should have qualified for the floating vote. Preston sent numerous cables to Laurier pointing out the abuses. These were intercepted by the censor, forwarded to A.E. Kemp, overseas minister of militia, who then sent them on to Borden. See PAC, Kemp Papers, v. 5. A.R.M. Lower, an eyewitness at a poll at Dunkirk, found the number of voters who turned up calling themselves 'Canadians' was 'distinctly surprising.' *Colony to Nation* (4th ed., Don Mills, 1964), 469n.

30 Borden, *Memoirs*, II, 765.

TABLE 10.1

Comparison of prediction and results of general election of 1917

	Prediction*		Results		Percentage of popular vote	
	Union	Liberal	Union	Liberal	Union	Liberal
Prince Edward Island	2	2	2	2	50	50
Nova Scotia	8	6	12	4	48	46
New Brunswick	6	5	7	4	59	41
Quebec	5	60	3	62	25	73
Ontario	72	10	74	8	62	34
Manitoba	10	4	14	1	80	20
Saskatchewan	12	4	16	0	74	26
Alberta	8	4	11	1	61	36
British Columbia	11	2	13	0	68	26
Yukon			1	0		
Total	134	97	152	82	57	40

*Four seats were omitted from the prediction because of deferred votes − one in Manitoba, two in Nova Scotia, and the Yukon seat. All were expected to go Unionist and all did.
Source: The prediction was given to the *Manitoba Free Press* by one of the Unionist organizers, probably Calder, and was published on 15 Dec. 1917. The results are taken from Hugh Thorburn, ed., *Party Politics in Canada* (Toronto, 1963), 155-67.

days before the election, the Unionists' own predictions had foreseen 134 Unionist seats and 97 Laurierite seats, a relatively close guess. The predicted distribution is worthy of comparison with the actual results (see Table 10.1). The relative accuracy of the prediction suggests that the Unionists realized that the election could be more accurately forecast than most because of the one predominant issue, conscription, and the clarity of the choice. The landslide in Quebec for Laurier and in Ontario and the west for Borden were both anticipated. Eighty per cent of the Quebec population was French Canadian; 73 per cent voted for the Liberal party.[31] In the 1942 plebiscite on the government's pledge of no conscription, approximately 74 per cent in Quebec voted against freeing the government from the pledge; in the 1917 general election, 73 per cent in Quebec cast their ballot against the Union government. The results starkly illustrate the dilemma of

31 *Sixth Census of Canada, 1921* (Ottawa, 1924), I, 406-7. In dealing with the Quebec vote in 1917, we must remember that English-Canadian women in Quebec were far more likely to be enfranchised in 1917 than French-Canadian women because their relatives were more likely to have enlisted.

Unionism. While maximizing support in English Canada by emphasizing conscription, Unionists knowingly assured a solid Quebec for Laurier and his successor.

The impressionistic or, perhaps more accurately, the qualitative evidence cited above clearly indicates why the Unionists and the Liberals regarded the election as a conscription plebiscite. Before 17 December the leaders of both parties anticipated that the results of the election would reflect a split on racial and, to a lesser degree, rural-urban lines. But did this in fact occur? Although the pattern of representation suggests that it did, further inquiry is necessary. Two questions are therefore proposed: first, where did the Unionists derive their support and, secondly, what type of members did Unionist voters elect?

A modern election study would employ survey data and aggregate data on the characteristics of the electorate to determine why citizens voted as they did. Unfortunately, the election of 1917 is not amenable to such an inquiry. Not only is survey data unavailable for 1917 but also the 1917 election featured constituencies so altered through the devices of the War-time Elections Act and the Military Voters' Act that aggregate data is of minimal use.[32] Neither before nor later did the electorate possess the strange contours it possessed in 1917. We are therefore limited to two relatively straightforward topics: the kind of ridings the Unionists won; and the impact of the special regulations of 1917 upon the results.

Canada in 1917 was on the point of emergence as an urban nation, but politically it remained a rural nation to an astonishing extent. The 1921 census indicated that 49.42 per cent of the population lived in cities, towns, or incorporated villages, but this was not reflected in the make-up of political constituencies. Thus, fully 117 of the Unionists' 152 seats were rurally controlled. This anomaly is best seen in Ontario. In 1921 over 56 per cent of Ontario's population lived in incorporated areas, but, at that same time, 50 of Ontario's 82 federal ridings were 'rural ridings.' This pattern was followed across Canada, more extremely in some provinces than in others.[33] Here we can see why Sifton and Borden were so fearful of the alienation of the farm vote: each ballot cast by the farmer could equal two or more cast in the city. Unionism, a

---

32 The effect of these acts is shown in the percentage of the total population of each province which was enfranchised:

Prince Edward Island	33.3	Manitoba	29.3
Nova Scotia	29.7	Saskatchewan	22.9
New Brunswick	29.9	Alberta	32.5
Quebec	20.6	British Columbia	38.4
Ontario	39.4		

Note the total for Quebec; disfranchisement explains the low figure for Saskatchewan. Roman March, 'An Empirical Test of M. Ostrogorski's Theory of Political Evolution in a British Parliamentary System,' unpublished PhD thesis, Indiana University, 1968, 90.

movement emanating from urban English Canada and reflecting its values, found itself forced to consider the increasingly exclusive aims and needs of rural Canada.

Town and country were an obvious division in Canadian life in 1917, but to most contemporary observers racial differences were thought to be a more fundamental source of conflict. Having examined the Unionist appeal, one is not surprised to learn that Unionist constituencies were overwhelmingly British in composition:[34]

	Unionist	Liberal
British majority	134	11
French majority	2	65
German majority	0	2
Mixed	16	4

The age-worn cliché that the 1917 election arrayed French Canada against united English Canada apparently underscores a basic truth. Of the 67 French-Canadian seats, 59 of them in Quebec, Liberals won 65, nearly all with solid majorities. Liberals also won the two predominantly German seats in Canada, Waterloo North and Lunenburg, which were two constituencies whose German population had long ago settled in Canada. That voting behaviour was influenced greatly by racial background is undeniable.

33 The following indicates for each province the number of urban seats as a percentage of the total number of constituencies in the province:

	Urban seats	Total seats	Overall percentage of population in urban areas
Prince Edward Island	0	4	22
Nova Scotia	3	14	43
New Brunswick	1	11	32
Quebec	24	65	56
Ontario	32	82	56
Manitoba	3	14	43
Saskatchewan	2	16	29
Alberta	3	12	38
British Columbia	4	13	47

Sixth Census of Canada, 1921, I, 11-218 passim, 346. Percentage in final column are rounded. There are some cases, particularly in British Columbia, where areas not yet incorporated are nevertheless urban in character and are considered as such. All calculations are my own.

34 Ibid., 346-81. It should also be noted that although British Canadians made up 55 per cent of the population they controlled 62 per cent of the seats. French Canadians controlled 28 per cent of the seats and were almost exactly the same percentage of the population.

The 'mixed' ridings are most difficult to evaluate because of the War-time Elections Act. In a study of the impact of this act Joseph Boudreau suggested that four Alberta seats — Battle River, Bow River, Edmonton West, and Strathcona — would probably have gone Liberal in the absence of the special franchise. In Saskatchewan, Boudreau found that Mackenzie, where 42 per cent of the population was of German-Austrian-Ukrainian origin, Saltcoats, Prince Albert, Swift Current, and Humboldt might also have been affected. In Manitoba, only Selkirk and Springfield were greatly influenced by the operation of the act. In Boudreau's view, then, the War-time Elections Act transferred as many as eleven seats from the Liberal to the Unionist columns.[35]

This argument is unconvincing, primarily because it fails to take into account the overall size of the electorate, voter turnout, and the impact of the enfranchisement of soldiers' relatives. In Battle River, for example, the Unionist candidate secured 5733 votes and the Liberal 4195 in a constituency whose total population was 49,173 (1921 census). Only 20 per cent of the total population therefore cast a ballot. It would be unreasonable to assume that more than one-fifth of the 5344 enemy aliens in the constituency would have voted, that is, approximately 1070 voters, considerably less than the Unionist majority even if unanimous support for the Liberals can be granted. Of course, this argument belies Boudreau's handling of other constituencies as well. Furthermore, turnout would likely have been considerably lower among German-Austrians than among Canadians of British extraction, since the enlistments which were the *sine qua non* for female registration came much more frequently in British-Canadian areas than in German-Canadian ones. The War-time Elections Act may have been the midwife of Union government in bringing out the western Liberals, but it was most certainly not the device which assured Unionist victory. In fact, it probably guaranteed not a seat.

When the effect of the War-time Elections Act is combined with that of the Military Voters' Act, however, one must admit considerable impact. Contemporary journalists unanimously agreed that the turnout of soldiers' female kin was extremely high, with estimates of their numbers ranging anywhere from 500,000 to one million.[36] Senator Foster's tribute to the Unionist women in

35 'The Enemy Alien Problem in Canada, 1914-1921,' unpublished PhD thesis, University of California at Los Angeles, 1965, 150, 162. Battle River had 5433 enemy aliens, 5733 Unionist votes, and 4195 Liberal; Bow River, 3311 aliens, 3737 Unionists, 2996 Liberals; Edmonton West, 6042 aliens, 9367 Unionists, and 6939 Liberals; and Strathcona, 6251 aliens, 5777 Unionists, and 3178 Liberals.
36 Hopkins, *Canadian Annual Review, 1917*, 631; *Manitoba Free Press*, 19 Dec. 1917; and the *Globe*, 20 Dec. 1917.

Montreal has already been noted. In Toronto, too, Main Johnson exuberantly noted the long lines of women at the polls as 'the first actual evidence which we had that the situation was favourable.' No one doubted how the women would vote, and one angry Liberal listed women as second only to preachers as the 'curs' who defeated his beloved Laurier.[37]

Fortunately, the examination of the soldiers' vote need not be so impressionistic. Of the entire vote for Union, slightly over one-fifth (20.41 per cent) was cast by Canadian soldiers. An astonishing 92.1 per cent of these ballots were marked for the government candidate, a percentage which probably exceeded the wildest imaginings of Unionist organizers. The soldiers' vote determined the outcome in fourteen ridings, and is perhaps the strongest testimony of the extent to which the election was narrowed to become a plebiscite on the war.[38] In January 1917 both Tories and Liberals sensed a general disgust with the government among the soldiers. Eleven months later, disillusion undoubtedly remained, but it was not expressed by an opposition ballot in the polling station.

Another topic which we must consider is what type of men the Unionist voters elected. Any parliamentary party is an exaggerated reflection of its much broader national support. In Canada with its characteristic diversity, the racial, religious, and professional character of the parliamentary party is of particular interest. In this light, the most remarkable feature of the Unionist parliamentary party was its homogeneity. The Unionist boast was ominously true; it was not a party like other parties.

It is only appropriate that racial background should be the first aspect of our inquiry. The census of Canada in 1921 revealed that 55.40 per cent of the nation's population was of 'British race,' 27.91 per cent 'French,' and 14.16 per cent 'other European.' Only three Unionist members could possibly be considered 'other European,' and all three were descendants of immigrants who had come to Canada in the early nineteenth century. In Saskatchewan where 'other European races' made up approximately 45 per cent of the population, all the Unionist candidates were of British background. Even more indicative of the British-Canadian constitution of Unionism is the lack of French-Canadian membership in the caucus. Although 28 per cent of the Canadian population was French Canadian, only one Unionist member was a French Canadian. He was

37 Senator James Domville to Laurier, 18 Dec. 1917, Laurier Papers, v. 718. Johnson Diary, 17 Dec. 1917.
38 'Return of the Thirteenth General Election,' *Sessional Papers,* 1920, no. 13. The fullest account of the effect of Military Voters' Act is Desmond Morton, 'Polling the Soldier Vote: The Overseas Campaign in the Canadian General Election of 1917,' *Journal of Canadian Studies* (Nov. 1975), 39-58.

TABLE 10.2

Religious background of Unionist members 1917

	Number	Percentage of total caucus	Percentage of group in the population	Percentage of 1909 Conservatives*
Anglican	37	24.3	16.0	37.9
Presbyterian	58	38.2	16.0	19.5
Methodist	31	20.4	13.1	20.6
Roman Catholic	5	3.2	38.6	13.7
Baptist	7	4.6	4.8	2.0
Other Protestant	6	3.9		5.0
Unknown	8	5.2		0

*For the 1909 Conservative analysis see Table 2.2. Individual percentages do not add up to 100 per cent because of 'rounding.'
Source: *Sixth Census of Canada, 1921*, I, 571; and *The Canadian Parliamentary Guide, 1918*.

J.L. Chabot, an Ottawa physician who, in his biographical sketch, called himself an imperialist. Ninety-seven per cent of the Unionist members, 148 of 152, were British Canadian in background.[39] Racially, Unionism was a monolith.

Chabot, the sole French Canadian, also had the distinction of being one of the few Roman Catholic Unionist members. Although Roman Catholics comprised almost 39 per cent of the Canadian population (21 per cent of the population outside of Quebec), they were virtually unrepresented in the Unionist party. Even more striking is the extraordinary preponderance of the two established churches of Great Britain as well as Methodism among the Unionists. The figures in Table 10.2 deserve some comment. First, the relative decrease in the number of Anglicans in the Unionist caucus compared to the 1909 Tory caucus is a reflection of Unionist strength in areas such as the Canadian west where Anglicanism was not so strong as in Ontario.[40] The surge, relatively and absolutely, in the Presbyterian total is largely attributable to the

39 James Bowman and J.J. Merner both appear to have been of German extraction and from the Berlin area in Ontario. W.A. Griesbach was of Austrian and German extraction. The latter had become an Anglican; the other two Methodists. The sources for biographical information are H. Morgan, *Canadian Men and Women of the Time* (Toronto, 1912); J.K. Johnson, *The Canadian Directory of Parliament* (Ottawa, 1968); and E.J. Chambers, ed., *The Canadian Parliamentary Guide, 1918* (Ottawa, 1918). Statistics are from *Sixth Census of Canada, 1921*, I, 353, 355.
40 There were fewer Anglicans than either Presbyterians or Methodists in the west. See *Sixth Census of Canada, 1921*, I, 573.

The plebiscite on conscription 201

TABLE 10.3

Occupations of Unionist members 1917

	Number	Percentage of total	Percentage of 1909 Conservatives*
Lawyers	41	27.0	29.9
Farmers	28	18.0	11.5
Manufacturers	23	15.2	11.5
Merchants	15	9.9	14.9
Doctors	15	9.9	11.5
Financiers	10	6.5	6.8
Others	10	6.5	6.8
Journalists	9	5.9	3.4
Unknown	1	.6	3.4

*See Chapter 2, p. 40. In both 1909 and 1918 mining entrepreneurs were included as manufacturers.
Source: *The Canadian Parliamentary Guide, 1918*, and *Who's Who and Why, 1917-18* (Toronto, n.d.).

influx of Liberal Unionists (Presbyterians in Canada as in Scotland normally voted Liberal), and to the Unionist success on the prairies where so many hardy Scottish pioneers had made their homes. For example, ten of the sixteen Unionist members from Saskatchewan were Presbyterian. Overall, the Presbyterian and Methodist majority which existed in the caucus seemed a guarantee of government support for the 'social gospel,' and especially for prohibition, a cause strongly endorsed by both churches. In religion as in race, Unionism overwhelmingly represented the British-Canadian segment of the population.

Race and religion are easier subjects to discuss than the social and economic backgrounds of the Unionist members. The quality of this information is not always reliable. The minister of agriculture, Thomas Crerar, for example, listed himself as a farmer and a teacher when, in reality, as president of the United Grain Growers, he was a large businessman with an annual income of $25,000.[41] Common sense must be one's guide in such matters. On the surface, the general pattern of members' occupations (see Table 10.3) conforms fairly closely to that of the 1909 Tories. In general, however, the 1917 members tended to be more notable within their respective fields than those in 1909.[42] Thus, while in 1909

41 I am indebted to R. Craig Brown for this information.
42 A conclusion such as this is necessarily impressionistic. However, anyone examining the professions of the 1917 members in a biographical dictionary cannot fail to note this fact. The 'self-made man' is especially prevalent in the Unionist ranks.

'manufacturers' were usually owners of a moderate sized industry within their own constituencies, in 1917 they controlled industries of considerable scale. Farmers, too, were now not merely individuals who had moved from the county council to reeve to the House of Commons, but individuals such as Crerar and J.A. Maharg, leaders of nationally known agricultural organizations. In short, the members of 1917 were more prominent figures, better educated and wealthier, but with little previous political experience.

The great increase in the number of farmers was the product of the victory in the Canadian west. Their presence promised to be a disruptive one in a caucus that included so many manufacturers and financiers, their avowed enemies. When the war ceased to bind these individuals together, serious conflicts were certain to occur. But to conclude on this note would be misleading since the homogeneity of the Unionists is the most significant fact. In every aspect – race, religion, and profession – the Unionists represented the upper middle class of Canada. Only one worker, skilled or unskilled, sat on the Unionist benches, and only one French Canadian sat with him. Nor were there many merchants, the men of the small town, so common in earlier Parliaments. The Unionist caucus was not representative of the broad socio-economic character of Canada, but was most certainly representative of the class which controlled and, according to John Porter, has continued to control, the majority of the nation's economic resources. The wartime Union government was the high tide of political involvement of this nationalist,[43] Protestant, and British sector of the population.

For all their similarities, the Unionists nevertheless lacked homogeneity in one crucial aspect: their political backgrounds. They continued to identify themselves and to be identified as Liberal Unionists and Conservative Unionists long after the election. Even new members who had never sat in Parliament would associate themselves with one faction or the other. The practice of holding separate caucuses exacerbated the differences between the two groups.[44] Some acute observers noted that, if they chose to act together, the Liberal Unionists held the balance of power in the new Parliament.[45] An examination of the 1917 results largely validates this view (see Table 10.4). The Unionist leaders knew these statistics well and they were troubled by them. Should the Liberal

43 The usage of 'nationalist' here is similar to that of Carl Berger in *The Sense of Power* (Toronto, 1970).
44 Separate caucuses continued to be held throughout the life of Union government, usually prior to a caucus of the entire party. They were publicly reported. See, for example, the *Globe*, 19 March 1918.
45 R.M. Dawson, 'The Political Situation in Canada,' *New Republic*, XIII (12 June 1918), 304-5; and Anon. 'Canada, The General Election,' *Round Table*, VIII (1917-18), 356-63.

TABLE 10.4

Results of Canadian general election of 1917

	Liberal Unionists	Conservative Unionists*	Liberals
Prince Edward Island	0	2	2
Nova Scotia	3	9	4
New Brunswick	4	3	4
Quebec	1	2	62
Ontario	12	62	8
Manitoba	6	8	1
Saskatchewan	7	9	0
Alberta	4	6	1
British Columbia	2	11	0
Yukon	0	1	0
Total	39	113	82

*Many non-partisans were included in the Tory total. In Saskatchewan, for example, such new Unionist members as J.F. Reid and J.A. Maharg, prominent Grain Growers' officials, were really independents rather than Conservatives.
Source: M.C. Urquhart and K.H. Buckley, eds. *Historical Statistics of Canada* (Toronto, 1965), section W.

Unionists defect *en masse* after the war the Unionist majority would be seriously threatened and could even disappear. For good reason, Liberal Unionists generally declined to indicate their post-war political posture. Were they to remain in a new and permanent Unionist party or to return to their old loyalties? Were they to become an independent group, the nucleus of a long-expected third party in Canada? The answer would surely depend upon the success of the government and on the construction of the necessary apparatus for a new party.

But still there was great hope: never had a Canadian parliamentary party had such a homogeneous social structure. Never had the electorate spoken so clearly. Yet the campaign with its lack of organization and its bitter internecine quarrels gave little evidence that this homogeneity could be translated into close co-operation. Even in the flush of victory, the doubts lingered.

11

A union divides

When Sir Robert Borden revised his biographical sketch in early 1918 he stroked out 'Liberal-Conservative' and wrote 'Unionist.' Few others did. By 1922 no Unionists remained, and J.W. Dafoe could find no 'tangible and visible manifestations' of Union government's power. 'The spirit behind the movement,' he concluded, 'passed with the war ...'[1] Within four years of the triumph of 1917, Union government was quietly interred, without a ceremony and with few mourners. What brought this fate upon a government which promised to carry through 'policies quite Utopian in normal times' and whose majority spread over both sides of the Commons chamber?

Ramsay Cook and R. Craig Brown have emphasized the superficiality of wartime unity. Wartime emotion, they wrote, muted 'conflicting views' and 'a host of ethnic, regional, and class discontents.' But by the war's end, the 'government's successes were quickly forgotten, and its failings constantly held before the public. Governing had become a thankless, perhaps even a hopeless, task.'[2] This, the traditional view, has considerable merit, yet it is misleading to focus mainly upon the evanescence of patriotic fervour. There are technical and practical explanations for the Unionist decline which are usually ignored but are exceedingly important.

In the previous chapter we primarily considered the sources of Unionist strength. Let us now examine the Unionist weaknesses – perhaps best illustrated in Table 11.1. Clearly the size of the Unionist majority depended greatly upon the military vote. It is equally apparent, in light of the character of the soldiers' vote, that the almost twelve-to-one Unionist margin could not be sustained in any future election. Moreover, the female vote, which all agreed was strongly

1 *Laurier: A Study in Canadian Politics* (Toronto, 1922), 180.
2 *Canada, 1896-1921: A Nation Transformed* (Toronto, 1974), 321.

TABLE 11.1

Civilian and military support for the government and the opposition in the Canadian
general election of 1917

	Civilian votes for		Military votes for	
	Government	Opposition	Government	Opposition
Prince Edward Island	10,450	12,224	2775	434
Nova Scotia	40,985	49,831	10,699	1474
New Brunswick	35,871	32,397	9934	919
Quebec	61,808	240,504	14,206	2927
Ontario	419,928	263,300	95,212	5793
Manitoba	83,469	26,073	23,698	1157
Saskatchewan	68,424	30,829	12,996	2672
Alberta	60,399	48,865	19,575	1055
British Columbia	59,944	40,050	26,461	2059
Yukon	666	776	293	32
Total	841,944	744,849	215,849	18,522

Source: Desmond Morton, 'Polling the Soldier Vote: The Overseas Campaign in the
Canadian General Election of 1917,' *Journal of Canadian Studies* (Nov. 1975), 55.

Unionist in 1917, would definitely change when females unrelated to soldiers
could vote. Indeed, the result might have been quite different in 1917 had these
other women possessed the franchise. Finally, we have the disfranchised of
1917. In the future, they were perhaps the strongest opponents of Unionism and
its legacy. In 1917 manipulation of the franchise was unnecessary, but it was
possible; in the next election it might well be necessary, but it would most
certainly be impossible.

The opposition, then, was stronger than it appeared to be, and, as Cook and
Brown point out, Unionism was weaker. Neither in the election campaign nor in
the Union government did the Liberal Unionists and the Conservatives coalesce.
For the Liberal Unionists, coalition was expedient in the fall of 1917. As one
Nova Scotia Liberal wrote to W.S. Fielding in 1918, entering the Union govern-
ment 'saved the Liberal party from a very undesirable defensive attitude which
they would be called upon to face and explain for a generation to come ...'[3]
Liberal Unionists held separate caucuses, maintained Liberal friendships, and
thought themselves distinct. When, therefore, Unionism attracted heavy fire, the
Liberal Unionists were, on the whole, quite willing to abandon the front lines,

3 Robert Trevill to Fielding, 16 Dec. 1918, PANS, Fielding Papers, box 525.

even if their erstwhile Liberal colleagues left 'no light in the window.'[4] Was this inevitable? What responsibility for the decline of Unionism does Borden bear?

LEADERSHIP

Historians have never disputed the charge, so frequently made by contemporaries, that the Unionist crisis was primarily one of leadership.[5] In the parliamentary system the leadership of a party lies mainly with the prime minister. For this reason, nothing illustrates the Unionists' problem so well as a tale related by the former parliamentary correspondent, Arthur Ford: 'After the Unionist election of 1917 Sir Robert never learned to know by name or by sight half of the supporters of the new government.' On one occasion, a flabbergasted new member of Parliament, undoubtedly intoxicated with the eminence of his new office, had a letter thrust into his hands by Borden with the instruction that he should deliver it to a minister.[6] Seldom has a member been mistaken for a Commons page boy, but then seldom was a party leader so remote from his party as Borden was after 1917.

This neglect of Parliament must have seemed incomprehensible. After all, was not the Unionist party Borden's most significant personal achievement and did it not represent the kind of political transformation which he had so long craved? The campaign had led to too much bickering, but it had also ended in triumph, and the possibilities for Union seemed unlimited. Borden, however, did not think of the future in parliamentary terms. He had promised decisiveness both in his post-election message and in his post-election correspondence. The people, he announced, 'have realized and splendidly fulfilled their duty'; the government would now perform its.[7] To those who had shirked responsibility and who now stood alone, Borden promised nothing other than 'an opportunity of seriously considering the position in which they have placed themselves.'[8] Rejecting calls to move deliberately, Borden moved to take advantage of the Unionist mandate. In rapid succession he acted to abolish patronage, to take over the national

---

4 Margaret Prang, *N.W. Rowell: Ontario Nationalist* (Toronto, 1975), chap. 18, title.

5 Among the best known of the contemporary analyses were Arthur Hawkes, *The Birthright* (Toronto, 1919); and 'Domino' (Augustus Bridle), *The Masques of Ottawa* (Toronto, 1921), 27-38.

6 Arthur Ford, *As the World Wags On* (Toronto, 1950), 141. Robert Manion in his autobiography tells how Laurier would take the care and the time to congratulate the new members on their speeches while Borden was aloof. *Life Is an Adventure* (Toronto, 1936), 237-8.

7 Cited in the *Toronto Star*, 18 Dec. 1917.

8 Borden to Hume Cronyn, 18 Jan. 1918, PAC, Borden Papers (BP), v. 101.

railways, to bring more order into the Canadian war effort, to step more boldly into the international arena with the establishment of a Canadian war mission in Washington, and to reward Unionism's strongest supporters by the grant of the franchise to women. He correctly noted in his *Memoirs* 'the tremendous variety and volume of important questions that continually surged upon [him].'[9] In dealing with all these questions, his actions reflected his belief that the election had given him a mandate for strong government, committed to the European war and to national reform.

Further evidence of Borden's early determination was his rapid decision to abolish the farmers' exemption when told that the war situation was 'desperate.'[10] Similarly, when riots erupted in Quebec City over the Military Service Act, he announced that anyone who obstructed federal authorities would be 'forthwith enrolled in the military forces of Canada.'[11] An even more telling symbol, perhaps, was the extraordinary order-in-council requiring that every able male between sixteen and sixty should be gainfully employed or face imprisonment.[12] Borden had always profoundly believed in the need for structure, form, and discipline in Canadian life, qualities which he felt were lacking in pre-war Canada. Now the war offered the opportunity to provide education 'by the current event,' as Jane Addams once said in another context. Part of that education must necessarily be such didactic legislation as the 'anti-loafing law'; and since, in Borden's view, the state finally possessed the moral authority to pass such legislation, it should employ this authority to the fullest extent.

Characteristically, Borden never clearly articulated his notion of leadership after 1917, but his actions nevertheless provide an excellent chart. At first, he appeared to be carrying the logic of the campaign to its conclusion by the formation of a forceful English-Canadian party. His concern was with the domestic situation; his posture was surprisingly aggressive. So important did he consider the task of remaking the Canadian state that he told Sir Thomas White

9 See Henry Borden, ed., *Robert Laird Borden: His Memoirs* (Toronto, 1938), II, 786-8. See also BP, Borden Diary, 14 Jan. (railways) and 28 Jan. 1917 (civil service reform).
10 Borden Diary, 12 Jan. 1917; 'Memorandum on Operation of Act,' and Rowell to Borden, 24 March 1918, PAC, Rowell Papers, v. 4; Sifton to Borden, 24 March 1918, BP, v. 101; and Prang, *N.W. Rowell*, chap. 14.
11 Borden also became involved in a bitter dispute with the local authorities whom he felt were not upholding the law. See his *Memoirs*, II, 791-2.
12 Borden, *A Speech before the United Kingdom Branch of the Empire Parliamentary Association, London, England, June 21, 1918*, PAC, pamphlet in library. Borden told this group that the 'anti-loafing law' was a very good law in wartime and probably 'an equally good law in time of peace.'

in February 1918 that he did not want to go to the Imperial Conference. To P.E. Blondin he wrote: 'it is open to question whether I can be of more use to Canada and to the Empire by remaining at home than by any work which I can accomplish overseas.' Yet on 24 May 1918 Borden left for England for the Imperial War Conference and the Imperial War Cabinet. Evidently, he had changed his mind. Perhaps he had, as he later claimed, 'measurably overtaken every matter that required [his] personal attention.'[13] There are, however, other, more convincing, reasons.

On 3 May Borden sent out a 'Confidential Memorandum to the English Press' suggesting that 'there is the best reason for believing that a remarkable change of sentiment is beginning to develop in the Province of Quebec in respect of the attitude of that Province towards the war. The recent drastic change in the Military Service Act [the ending of exemptions] has been received in excellent spirit by the French-Canadian population.'[14] A few days later Borden asked his bitter enemy of 1917, Sir Lomer Gouin, to join his government. When the Quebec premier pleaded age as an excuse (this must have shocked Borden who was older than Gouin), Borden told him that during his absence 'Quebec would be in his charge both provincially and federally.'[15] This surely is an astonishing statement in the light of Borden's own attitude less than two months earlier. It parallels a marked change of mood which is also reflected in his diary, from a determination to remake the nation to, almost, a disinterest in domestic affairs.[16]

One reason for the transition was simply the exhaustion of the sixty-three-year-old prime minister.[17] More important, however, was Borden's realization that the 1917 election had not created a *tabula rasa* upon which a new political system could be composed. Frankly, he misread the results, and the old problems reappeared very soon. The nation seemed unwilling to accept the responsibility thrust upon it. Borden himself believed that '... he who performs willingly

---

13 Borden to White, 19 Feb. 1918, BP, v. 96; Borden to Blondin, 13 March 1918, BP, v. 232; *Memoirs*, II, 806.
14 3 May 1918, BP, v. 101; see also Borden to W.R. Givens, 6 May 1918, *ibid.*
15 Borden Diary, 11 May 1918; and Borden, *Memoirs*, II, 805. Gouin's brilliant speech in opposition to the Francoeur motion which proposed the secession of Quebec won him much favour in the previously hostile English-Canadian press. See, for example, *Toronto Mail and Empire*, 25 Jan., and *Quebec Chronicle*, 18 Jan. 1918.
16 Borden Diary, Feb.-May 1918, *passim*. Borden even left Ottawa without giving his ministers instructions. An angry Foster wrote in his diary on 24 May: 'the usual haphazard leavetaking.' PAC, Foster Diary.
17 On Borden's health problems, see 'Interview with Dr. Campbell Laidlaw' (Borden's physician), PAC, Oral History Section.

and earnestly the service to which his duty calls him helps to hold the line against the enemy; he who shrinks from that duty, or neglects it, strengthens the enemy's line.'[18] But neglect soon became apparent everywhere, not only among the young men who defiantly pressed for exemptions and among the French Canadians, but in the heartland of Unionist strength and in the cabinet itself. There was, almost immediately after the election, a sense that a more interventionist government did not mean a more obedient population. Old doubts resurfaced; new fears thrived.

The atmosphere in the cabinet is described in the early 1918 entries in Sir George Foster's diary:

Jan. 15. Canada is waking up to the food question and the necessity of our saving and sending overseas — at a good price. Really how little we sense the reality of war suffering. Our country farming people deny themselves little or nothing — demand the most extravagant prices for all they produce, and yet they think they are helping to win the war! ... the well to do in towns and cities deny themselves little or nothing — they give liberally many of them, but sacrifice nothing.

Jan. 23. The C[ivil] S[ervice] Board has done nothing yet ...

Jan. 28. The M[ilitary] S[ervice] Act goes slowly and results are doubtful so far as our getting the 100,000 men.

Jan. 29. The Russian Revolution had started the world movement for war between the proletariat and other classes.

Feb. 6. Yet how little we sacrifice! Of nine women more or less prominent in the Can. Club here, it transpired during a conversation that only one was observing meatless days. Other Red Cross workers use coal to keep their motorcars warm. I often ask if in Britain and Canada class and labor upheavals could result in murder and [revolution]. Dare one say 'impossible'?

March 6. Truly the world is in ferment. In Canada the public nerves are on edge and ready to respond to every critical or querulous touch. There are doctors or quacks innumerable.[19]

18 Borden, *Canada at War* (n.p., 1918), 16.
19 This is a handwritten diary and, although the gist of Foster's remarks is clear, punctuation and individual words are often illegible.

The world was indeed in ferment, and Borden knew no panaceas for its sores. Statistics on strikes and cost of living as well as enlistment were symptoms of an ailment whose causes remained inscrutable.[20] There is no need to detail here the varieties of dissent and public recalcitrance; our concern, rather, is their impact upon Unionist leadership. This was profound and prompt. As the Unionists perceived that their conception of their authority was erroneous, their resolve diminished, and ministers became uneasy and irritable. Backbenchers joined some ministers in an unseemly squabble over civil service reform, a showpiece of the Unionist platform during the campaign.[21] Others retreated in the face of the farmers' wrath.[22] Rivalries plagued the cabinet. James Calder accused White of covertly seeking Borden's office; Frank Carvell asked that his fellow Liberal Unionist N.W. Rowell be given a seat in the second row in the Commons.[23] Borden initially believed that Unionism brought a 'revolution' in Canadian politics, and indeed the Unionist régime was a productive one. But he soon realized that the 'revolution' would be incomplete, forever lacking the richness of its promise. Borden, weary of the battle and with a concern for posterity, turned his attention to what he believed could be another, more successful, revolution – a revolution in constitutional practice.

To this end, he devoted virtually all his talents, energies, and time. In the hundred weeks from 24 May 1918, when he left for Britain, until his official retirement on 7 July 1920, Borden spent approximately seventy-eight weeks

20

	Strikes	Wholesale price index (1900 = 100)
1915	63	142.3
1916	120	176.6
1917	160	236.7
1918	230	256.5

M.C. Urquhart and K.H. Buckley, eds., *Historical Statistics of Canada* (Toronto, 1965), 107, 291.

21 Borden Diary, 11 May 1918; Foster Diary, 12 March, 11 May 1918, Foster Papers; and Roger Graham, *Arthur Meighen: The Door of Opportunity* (Toronto, 1960), I, 196.
Graham notes that Meighen, who was considered progressive by many at the time, was not favourably inclined towards civil service reform. Undoubtedly, Meighen felt that he needed patronage for his forthcoming struggle with Robert Rogers for party dominance in the west.

22 Borden Diary, 14 April 1918; T.A. Crerar to W.R. Motherwell, 3 and 20 April 1918, PAC, Motherwell Papers, M 12; The *Weekly Sun*, Toronto, 22 May, described Crerar's action during a mass farmers' protest: 'Crerar was the most restless of the lot, and frequently looked at his watch or shifted in his chair, at times hiding his eyes with his hand...'

23 Borden Diary, 1 Feb., 22 March, 7 May, 23 Aug. 1918; and Foster Diary, 20 March, 10 May, 18 May 1918.

outside Ottawa, most of these in Europe.[24] In his absence, few instructions were left. One notes with interest that he considered his role in the creation of an international personality for Canada to be his greatest achievement, and Canadian historians, accepting his judgment, have accorded him high praise for his accomplishments.[25] On the other hand, his domestic achievements customarily receive short shrift. Borden never translated his external policy triumphs into domestic political capital as Unionists hoped he would. In fact, he scarcely seems to have tried. Few shared in the formulation of foreign policy; few shared in its successes.[26] Perhaps Borden thought that an attempt to employ his European victories for political gain would only devalue them and open them to partisan sniping. He seemed certain that posterity would regard his external achievements as the most significant work of Union government.

While the successful Canadian prime minister must be and appear to be, to borrow O.D. Skelton's term, 'the master of the administration,' leadership is not solely his prerogative or responsibility.[27] Administration necessarily rests largely with the ministers, and because of the regional, religious, and racial representation found within a Canadian cabinet, so does much of the obligation of leadership. When a prime minister lacks a strong personality, a strong cabinet can exert an unusual degree of leadership. Similarly, if a prime minister is absent, the cabinet acquires great importance. Initially, there was little concern that Borden's presence in Europe would have serious ill effects. After all, had not the *Toronto Star* declared on 18 December 1917 that no 'government in Canadian history ever possessed the moral and physical forces of Union Government?' For this reason, the collective failure of the cabinet was much more striking. Nevertheless, the cabinet from its formation possessed more flaws then the press, the Unionists, and even the opposition imagined. We have already seen some of the pre-election difficulties when jealousies and feuds threatened to undermine the Unionist effort. Rather then arresting these destructive forces, victory exacerbated them.

24 This is my own calculation. A scrap of paper found in PAC, Arthur Sifton Papers, v. 2, claims that Borden spent 55 weeks in Europe.
25 One article suggests, however, that Borden was more concerned with the externalities of Canadian autonomy rather than practical application. See S.F. Wise, 'The Borden Government and the Formation of a Canadian Flying Corps, 1911-1916,' in R. Bothwell and M. Cross, eds., *Policy by Other Means* (Toronto, 1973), 123-33. Borden's own views are found, *inter alia*, in his *Canadian Constitutional Studies* (Toronto, 1922), especially 115-38. Two 'Whig' historians who have praised Borden are Frank Underhill, 'Canada and the Last War,' in Chester Martin, ed., *Canada in Peace and War* (Toronto, 1941), 120-49; and A.R.M. Lower, *Colony to Nation* (4th ed., Don Mills, 1964), 476.
26 Among the cabinet ministers only Rowell seems to have taken an interest in foreign policy. Borden Dairy, 1918-20.
27 *Life and Letters of Sir Wilfrid Laurier* (London, 1921), chap. 13, title.

The main political task of the Union government was to weld together two political factions. To accomplish this required the identification of a Liberal spokesman who could defend Liberal interests against the Conservative preponderance until a definite *modus vivendi* could be found. N.W. Rowell served this function in the campaign, by aggressively fighting for seats in both the Commons and the cabinet. After the election, however, his role constantly diminished.[28] His place could probably have been taken by Frank Carvell, talented, relatively young, and effective in the Commons, but Carvell's bitter attacks on the old Conservative government were not forgotten. Another possibility, A.K. Maclean of Nova Scotia, Borden thought 'of little use, very slow, not very clear and not very active.'[29] C.C. Ballantyne's narrow base of support, English Quebec, made him obviously ineligible while S.C. Mewburn's inexperience was too great a liability, even for a highly popular and able minister. T.A. Crerar was too much the representative of agriculture, and Arthur Sifton was an enigma to Borden and his colleagues, a highly competent individual who seemed almost indifferent to the fate of the government.[30] The mantle therefore was placed upon the shoulders of James Calder whose qualifications were many: he had been an excellent administrator in Saskatchewan as well as a brilliant political organizer; moreover, he appeared to have the support of Saskatchewan's Premier W.M. Martin and of many other prominent western Canadian Liberals.[31] To Borden, Calder was the practical 'man of affairs' that the crusading Rowell was not.

Still, Calder was a peculiar choice, since he had insisted that his duties in the Union government should be limited, a wish he believed to have been granted when he was appointed as minister of immigration, a portfolio 'not wanted by anybody else.' Calder, weary from the provincial wars, had determined to retire from politics when Borden's call came, a call he accepted most reluctantly.[32] He

28 Rowell was personally unpopular with his colleagues. After a vicious attack on him by Charles Murphy in the House, some Tories applauded and many Liberal Unionists expressed their pleasure. See *Can. H. of C. Debates*, 19 March 1918, I, 35-44; Foster Diary, 20 March, 10 May, 20 May 1918; and Borden Diary, 7 May, 4 Nov. 1918; and Prang, *N.W. Rowell*, 240.

29 Carvell was widely believed to be 'on friendly terms with certain leaders of the opposition ...' His defection was expected from the moment the war ended. See Borden Diary, 19 June 1919, and, on Maclean, 4 Feb. 1918.

30 Even Sifton's brother could not understand his inaction. See Clifford Sifton to Dafoe, 3 Feb. 1921, PAC, Dafoe Papers, microfilm copy; Harold Daly, 'Memoirs,' PAC, Daly Papers; and Laurier to Walter Scott, 9 Aug. 1918, Motherwell Papers, file 109.

31 See Allan Turner, 'Reminiscences of the Hon. J.A. Calder,' *Saskatchewan History*, XXV (Spring 1972), 55-75. Thomas Crerar considered Calder probably the ablest in the cabinet. Crerar to author, 23 Nov. 1970. See also David Smith, *Prairie Liberalism: The Liberal Party in Saskatchewan* (Toronto, 1975), 153.

32 Turner, *ibid.*, 74-5; and Scott to Motherwell, 30 May 1918, Motherwell Papers, file 109.

himself believed that Union government was only a temporary phenomenon unless a dramatic realignment occurred in Canadian party life. This would only happen if the Conservatives became liberal and the Liberals 'extremely radical and socialistic,' hardly a likely prospect.[33] The selection of Calder does not reflect upon his own merits so much as upon the difficulties and weaknesses of the other Liberal Unionists in the cabinet. The rich lode discovered in 1917 had proven to contain much fool's gold.

Ironically, the Liberal Unionists were considered to be by far the stronger element of the cabinet. Arthur Ford wrote in March 1918: 'The Liberals have the younger men, the enthusiasm and the energy. While Conservatives are in the majority they are in reality in the minority.'[34] Time did not heal the Tory ailments as absence, sickness, and lethargy cut deeply into their ranks. Arthur Meighen and J.D. Reid were often forced to administer as many as four portfolios. The two senior ministers, White and Foster, were the worst offenders. The former was indecisive, periodically submitting his resignation and then withdrawing it,[35] while the latter passionately extended 'the jurisdiction of his department in every possible direction, although its original scope was quite sufficient to absorb his whole energies.'[36] Frank Cochrane had a stroke immediately following the election, and Thomas Crothers proved, in Borden's own words, 'useless.'[37] Sir Edward Kemp remained abroad as overseas minister of militia, and Charles Doherty usually accompanied Borden for work in Europe. Not only did the Tory ministers retain an intense distrust of their Liberal colleagues which greatly impaired cabinet efficiency, but they were themselves disunited, dispirited, and unable to fulfil their responsibilities.

The highly touted committees for co-ordination and direction of the cabinet, the war committee and the reconstruction committee, contributed little. An irate Loring Christie informed Borden that Newton Rowell's war committee had met only once between 21 February and 9 April, a period when the war crisis was at its worst.[38] The associate secretary of the war committee, Vincent Massey, similarly found the machinery of Union government imperfect: 'The role of secretary seemed to be imperfectly understood. As a secretary myself I

---

33 Calder to Scott, 6 Jan. 1918, cited in Smith, *Prairie Liberalism*, 153.
34 Ford to Willison, 5 March 1918, PAC, Willison Papers, v. 30.
35 White first sent in his resignation on 23 Jan. 1918, withdrew it temporarily on 25 Jan., had it accepted on 23 March, withdrew it again on 25 March, told Borden he 'wanted to get out' on 1 Sept., and finally on 5 May 1919 said he must get out immediately and did. Borden Diary, 1918-20, *passim*; and White to Borden, 22 June 1920, BP, v. 16.
36 Borden, *Letters to Limbo*, ed. Henry Borden (Toronto, 1971), 69.
37 Borden Diary, 2 Jan., 21 April 1917. Why Borden reappointed Crothers in light of such comments is inexplicable.
38 'Memorandum for the Prime Minister,' 9 April 1918, BP, v. 96.

acquired a professional point of view on this subject. Secretaries of Ministers were often chosen without either experience or training, which meant that they were not able to help their chiefs as they should. As a consequence, the chiefs had too much, their secretaries too little, to do.'[39] Whatever the cause, little was done. No evidence exists that, apart from individual initiatives in certain areas, these committees succeeded in their announced purpose of throwing 'the full power of Canada into the national endeavour.'[40] They gave an air of planning and of organizational sophistication so fashionable in the late war years, but the broadness of their task and the inexperience of their members made this air nothing more than fatuous pretension.

Reorganization of the government was planned, postponed, and then finally forced by resignation of death. Foster's departure, for example, was considered imminent and necessary in January 1918. Yet this relic of the age of Macdonald remained until 1921, primarily because no one of appropriate stature could be found to replace him. No French Canadian would consent to enter the government although several prospects were sounded. Even F.F. Pardee, who had clamoured to come in only a few months earlier, refused to join the government on 5 November 1918: understandably, he was unwilling to climb aboard a ship tossing about in a political storm.[41]

DEFECTION AND DISILLUSIONMENT

The Liberal Unionists in Ottawa were both reflections of and victims of the actions of provincial Liberal governments. This, of course, is not surprising since so many of them either came from provincial Liberal parties or were their delegates. Prior to December 1917, these Liberals as well as Borden regarded the nascent Unionist movements within the provinces (especially in Ontario and Manitoba) as the guarantee of Unionist security and endurance. But this was not to be; the provincial governments methodically broke their Unionist bonds after 1917.

The Maritimes, the section of English Canada least entranced by the Unionist siren in 1917, found it relatively easy to disavow the 1917 flirtation. New Brunswick's Liberal government had never supported Union, although Premier W.E. Foster was himself sympathetic. Here, then, there were no ties to breach. In Nova Scotia, however, the matter was more complex. Premier G.H. Murray

---

39 *What's Past Is Prologue* (Toronto, 1963), 51.
40 Borden, *Memoirs*, II, 759.
41 For Foster, see Borden Diary, 21 Jan.; the decision to add French Canadians, 31 Oct.; and Pardee, 5 Nov. 1918; see also Pardee to Rowell, 6 Nov. 1918, Rowell Papers, v. 4.

did remain Unionist after 1917, but he found it increasingly difficult to maintain a united provincial party while he clung to the Unionist banner.[42] He therefore became silent while, in Laurier's words, continuing to be 'more Unionist than he dare avow.'[43] By early 1919, however, Murray saw that Unionism was politically dead and that he must find a place for himself and other Liberal Unionists in post-Laurier Liberalism. Thus, at the Liberal convention in August 1919, Murray consented to be co-chairman (with Gouin) and keynote speaker. Rowell has left us a fine description of his performance on that occasion: 'I do not believe the keynote speech could have been a very congenial task. I was a little surprised that he went as far as he did in speaking of Union Government, when he declared that they were all agreed that Union Government should cease and that it was the duty of Liberals to oppose it. The principal part of his speech, however, was an attack upon the former Conservative administration and particularly on their attitude toward Reciprocity.'[44] It was as if Murray wanted to efface all traces of Unionism from his own and the Liberal record.

Rowell understood Murray's situation very well because it was quite similar to that of Ontario's Liberal Unionists. In early 1919 the provincial Liberal party cast off Rowell's hand-picked successor, William Proudfoot, in favour of Hartley Dewart, an opponent of conscription and of Union government and, according to the *Christian Guardian* (which Dewart's father once edited), 'the chief representative of the liquor interests in the Ontario legislature.'[45] The Hearst Conservatives, who remained faithful to Unionism, sought to crush the upstart Dewart in a general election in October 1919; but the desired revenge was not obtained. Dewart was defeated, but so too were the Conservatives as both parties were the surprising victims of the United Farmers of Ontario. There is no need to trace here the fall of Sir William Hearst's government.[46] What is significant for our purpose is the enormous shock which the 'UFO' victory caused in Ottawa. The first third-party government in Canadian history had been elected in the

---

42 E.M. Macdonald, *Recollections: Political and Personal* (2nd ed., Toronto, n.d.), 328-50; Macdonald to Laurier, 31 Dec. 1918, PAC, Laurier Papers, v. 728; and PAC, King Papers, King Diary, 1919 (the latter is a series of essays covering months at a time); F.B. McCurdy to Borden, 11 Sept., 9 Nov. 1918, BP, v. 114.
43 Laurier to J.H. Sinclair, 23 Nov., Charles Murphy to Laurier, 25 Nov. 1918, Laurier Papers, v. 727.
44 Rowell to Maclean, 18 Aug. 1919, Rowell Papers, v. 5.
45 *Guardian*, 27 July 1919. Rowell publicly dissociated himself from Dewart in a public letter. See *Toronto Star*, 15 July 1919 and Prang, *N.W. Rowell*, chap. 18.
46 See Peter Oliver, 'Sir William Hearst and the Collapse of the Ontario Conservative Party,' *Canadian Historical Review*, LIII (March 1972), 21-50; and W.R. Young, 'Conscription, Rural Depopulation, and the Farmers of Ontario, 1917-19,' *ibid.*, 289-320.

Unionist stronghold of Ontario. Some ministers immediately identified the United Farmers with Bolshevism and Sinn Fein.[47] Upon mature consideration, however, the Unionists saw that they were in serious trouble not only in Ontario but throughout Canada, and one shrewd political analyst assessed the chances of a federal farmers' government as 'at least even.'[48]

The main support for this judgment was the strong anti-Unionist sentiment upon the Canadian prairies. The 1917 victory in the west had been deceptive: numerous aliens were disfranchised; agricultural prices were the highest ever; and farmers' sons were exempted from conscription. The following year, however, the farm labour shortage became acute as conscription took effect, and the farmers' exemption was abolished. Once again, as in the decade before the war, the western Canadian farmer felt himself at the mercy of an eastern policy which disregarded his particular needs. Union government seemed different only in name from earlier party governments. Thomas Crerar, the minister of agriculture, whose presence in the cabinet was intended to maintain the allegiance of the powerful farm organizations, faced intense pressure. His loyalty, in fact, had never been strong; he had written in October 1917 to a correspondent who chided him upon his entry to the Union government: 'I think probably your estimate as to the future of the old Liberal and Conservative Parties is correct, and I should not wonder if your forecast as to the development of a Progressive Party somewhat later is also correct. Your letter expresses a hidden fear that I might not be found in the Progressive element when that time comes. In this respect your judgment will prove wrong.'[49]

Twenty months later Crerar kept his word. He resigned in the spring of 1919 when White introduced a budget without an extensive tariff revision. Crerar's move provoked a sympathetic reaction among other western Liberal Unionists, especially at the provincial level. In a letter to Sir Clifford Sifton, J.W. Dafoe explained the actions of his close friend, Crerar, and speculated upon the political future of the Canadian west. According to Dafoe, Crerar had long since given up hope of the Unionists becoming a 'progressive' body. He particularly feared the Unionist flirtation with Gouin and the Quebec Liberals who, together with Ontario Unionists, could form a central Canadian coalition representing those economic interests which were anathema to the Canadian west. Crerar had little in common with eastern Liberals, either the industrial and financial interests or

47 F.H. Keefer to Borden, 12 Nov., Foster to Borden, 23 Oct. 1919, BP, v. 114.
48 Thomas B. Costain, 'The Farmer in Politics,' *University Magazine*, XVIII (Dec. 1919), 454-8.
49 Crerar to R.J. Deachman, 15 Oct. 1917, Queen's University Archives, Crerar Papers, box 37.

'the bi-lingual group.' A revived Liberal party 'on the old lines' would be 'organized hypocrisy.' He did not know where to turn. He admitted that his Unionist connection had meant that he had 'lost control of the Farmers' Movement.' For the moment, Dafoe claimed, western Liberals like himself and Crerar should take refuge in political limbo.[50]

With the 20 October 1919 Ontario election these western politicians returned to active political involvement. But their return was neither to Unionism nor to Liberalism but to a new Progressive party which became 'a no man's land for defecting partisans.'[51] Crerar became the leader of the Progressive group in the House of Commons and the provincial governments of Manitoba, Saskatchewan, and Alberta tried to accomodate the farmers' quite exclusive demands which were expressed in a significantly titled 'New National Policy.' Some resisted the Progressive magnet. Calder remained in Ottawa, but those who had been most active in placing him there would have nothing to do with him. As David Smith remarks in his history of Saskatchewan Liberalism, 'From all sides Calder was agreed to be persona non grata.'[52] Facing an internal threat and sincerely troubled by economic pressures, the Liberal governments of the Canadian west completely abandoned Unionism with great flourish, little trouble, and no apology.

There was to be one final, ironic attempt to bolster Unionism through garnering provincial support. On 23 July 1919, at Murray's Bay, Quebec, Borden joined William Howard Taft in a golf twosome with the opposition, Henry Drayton and Sir Lomer Gouin.[53] No record of the result of this match exists, but we do know that Borden failed to score in the political game. On the advice of Lord Atholstan (Hugh Graham) and James Calder, Borden had decided to gamble upon acquiring Gouin, the master of Quebec provincial politics, or, failing Gouin, Ernest Lapointe, Rodolphe Lemieux, or Jacques Bureau for the federal cabinet. In his conversation with Lapointe, Borden set out the 'community of interest' which he felt the Quebec politician shared with his own beleaguered ministry: 'I observed that there was a tendency throughout the world, from which Canada was not immune to lose respect for constituted authority, to disregard law and order, and to attempt the redress of alleged grievances by violent and unconstitutional methods. The people of the Province

50 Dafoe to Sifton, 21 and 24 July 1919, Dafoe Papers. See, generally, W.L. Morton, *The Progressive Party in Canada* (Toronto, 1950).
51 The phrase is J.J. Morrison's in 'Memoirs,' PAC, Morrison Papers, p. 67. Morrison was the secretary of the United Farmers of Ontario. According to him, 55 per cent of the UFO members were former Conservatives; 45 per cent former Liberals.
52 Smith, *Prairie Liberalism*, 153.
53 A full description of this match, complete with photographs, is found in BP, v. 114.

of Quebec, through their habit of mind, their traditions, and their training formed an element of the population which should be of invaluable assistance in resisting.'[54] Lapointe, denounced as a traitor himself by many Unionists less than two years earlier, undoubtedly saw much irony in Borden's remarks. He failed to see much logic; neither did the others and no French Canadian would enter Union government.[55]

Borden's comments to Lapointe have a wider significance. The heir to a movement which fundamentally changed Canadian political methods and forms had become the leading opponent of change. Borden's hope that Union government could deny its own ancestry was unconvincing to all. From the cabinet to the constituency, all knew that Borden was the 'lame duck' leader of a rapidly disintegrating party. His indecision, in part the product of his limited range of choice, became the butt of the questionable humour of his oldest friends and allies. Sir John Willison wrote to Sifton: 'You have no doubt heard why the ship that Borden was to christen at Halifax slipped into the water before the ceremony could be performed. It could not wait for Borden to make up his mind.' Sifton replied: 'I had not heard that joke about Borden but it is extremely good. He will go down to posterity (as far as he goes) as Robert the Unready.' The coalition which had promised dynamic leadership for a feckless nation had provided none.[56] The epic of 1917 had ended as a farce.

The defection of the provincial parties symbolized a marked loss of confidence in Union government. Some, notably French Canadians and the disfranchised, never possessed confidence but, for others, the degree of disillusionment was closely related to their lofty visions of Union's promise in 1917. By 1920, the *Manitoba Free Press* reported, 'No matter what [the Union government] does it gets into trouble. Few thanks and plentiful kicks are its daily portion. In this it is in part the victim of circumstances; but it is also in great measure the architect of its own misfortunes.'[57] And indeed it was.

In 1917, as in 1911, Borden had succeeded by drawing prominent interest groups into direct political action. Yet those he assiduously courted at election time, he often ignored or even spurned afterwards. In some cases he had little choice; in others, however, he should have tried but did not. His actions may be

54 'Memo,' 20 July 1919, BP, v. 16.
55 See Borden, *Memoirs*, II, 982-5; 'Memo,' 24 July, 'Memo,' 25 July 1919, BP, v. 16 and Borden to Rowell, 28 July 1919, Rowell Papers, v. 5. Borden knew that Quebec feared the upcoming Liberal convention.
56 Willison to Sifton, 28 Dec. 1920, PAC, Sifton Papers, v. 208; Sifton to Willison, 29 Dec. 1920, Willison Papers, v. 74.
57 Cited in Brown and Cook, *Canada, 1896-1921*, 326.

ascribed in part to his Burkean view of the nature of political office. But indecision and neglect were also significant factors, and, in the view of erstwhile supporters, neglect meant betrayal. On the one hand, this bred cynicism; on the other, political activity directed against the betrayer. Ironically, the form of this political activity derived from the experiences these interest groups had obtained working with Borden. As one distinguished student of political behaviour has written: 'Although political movements begin in unrest, all social unrest does not find expression in political movements. Under some conditions, a community which is visited by plague may pray; under other conditions, the community will demand the retirement of the health commissioner.'[58] In 1918 and 1919, the age of praying had past.

Thus farmers, offended by the loss of their sons' exemptions, by the retention of the tariff, and by the indecision surrounding the Wheat Board, used those political skills acquired during wartime to forge a united front to challenge Unionist authority. The farmers, at least, chose traditional channels; labour, frustrated by economic inequalities and fearful of the government's restrictive policies, took to the streets — in Calgary, in Vancouver, in Toronto, in Sydney, but most of all in Winnipeg. This most fascinating chapter in Canadian labour history need not be retold here.[59] What is significant for us is the government response: force on a scale unprecedented in peacetime. Farmers, labour, and French-Canadian nationalists had little in common; but as Arthur Marwick has written of post–First World War Britain, there was 'one great denominator, a widespread impatience of authority as such.'[60] In Canada, it was not all authority but, specifically, Union government's authority. Because of Borden's protracted absences, because of the lack of a coherent, convincing policy (much less an ideology), and because of the Canadian state's disordered growth and ramshackle structure, authority could not respond to the diverse challenges. The Unionists overestimated their strength in 1917; two years later they exaggerated their weaknesses.

On 10 July 1920 Union government finally died, its remains passing to Arthur Meighen, the leader of the new National-Liberal-Conservative party.[61] There was not much left: after Crerar's resignation in 1919, Unionism was

---

58 Harold Lasswell, 'The Measurement of Public Opinion,' *American Political Science Review*, XXV (1931), 311-36.
59 See David Bercuson, *Confrontation at Winnipeg: Labour, Industrial Relations, and the General Strike* (Montreal, 1974). On this period and the protest movements, see Brown and Cook, *Canada, 1896-1921*, chaps. 15 and 16.
60 *The Deluge* (Harmondsworth, 1967), 322.
61 Borden had tried to resign in Dec. 1919, but the party refused to let him. Instead, they agreed he should take an extended vacation. See Borden, *Memoirs*, II, 1015-19.

'steadily ... dismembered.' 'We manage,' Sir Joseph Flavelle complained, 'to lose a cabinet minister about once a month.'[62] In this atmosphere the Unionists tried to develop a new policy, but, frankly, the attempt was pathetic as well as prolonged. As Rowell pointed out, the proposed policy statement was too general and, in certain respects, evasive and conservative. The policy prompted Rowell's resignation; he believed that it signalled future Conservative dominance in the Unionist coalition, and he was correct.[63] The Union, split in unequal factions, quietly divided. Was this precipitious decline inevitable?

Unionism was, it is true, the victim of circumstances and its own decisions. Its record, however, was not a negative one. It had nationalized and reorganized Canada's bankrupt railways, despite great opposition among its own supporters in Quebec.[64] It had tested the limits of the interventionist state, educating future generations of Canadian public figures on the limits and possibilities of state activity. A Department of Health, women's suffrage, federal assistance to technical education and to highway construction, and veterans' re-establishment were other valuable legacies. And yet the aura of indecision and decay pervades the Unionist years, obscuring its accomplishments and initiatives. It is necessary to move beyond individual achievements or failures to understand this impression. Part of the disappointment was the product of heightened expectations and overblown wartime rhetoric. More fundamentally, Union government's decline illustrates the confusion of Unionist thought and its misplaced confidence in the results of 1917. For its supporters, Union government was to be the instrument through which the 'new era' would be achieved. By demanding that the state become the agency of its interests and its social values, Unionism forced French Canada to choose between regional and national loyalties. For Unionists, no such choice was necessary: local and national loyalties seemed complementary. Thus, the state and political parties would not be moderators of conflicting interests but the expression of a particular interest. Borden, Loring Christie remarked in December 1917, was no longer disposed to play 'the national unity game.'[65] More bluntly, J.W. Dafoe warned a French-Canadian friend: 'You can do precisely as you believe; and we shall do whatever may be necessary.'[66]

'Whatever may be necessary.' The phrase evokes a certain view of a society, a belief 'in coherence by constraint and domination,' and as such it stands in

62 Flavelle to David Carnegie, 16 Feb. 1920, quoted in Cook and Brown, *Canada, 1896-1921*, 326.
63 See Prang, *N.W. Rowell*, 335-6.
64 See J.A. Eagle, 'Sir Robert Borden and the Railway Problem in Canadian Politics, 1911-1920,' unpublished PhD thesis, University of Toronto, 1972.
65 Main Johnson Diary, 28 Dec. 1917, MTCL, Johnson Papers, v. 9.
66 Dafoe to Thomas Côté, 1 Jan. 1918, Dafoe Papers.

contrast to the other major historical view, the belief in 'coherence by consensus.'[67] But while Unionism uttered the language of the coercive state, it also, necessarily, adopted the dialect of Western liberalism. The war, after all, was fought for freedom, for justice, for democracy. Janus-faced, Unionism never presented a distinct, full, and convincing image; it confused its followers and encouraged its foes who correctly saw that the tension between the two conflicting visions was Unionism's critical flaw. For the Unionists, coercion was never an enduring possibility, but neither, after December 1917, was consensus. Inarticulate and undefined, Unionism lurched towards its inevitable doom.

67 R. Dahrendorf, *Class and Class Conflict in Industrial Society* (Stanford, 1959), 157.

Conclusion

We cannot return to the days when the people and even the parliaments knew nothing of what was going on behind their backs until they were asked to give their lives to vindicate the bargains of the diplomats. All that is past ...
Craig Forrester in Douglas Durkin, *The Magpie*

J.W. Dafoe and Craig Forrester took their places on opposite sides of Winnipeg's barricades; nevertheless, both agreed in one respect: the Unionist experiment, however brief, had been a decisive moment in Canadian political and party history. The events of 1917, Dafoe later wrote, marked 'both an end and a beginning in Canada's political development. They brought to a definite close what might be called the era of the Great Parties.' The 'efforts at the realignment of parties, the attempt to newly appraise political values, and to redefine political relationships ... [were] testimony to the dissolving, penetrating power of the impulses of 1917.'[1]

Dafoe recognized that Unionism was a much wider stream than merely a conduit for Canadian pre-war sentiment. Even in the absence of war one might have expected a movement similar in tone if not in intensity. The rapid economic growth, the flood of immigrants, urbanization and the consequent depopulation of rural Canada, broke down traditional allegiances, disrupted local communities, and promoted social disturbance. The turmoil of 1914-18 accelerated these tendencies; it did not give birth to them. Writing on German unification in the nineteenth century, Robert M. Berdahl has argued: 'The process of economic modernization involves a radical transformation of the traditional structure of an agrarian society. It involves the destruction of an older social

---

1 J.W. Dafoe, *Laurier: A Study in Canadian Politics* (Toronto, 1922), 176, 180.

order in which the bonds of individual loyalty and dependency are based on personal and local obligation; it requires the creation of a new society in which individuals become highly dependent on many others from whom they are far removed personally and geographically.' In the face of the resulting disintegration, nationalism 'acts as a force for the reintegration of society.'[2] Berdahl further claimed that nationalism as an ideology as distinct from an idea is functional: 'It serves a definite purpose of elites, as, for example, furthering economic development or binding a community together during a period of social upheaval.' In David Apter's words, it forms 'the link between action and fundamental belief.'[3]

Union government reflected the aims of what Apter would term a 'nationalizing elite,' English Canadian in origin and deeply concerned with the need to bind together a fragmented Canadian community.[4] To attribute 'the clash' between French and English Canada solely to cultural differences is unsatisfactory. This cultural differential has been a factor since the beginning of the nineteenth century but the degree of antagonism has varied immensely. Moreover, modern studies of nationalism show that there is no intrinsic reason why regional loyalty must necessarily conflict with national loyalty.[5] Cultural reasons alone are therefore insufficient explanation for the variation in the degree of hostility between English and French Canada. The analysis of the preceding chapters suggests that prior to the First World War the community of interests, which in the absence of a common culture binds a nation together, no longer obtained in Canada.[6] Ontario had become an urbanized province with a new industrial élite which possessed close economic, cultural, and social ties with the 'new west.' French Canada, however, continued to exalt the values of a traditional society and, in response to the aggressive character of Anglo-Canadian nationalism, had developed its own kind of nationalist expression. As a result,

2 'New Thoughts on German Nationalism,' *American Historical Review*, LXXVII (Feb. 1972), 75, 76.

3 *The Politics of Modernization* (Chicago, 1965), 314.

4 *Ibid.* and Karl Deutsch, *Nationalism and Social Communication* (New York, 1953), 18-20.

5 The following is much influenced by David Potter, 'The Historian's Use of Nationalism and Vice Versa,' *American Historical Review*, LXVII (July 1962), 924-50. According to Potter, psychological research suggests that intense local loyalties may, in fact, strengthen national loyalty. See also Rupert Emerson, *From Empire to Nation: The Rise to Self-Assertion of Asian and African Peoples* (Cambridge, Mass., 1960), 60.

6 Potter writes, 'There is certainly at least one other important factor besides common culture which may bind an aggregate of individuals together, and this is community of interest, not in the narrow sense of economic advantage only, but the broad sense of welfare and security through membership in society.' *Ibid.*, 935.

the equilibrium which had permitted French Canadians to accept the existence of a community of interest with English Canada gradually disappeared. Yet not only French Canada shunned the new nationalism: the Maritimes, the oldest English provinces which the new immigrants avoided and where economic stagnancy seemed permanent, also baffled the Unionists.[7] So, too, did rural Ontario where only a blatant political bribe purchased the loyalty of the Ontario farmer in December 1917. These ineffable political realities punctured the integrative vision of Unionism's 'nationalizing élite,' but not before the Canadian party system was changed fundamentally.

The traditional party system, based upon, in Berdahl's terms, 'the bonds of individual loyalty and dependency,' could not survive the nationalizing influence of the 1917 campaign; no longer did constituency boundaries and interests define the party contest. National politics did matter: individuals, again in Berdahl's terms, became 'highly dependent on many others from whom they are far removed personally and geographically.' The venerable patterns of constituency politics, which industrialization, urbanization, and immigration already threatened, crumbled as new pressure groups and leaders replaced traditional party structures in the organization of the campaign. About this, Borden had few regrets, and, with the help of others, he moved to assure the endurance of this fresh political landscape. In accomplishing this, nothing was so important as the reform of the federal civil service. The fulfilment of this campaign pledge exceeded even its proponents hopes: '... The sense of the uniqueness of the opportunity this [coalition government] provided gave strength to the reformer's broom which swept in a wide and ruthless arc, to leave the newly constituted [Civil Service Commission] in full legal command of personnel administration throughout the entire civil service.'[8] In a stroke, the reformer's broom swept away what observers from Siegfried through Skelton had regarded as the lifeblood of the Canadian party system.

Local Conservatives and many members of Parliament regarded the sudden removal of patronage – the most potent lever at the constituency level – as sheer robbery, and Robert Rogers led them in a futile but persistent resistance to the theft. An illustration of what happened and what they objected to can be seen in the correspondence between Arthur Meighen and his Portage la Prairie

7 Census figures indicate this most dramatically (percentage of total Canadian population):

	1871	1881	1911	1921
Prince Edward Island	2.55	2.25	1.30	1.01
Nova Scotia	10.51	9.32	6.83	5.96
New Brunswick	7.74	6.65	4.88	4.41

Sixth Census of Canada, 1921 (Ottawa, 1924), I, 3.

8 J.E. Hodgetts et al., The Biography of an Institution (Montreal and London, 1972), 50.

'bagman,' Jack Garland. On 25 May 1918 Garland wrote to Meighen requesting a small favour of the type so readily granted by Canadian politicians since Confederation: 'I am told that Harry Johns has sent in his resignation as caretaker of the Post Office. If such is the case do you think there would be any chance for Chas. Gordon. Gordon, as you know, after he was dismissed by the [Liberal] local government, went out farming and met with an accident which has left him for all time unable to do hard work, was in Jacket for nearly a year and he is the very sort of man to look after a position such as this in his condition.' Here was a rich opportunity to reward a party man and to win goodwill, an important political commodity in a small town like Portage la Prairie. Meighen's private secretary therefore forwarded Garland's letter to Public Works Minister Carvell with a note asking him to do all that was possible to meet the request from 'a very close friend of Mr. Meighen.' On 29 May B.K. Dibbee, Carvell's secretary, replied: 'In the absence of Mr. Carvell, I beg to acknowledge receipt of your favour of the 28th instant regarding the position of Caretaker at the Post Office at Portage la Prairie. These positions are now filled through the Civil Service Commission, and Mr. Gordon should be advised to apply to them and take the necessary examinations.' Meighen's irritated secretary wrote at once to the chairman of the Civil Service Commission, W.J. Roche, a former Conservative minister and a fellow Manitoban. Roche's reply was friendlier than Dibbee's but the substance was the same: commission regulations could not be breached whatever Meighen's fate in Portage la Prairie might be. Charles Gordon did not become the caretaker of the Portage la Prairie post office.[9]

While Meighen did not join Rogers in the latter's implacable resistance to the new political order, he, like many other Conservatives, quietly lamented many of the changes, not least because of their impact upon his political future. To a friend he voiced his frustration with the constraints which Union government imposed upon its members: 'I am down here pretty much alone, so far as the west from our old standpoint is concerned. I cannot take the course that a Minister could take under old conditions, and consequently I cannot engage the party support which it has all along been possible to engage.'[10] Political men could not behave in what they thought was proper political fashion; the government of men seemed to have become mainly the administration of things.

9 Garland to Meighen, 25 May, Mitchell to Carvell, 28 May, Dibbee to Mitchell, 29 May, Mitchell to Roche, 30 May, Roche to Mitchell, 31 May 1918, PAC, Meighen Papers, v. 42.
10 Meighen to Staples, 21 Nov. 1918, *ibid.*, v. 2.

Without the tie of patronage, limited by the nature of coalition government, and with the party press almost mute, Unionist members found themselves isolated from their constituencies. But many Canadian politicians escaped these afflictions, and this fact more than any other fuelled Rogers' assault on Union government. On a very practical level, Liberalism in its various guises was the prime beneficiary of the Unionist reforms. Federally, Union government meant that the Liberals, for the first time since 1911, had a share of federal advertising, judicial work, and appointments, from the judiciary to the poll clerks. When they did not get their share, they complained vigorously.[11] What exasperated Conservatives was not so much the sharing of federal patronage but rather the Liberal control of patronage in the provinces where the dent of reform was almost invisible.

After the fall of the Hearst Conservatives in Ontario in 1919 the Tories held not a single province, and the importance of this in the collapse of the Conservative-dominated Union government should not be underestimated. In Nova Scotia, for example, most federal patronage passed through the hands of the Unionist minister, A.K. Maclean, into the control of the powerful Liberal machine of Premier George Murray. But although Murray received a share of the federal patronage, the provincial patronage was reserved exclusively for Liberals. Not surprisingly, the provincial Tories were outraged. Thus, when a Nova Scotia Tory was asked for his explanation for the Conservative débâcle in the 1921 federal election, he pointed out that his friends had been 'sullen and resentful because they felt the old Conservatives had been sacrificed.' This, 'even more than hard times and war discontent, was responsible for the horrible showing we made here.'[12] Another Nova Scotian, F.B. McCurdy, the public works minister in the Meighen ministry, echoed these complaints. Federal civil service reform, he gently chided Borden, 'is certainly unsuited to Nova Scotia where the local provincial government continues to care for its supporters.' McCurdy added, not as criticism but as analysis, that as much as 10 per cent of the electorate drew 'emoluments' or received 'recognition' in some way or another from the province.[13] It was, very simply, a way of life which Nova Scotians of both parties expected to continue. And, in a few years, McCurdy and his friends did reap their rewards.

What had changed, however, was both the rewards and the manner of their disposition, and it is in this respect that the Unionist experience left enduring

11 See, for example, PAC, Borden Papers (BP), Borden Diary, 15 Sept. 1918.
12 William Hall to Meighen, 10 Feb. 1922, Meighen Papers, v. 67.
13 McCurdy to Borden, 21 Dec. 1921, BP v. 277.

results. There are, Peter Clark and James Q. Wilson have argued,[14] three kinds of rewards which political parties can use to attract support and party workers: material, solidary, and purposive. The first describes patronage in the popular sense: jobs, contracts, career incentives, and the like, whether legally permissible or otherwise. The second refers to the 'sense of fellowship' one derives from association with like-minded individuals. The third is ideological reward: the party is seen to further or represent ideals to which an individual strongly adheres. In the case of material rewards, the provincial governments and, therefore, the provincial parties controlled most after 1917. This was in part the result of Union government and its reforms and in part a reflection of the character of Canadian social and economic development. Prior to the war, Clifford Sifton's 'army' — the immigration agents and officers — swarmed about the west performing public and party service. The railways, so dependent on the politicians' aid, threw themselves into the political fray, often on both sides. But during the war and after, immigrants no longer found much welcome on Canada's shores and plains, and the railways which had brought them here had, in many cases, been nationalized and 'politically purified' by the Union government. Inevitably, with the end of the war, the federal government ceased its dominant role in Canadian economic life. In the provinces, however, new tasks abounded. The proud owners of Buicks, Reos, and, of course, Fords demanded new and better roads; the millions who had made their homes in Canada's cities sought the amenities of modern life; and these were generally the responsibilities of the provinces. So too were the natural resources whose rapid exploitation continued in peace as in war.

As a result of these broadened functions, the provincial governments became, in Christopher Armstrong's words, 'semi-independent principalities treating with one another and the federal government.'[15] Provincial parties established a similar and related independence and, indeed, paramountcy. With the reduction of federal patronage, the breakdown of federal party lines, and the wider ambit of provincial governments, the opportunity for Ottawa to interfere with, much less control, provincial parties diminished. In comparison with pre-war days, one might say that the party's heart was cut off from the arteries and other vital organs. In this sense, one can appreciate Meighen's complaints that he felt 'all alone' at Ottawa, and McCurdy's yearning to return to the old system of

14 'Incentive Systems,' *Administrative Science Quarterly*, VI (1961), 129-66.
15 'The Politics of Federalism: Ontario's Relations with the Federal Government, 1896-1941,' unpublished PhD thesis, University of Toronto, 1972, 2. See also H.V. Nelles, *The Politics of Development* (Toronto, 1974). Nelles argues in a similar vein and concludes that the provincial government became a 'client' of business interests.

political appointment, 'a non-rigid system with a human touch ... in which all affected had a voice.'[16] Without adequate material rewards, Unionism depended upon 'purposive' incentives, and these, simply, were not enough.

Union government also broke down the 'solidary' fellowship of the Conservative party. The popularity of Bob Rogers' 'smokers,' at which, during wartime prohibition, one could find good whisky as well as good tobacco, is also explained by the opportunity which these occasions gave to Conservatives to feel comfortable and to have their prejudices confirmed while meeting with old friends. This was not the atmosphere of Unionist gatherings where suspicion mingled uneasily with solemnity. Many went elsewhere, some to the new political groupings where purposive incentives did apply. The most notable of these groupings was the Progressive party which harnessed western Canadian feelings of resentment and made a specific sectional appeal in contrast to the characteristically general appeal of the traditional parties. But the most significant and lasting example of party commitment born of a spirit of resentment, perhaps even of vengeance, occurred not in the west but in Quebec. Not long after Meighen replaced Borden, the former Tory organizer Sir William Price gave a melancholy summary of Quebec politics to his new leader: 'It must be understood that today in this Province the Liberal Party is looked upon by its adherents as the Party of French Canadians – in other words as a National Party.'[17] The emotion lingered, accompanied by a lasting distrust of 'centralization' and of Union government's heir, the Conservative party. Against a party commitment of this nature, material incentives could make no headway. This was, perhaps, Unionism's most fateful legacy.

In those earlier days when Borden was fashioning the Unionist coalition, he believed he was fathering a party which would transcend the variety of Canadian political cultures, a party which would define and indeed represent a definable national interest. Harking back to a tradition as old as the English Civil War which declared party and public interest to be antithetical, Unionism proposed to abolish party by declaring itself the embodiment of the public interest.[18] But between this idea and the reality fell far too many shadows – the bitterness of the disfranchised, the outrage of the French Canadian, the promises unfulfilled – and these shadows fell darkly along the path that future Conservative politicians would have to tread.

---

16 McCurdy to Borden, 21 Dec. 1921, BP, v. 277.
17 Price to Meighen, 29 Dec. 1920, Meighen Papers, v. 44.
18 On the anti-party tradition, see Richard Hofstadter, *The Idea of a Party System* (Berkeley and Los Angeles, 1969), chap. 1; and Austin Ranney, *Curing the Mischiefs of Faction* (Berkeley and Los Angeles, 1975), 22-57.

It was, however, not only the Conservative party but also Canadian federalism and the Canadian party system which bore the consequences. Rather than strengthening the nation state, the attempt to end partyism instead reduced the possibility for national action. 'National government' became, to too many Canadians, a symbol not of innovation and creativity but of domination by an arrogant majority. Thereafter they would prefer the muddle, the contradictions, and the ambiguities of brokerage and consensus politics. In this Mackenzie King had no equal. Thus the Union government which divided us most was succeeded by that prime minister who would divide us least.

Index

Abbott, John 33
Achim, H. 82n
Acworth, W.M. 127n
Addams, Jane 207
Advisory boards 75
Aitken, Max (Lord Beaverbrook) 51,
    93, 182
Allan, Alexander 180
Allison, John W. 98-100
Ames, A.E. 120
Ames, Herbert B. 20, 49, 51, 57-8,
    66n
Andrews, A.J. 155-6
Armour, J.D. 19
Armstrong, Elizabeth 91-2
Armstrong, J.A.M. 166
Arsenault, A.E. 175
Asquith, H.H. 160
Atholstan, Lord, see Hugh Graham
Atkinson, Joseph 118, 120n, 134
Autonomy Bills (1905) 13, 49

Ballantyne, C.C. 155-6, 176, 212
Banks: and politics 25n, 55, 64
Barnard, G.H. 40
Barrette, J.A. 82n
Beck, Adam 152

Bellemare, A. 82n
Bennett, R.B. 188, 188n
Birmingham, A.R. 96
Blain, Richard 40
Blair, Andrew 13
Blake, Edward 10, 146
Blondin, Pierre 40, 82n, 132-3
Blount, A.E. 128
Boer War 88, 93
Borden, Laura 34, 48, 60
Borden, Robert L. 3, 5, 6, 13, 15-16,
    34, 36, 39-41, 51, 91, 93, 96, 97,
    100-2, 104-5, 111, 114, 122,
    127-8, 140, 144, 162, 186; party
    leadership 31-3, 36, 36-8, 60-1,
    152, 184, 206-11; Halifax Platform
    35, 163; party organization 45-50,
    54, 80, 82-3, 173ff; party policy
    70-4, 84-5, 140-1, 161-3; reaction
    to WW I 94-5, 102-4; conscription
    124-5, 128-9; formation of Union
    government 133-5, 136-44, 147,
    149-60, 164-6; relations with
    Quebec 48-50, 54, 56, 60, 64-5,
    68-9, 77-87, 132-3, 176, 191-2,
    208, 217-18, 220-1; relations with
    'progressives' 52, 55, 68, 70; and